Sicknote Goes Cruising
An Occasional Diary

DENNIS RICHARDS

Copyright © 2014 Dennis Richards
All rights reserved.
ISBN-10: 1495957497
ISBN-13: 978-1495957499
This book may also be made available under the title "Cruising & Me"

To Mandy

You to me are everything,

the sweetest song that I can sing

(oh baby)

Sicknote Goes Cruising

Sicknote Goes Cruising - *An Occasional Diary*

Chapter 1 – A Real Headache

Chapter 2 – The Maiden Voyage

Chapter 3 - Keeping It Up!

Chapter 4 – Getting Hooked

Chapter 5 – Am I Going to Lose My Job?

Chapter 6 - The Pensioner in Amsterdam

Chapter 7 – An Adriatic Adventure

Chapter 8 – This Time I'm Going To Do It!

Chapter 9 – The Glass Ceiling

Chapter 10 – The Menace in Venice

Chapter 11 – My Worst Nightmare

Chapter 12 – Chemo-Brain and Going Radio Ga-Ga

Chapter 13 - The Little Ship with the Big Heart

Chapter 14 – An Emotional Rollercoaster

Chapter 15 – A Time to Celebrate

Chapter 16 – Reflecting

Sicknote Goes Cruising

Chapter 1 – A Real Headache

Tuesday 11 September
The large West Indian lady doctor, who marched at some speed into my curtained-off cubicle in the hospital's A&E wing today, was pretty scary in her own right. Combine that with the fact that she was a large West Indian lady doctor with the results of my brain scan in her left hand, and I was, frankly, crapping myself. Her opening line, which very nearly resulted in my other bodily fluids doing a runner for the exits too, was "tis a good ting you flew home whens you did young man".

Only yesterday, I was driving along under a gloriously blue Florida sky without a care in the world. Then today, there I was having a complete stranger bearing, it has to be said, a more than passing resemblance to Lenny Henry in drag, completely and utterly terrify me with one short heavily-accented sentence. I've just come back from my holiday, for God's sake. Yes, my head really started to hurt on the flight home; yes, it hurts even more now; and yes, I had lost count of the number of times a whole stream of doctors had subsequently poked, prodded or appeared to subject me to some form of perverse pagan ritual. But there was no way I was expecting a diagnosis, prognosis or any other nosis that began with "tis a good ting you flew home whens you did young man".

Only when Dr Lenny eventually caught the expressions of outright fear on my face, and that of Mandy, my wife, did she somewhat belatedly add "no, no-ting wrong wid your head man, your scan's fine". When this resulted in only marginal improvements in our expressions, and she eventually realised the full impact of her initial statement, she added "there's no flights man, some idjut gone flown an airplane into da World Trade Centre".

"Oh, is that all? Thank Christ for that!"

Friday 14 September
Back home from hospital now and reflecting on the fact that yes, here I am, probably the only person on the planet, outside of Bin Laden and his mates, who was actually pleased to hear the initial news of the events of 11 September 2001. I was so relieved that I didn't have a tumour the size of Pavarotti in the deepest, darkest, most inoperable area of my brain, that I can actually remember thinking "thank Christ for that". Self obsessed much? Me??

The last few days have been spent almost entirely in front of the TV watching the rescue attempts in New York. Although the severe headache I am experiencing is easing slightly, I can't do much but lie flat on my back waiting to feel better. As part of the deal with the hospital to allow me to come home, Mandy has had to take a few days off work to keep an eye on me. We have done little but watch TV, mostly in stunned silence, my own health pushed to the back of my constantly throbbing mind, as the aftermath of 9/11 fills the screen.

The strange thing is none of this feels real. My head is killing me, I feel like I have the mother of all hangovers in spite of not having drunk any alcohol, and I have this strange "woolly" feeling. It's very difficult to describe, but the best comparison I can make is that it's akin to wearing a crash helmet full of cotton wool, while everybody else seems like characters on the screen of a poorly-tuned TV. Also, not one, but two aeroplanes have flown into one of the most iconic buildings in the world, on top of which Mandy and I were stood just last Christmas. The whole thing seems surreal.

Wednesday 3 October 2001
God I'm bored. My headache, although less severe now, is still there and is, literally, a pain. Trouble is, I'm bored to tears with the amount of lying around the house I have found it necessary to do, and whilst our three cats have been constant and welcome companions, I think even they want rid of me now. I am itching to get out and about and back to work. Aside from the old head still giving me problems, the main trouble now is this foggy feeling which has left me very slow mentally, and verbally inarticulate, to say the least. I've taken to saying completely the wrong word to the one I thought I had said, and my short-term memory has gone haywire. The strangest, most comical result of this is that when I mean to carry out two particular actions, I end up doing these in the exact opposite way to the one I intended – e.g. a just-made cup of coffee will find itself placed in the fridge, whilst the milk carton sits on a coffee table in the front room.

Also, although it's fair to say I've never had the grace of a ballet dancer, this fogginess has turned me into this clumsy liability of a man. Walls and doorframes, whose locations I have been familiar with for years, suddenly seem to jump out in front of me. And I'm dropping things, knocking them over, or both, on a regular basis. Even our cats, who have rarely left my side when I am horizontal, have learned that the vertical me is a whole other ball game, and give me a wide berth. Walking, to be fair, isn't too bad, but standing still for any length of time is really hard and, when I try, I start to wobble. A lot. I reckon I'm the only man on the planet whose wife <u>does</u> want him to pee on the toilet seat, as at this stage it would mean a marked improvement on my part.

Thursday 11 October 2001
I met with a neurological specialist today, to whom I was referred due to my ongoing headache. When I walked into his office the neurologist immediately introduced himself as Dr Dym. He then took me through what had become a very familiar routine over the last few weeks. In short, everything from going over my symptoms to scratching the soles of my feet with a sharp implement. The physical examination having gone well, Dr Dym then discussed with me the events to date and reviewed the various notes and scans. His conclusion was that there was probably little, if anything, wrong with me.

The meeting with Dr Dym was clearly therefore, a big relief. But it was also tinged with frustration because I was hoping for at least some explanation of what had caused me the problems I had been encountering. Still, I told myself he's the expert and, despite his unfortunate surname suggesting the contrary, clearly a very intelligent man. I should just be grateful I'm not seriously ill. He did prescribe me some tablets which he thought would help ease the headache, but as they were quite strong, he said I should initially start at a very low dose and then gradually increase them. I just thought, hey, if they can shift this headache, hand me some water and I'll take some right now.

Friday 26 October 2001
I tentatively returned to work this week on a part-time basis. This was as much to do with the sheer boredom I was suffering at home, and my impatience to get back to normal, than it was to do with me feeling better. However, the tablets Dr Dym prescribed seem to be easing the headache, and I am sleeping much better, too. I still feel unbelievably foggy, but I am desperate to get back to work, so hopefully it's just a case of blowing the cobwebs away.

Dave, my boss, has been fantastic and basically said "just do what you can, when you can do it, and keep me posted with how you're feeling". This means I can start off on a few hours work a day and then slowly increase my activity levels in order to - fingers crossed - get back to operating at a reasonable level of competency in the not-too-distant future. However, there is no hiding the fact that I don't feel myself. I seem to be missing my old sharpness and razor-like wit (okay, maybe more butterknife-like wit than razor-like, but you get the idea) and, as soon as I come home from work, my entire evening is spent prostrate on the sofa. That can't be right.

Wednesday 28 November 2001
With work going okay, and armed with another couple of "there's nothing wrong with you" statements, or words to that effect from my doctors, I recently returned to my first love, playing football, in the hope of convincing myself I am okay. It's clear the full eleven-a-side game is physically beyond me at this stage, but my weekly six-a-side games aren't going too badly. I love playing football again, and even the agony of my amazingly stiff muscles in the days after each game does not detract from the enjoyment: I absolutely love it. Those stiff muscles are still present when the following week's game comes around, which isn't good, but logic tells me that should improve.

A more pressing concern is that the brain-fog may still be affecting my balance and perspective as, in last week's game, I managed to run into the side wall, which until the point of impact I had believed to be running parallel to me, a good few yards away. The peripheral vision of a hoody-wearing Stevie Wonder would have spotted this wall, and taken evasive action, but somehow I found myself flat on the astroturf, with blood pouring from a three inch gash on my forearm. The nearest player to me, JD, was a good ten feet away and briefly looked as confused as me, before he too collapsed to the floor as he completely wet himself laughing. I considered blaming the git for giving me a crap pass, but this clearly wasn't an option as he hadn't yet released the ball to me. So I just got on with the game, albeit with blood trailing my every move.

Still, on the positive side, the result of my increased football activity is, I believe, twofold. Firstly, by hook or by crook (if hook = getting the trots after every game and crook = walking round like John Wayne for days afterwards), I am both thinner and fitter. Secondly, psychologically I feel loads better, I really do love playing football and despite more often than not playing slowly/badly/incoherently, my enthusiasm is, I think, carrying me through. In fact, feeling a pressing need to prove those "there's nothing wrong with you" statements true, I have made the decision to play twice a week.

Wednesday 12 December 2001

I was sat in my office this morning – well, when I say office, I mean I was sat behind the five foot high perspex partition situated between me and my team, aimed at magically allowing me to have confidential, manager-like conversations whilst still being able to witness every member of my pimple faced, sex starved team individually trying to chat up the young temp from the seventh floor – when Dave, my boss, phoned to call me down for a chat. On the walk down the stairs to his office, I was a little concerned about what this chat was going to be about, as although I felt I was still doing a decent job, in my own mind I knew my normal sharpness still hadn't returned. Don't get me wrong, Dave is a good boss who I trust completely, and someone for whom I enjoy working. I also still enjoy the job and, if anything, I have been working my nuts off to ensure my team continue to perform at the high level they had prior to my health problems. It was just that the company I work for have become more and more cost-conscious in recent years, and have certain "must-hit" targets to achieve, so I was concerned.

I needn't have worried. Dave was his normal relaxed self when I entered and he quickly explained that my previous boss, Jo, had been in touch to offer me a job in her department over the road. Now, Jo is someone who I have worked with, and for, on and off for a number of years, and so is someone who I know well. As with Dave, she has also become a good friend and so I was really chuffed with this job offer, particularly as my current department will start to be wound down next year. Dave feels it would be a good step for me and, although the opportunity has come much earlier than either of us expected, I was feeling pretty positive as I left Dave's office with a promise to think things over.

Friday 15 December 2001

I've obviously been thinking a great deal about the job offer. The new position offers a new challenge, with better long-term prospects, and working for Jo would be a bonus. On the other hand, am I ready? Do I really want to leave a position I enjoy, and am still growing into, earlier than is absolutely necessary? In short, the normal thought process I suspect most people go through in my position and, as is the norm for anyone with even a relative amount of confidence in their abilities, I've pretty much decided I have to go for it. I just have one nagging doubt that remains.

You see I have this little voice in my head that won't go away, which is raising one very valid point: How can I take a new job, working for a friend no less, when I have doubts over my health? The devil on my other shoulder is also, quite rightly, pointing out that I have been given the all-clear by every doctor I have seen and, if I make too much out of this, I could lose out on not just this opportunity, but possibly others too. Having mulled this over for a while, I don't think I can accept the job without first having a thorough medical, or MOT if you like, by someone who could and would take the time to do the job properly.

Thursday 20 December 2001
I went to a local private hospital today where I have been able to arrange a medical at just a few days notice, with the results to follow quickly afterwards. At £350 a pop it's not cheap, but it will be well worth the money if I can get the assurance I am looking for.

As I arrived at the hospital I was fairly relaxed. I have been there a few times over the years for operations on various football injuries, so know it well. I have had a good run health-wise too, with the tablets the neurologist had given me continuing to take the edge off the headache. I therefore felt positive, and very much looking on the medical as confirmation that I was okay. In fact, even when it became clear that a (very) attractive lady doctor was going to carry out some (very) personal aspects of my medical I was still reasonably relaxed.

The medical itself started well, a very nice nurse taking from me the samples I had been asked to take along with me although, I have to say, a very transparent plastic container is the very last place such samples should find themselves. She then took down a medical history before taking some blood and asking me to carry out a few tests to check things like lung capacity. All in all, very easy, and aside from samples in clear plastic containers, a very pleasant experience. The nurse had also said enough in between the various tests for me to know things were going well. So far so good.

It's fair to say that the second part of the medical wasn't quite as enjoyable, which you may find strange given my previous comments vis-à-vis the attractiveness of the lady doctor concerned, and that she would inevitably need to cup my testicles at some point. Had she been an older, less attractive doctor I'm sure I wouldn't have thought twice about the impending "cupping", but as she was what I believe is technically referred to in medical circles as "a babe", I suddenly became concerned about the whole cupping process. If that wasn't bad enough, I also started to think through the implications of her earlier throw-away line "and we'll end up by examining your prostate", which as the penny dropped, I realised she was shortly going to stick her finger up my bum. In short, the kind of treatment some fellas regularly pay good money for, from ladies much less medically qualified.

In practice, I found the constant reciting in my head of the mantra "don't get a stiffy, don't get a stiffy" worked perfectly throughout the cupping stage of the deal. Although by the slight smile on the doctor's face as she released her grip on my "boys", it did briefly cross my mind whether my mental mantra did in fact, unknowingly verbalise at some point. However, I have no other evidence of this and so prefer to think on her smile as a medical professional just enjoying the opportunity to work with good material. Nonetheless, I think she must have detected a certain amount of nervousness on my part, as she kindly offered me an "out" on the prostate test by stating that someone of my age and fitness needn't really have this if they didn't feel it was necessary. I'm not sure if it was the pulling up of my trousers at three, possibly four times the speed of light that came first, or the high-pitched falsetto, Joe Pasquale-esque "fine" that shot from my mouth, but either way I was a fully clothed, prostate test cancelling guy, with places to go and people to see, in next to no time. And boy I felt the better for it.

The main thing was that everything went very well medically, and from the initial comments of the health professionals concerned, I seem to have come through all of the tests very well. Compared with the half-cocked attempts of some of the previous doctors I had seen – in fact, half-cocked probably suggests around 50% more cock than their efforts actually equated to – this medical felt both more thorough and professional and was exactly what I needed. Now, I just needed to wait for the full results in about a week.

Wednesday 2 January 2002

The full report from my medical arrived today, and it very much confirmed their initial positivity. I had passed with flying colours, and although they said my headache wasn't something that they could investigate in any depth through the medical itself, every test they had done had suggested I was very fit and very healthy. This meant that, combined with the earlier reassurances from Dr Dym, I could now confidently accept Jo's offer to move over to her team.

So, I am going to have a new job, a new boss and a whole new team to manage. I went over to meet the team this afternoon (I think Jo was worried I might change my mind if she left it for another day), and although the team were very much younger than my current team, they seemed a good bunch. It will be another month before I will be working with them, but most seemed genuinely pleased to have a new boss and, although one lad was very much giving off an "I only work here to fund my partying, dude!" kind of vibe (and looked and smelt like he had just come straight from the latest one), collectively this was a team I could work with, and we could hopefully enjoy ourselves at the same time.

I also got to see my new management team headed up by Jo. A few faces I knew already, most notably Skelts (a good mate and fellow attendee at our regular Curry Nights) and Sally, the other half of Barney who I kick lumps out of every week at Monday night football (purely reciprocal). Again, a good bunch that I'm sure I'm going to enjoy working with.

Saturday 16 February 2002
I'm doing okay health-wise now but still find, come the weekend, that I don't feel up to doing much, which is a shame as Mandy and I have an anniversary of sorts this weekend. I say "of sorts" because mid-February is when we first met (in 1988), and after four subsequent years of flirting, joking, and me finally building up the courage to ask her out, it was also the time of our first date in 1992. But even then there followed a period of some months where we told ourselves, and others, we were just friends. Still, as it turned out, the sort of friends that flirted a lot, saw each other most days, and regularly talked into the early hours on the phone at night, but just friends. So, you see, even though, in hindsight, we were clearly kidding ourselves over the friendship thing, it does make the start of our relationship a little tricky to pin-point.

The signs were there of course, right from Day One of my new job at the company that Mandy herself had only joined as a secretary a few months before. It was all quite exciting for a small-town boy, commuting in on the train the 20 miles from my home town, and seeing hundreds of fresh-faced lads and lasses, just like me, filing into the numerous buildings with my new employer's name emblazoned across them. When, an hour or so later, the most gorgeous-looking one of those lasses asked me into the Divisional Director's (temporarily vacant) office to take my photo for our department's photo board, I knew I was going to like it there.

"I like your tie" said Mandy from behind the camera, and gave me this huge smile. I mumbled something about that being marriage talk where I come from, and do you know it's only now, 14 years later, I realise how prophetic that statement was. Or do I mean pathetic? Either way, I blushed so much I had the pinkest, shiniest face on that divisional photo board for years to come.

Monday 11 March 2002
I've been with the new team for a couple of months now and it's proving a challenge, but one which I am enjoying. The main test with this team, so far, has been more about the volume of tasks that need to be completed, and how accurately, rather than their difficulty. Given the poor quality and low quantity of the work that was being carried out in the team before I joined, and the flak the team had got as a result, morale was initially a big problem, too. However, I'm pretty confident I know what is needed to improve our work standards and my normal, very honest, but (hopefully) fair approach seems to be going down well with the team, even if it's not always what they want to hear.

Things seem to be going okay health-wise, or so I'm trying to convince myself. You see, although things still don't feel quite right, the twice-weekly six-a-side football is still acting as my own personal, very enjoyable, confirmation that there can't be much, if anything, wrong with me. Even the aforementioned post-match trots have reduced to just every now and again and, with me pushing myself physically in these matches to prove I am alright, I am now fitter than any time since I was a teenager. Also, the tablets the neurologist has prescribed to me are still doing the trick by taking the edge off the headache, and helping me sleep. I do feel like a zombie some days, but work is going well, and I love the football, so it seems a small price to pay.

Tuesday 26 March 2002
I had a very odd experience last week. Last Friday I joined some mates for one of our regular "Curry Nights", which I was chuffed to be doing as I hadn't been out properly since my health issues started in September. Things started off really well and I remember having a great time, but it went pear-shaped at some point, with me ending up in A&E,

and before the curry part of the evening had even occurred. It's all a bit hazy to be honest, but I know my head really started to hurt, then there was some form of collapse on my part and a semi-conscious period where my concerned, but inebriated, mate Macca repeatedly told me I was okay and he loved me. Also an ambulance ride to the hospital, during which a now unconcerned, but still inebriated, Macca repeatedly told the lady paramedic he loved her. And eventually, some hours later, after A&E could find no obvious reason for my problems, I was allowed to go home after I assured all and sundry I felt fine, or at least no worse than I feel most of the time.

Even now, I still haven't a clue what happened, but other than my now semi-normal symptoms of headache and mental fogginess, I feel okay. I wondered if someone had slipped something in my drink, or if it's something to do with the tablets I'm on, even though, as instructed I deliberately stopped them for a few days prior to having any alcohol. One of the conditions of A&E letting me go was that I would arrange a follow-up appointment with my doctor. However, as I'm feeling relatively okay now, and I'm shortly due to have Dr Dym say there's nothing wrong with me, I'll wait until then I think. I know in myself that I'm not right as there are too many strange things happening to me, but nobody seems to be able to find anything wrong. It's frustrating as hell.

Thursday 25 April 2002
Met with Dr Dym today after four really good weeks. The headache has eased off a lot, and cognitively my head feels pretty clear, except for first thing in the morning when it takes a while to shake the cobwebs away. Physically things are going well also and, as a result, I have been advised to reduce the tablets I'm on with a view to stopping them completely over the next few weeks. I'm quite pleased about that because, as much as they may have helped with the headache and sleep, I want to know how much the ongoing issues I've experienced may be due to the tablets themselves. And with things going better than they have for a long while, I think now is the time to find out.

Work is also going very well, I'm pleased to say. The team has improved immensely now, and whilst we still have a way to go to be performing at the high level I want us to be at, I'm confident this is in sight. I hate to say it but, if anything, this new role hasn't proved quite as testing as I had hoped. But that could be just because I'm feeling much sharper now, so it's sensible to see how things go for a bit I think.

Monday 27 May 2002

Today was the day I thought I was going to die. Well not actually today as I am writing this some considerable time later but, for the purposes of this diary format (which in retrospect was somewhat ambitious) let's go with "today". Yes, 27 May 2002 was the day I thought my time was up which, from my point of view, would have been a shame. I mean for starters, I was at work, and whilst it was a Monday (so the right side of the weekend to pop your clogs), let's face it nobody should leave this mortal coil when at work. Kick the bucket while playing football? Or having a pint with a mate? Maybe at home with my beautiful wife? Yes, yes and yes, but at work? Absolutely not, so it's just as well I'm still here talking like a jessie about thinking I was going to die. But let me at least elaborate on what happened.

I can't elaborate on what happened, I was barely conscious. Or at least if I was, I wasn't really with it. It was as if someone had turned off the lights. What I do know is that, all of a sudden, I had felt really strange and I had the mother of all headaches. At some point I went over to the team adjacent to mine to tell my mate, and fellow member of my management team, Skelts, that I was going home. Apparently when talking to Skelts, I initially crouched down, wobbled a bit, and then collapsed on to the floor next to him. When I opened my eyes it was like I was in a dream. But not a nice dream. My head felt really fuzzy, I didn't know where I was, and when I tried to lift my arm to fend off the blurry army of people around me, my arm wouldn't co-operate. I tried to get up, but just felt completely weak and couldn't raise myself off the ground or even make myself understood. I remember Mandy being there after a while, and some bloke in a green outfit talking very loudly to me, but very little else. I don't know at which point, and if I heard someone say as much, but I distinctly remember thinking I've had a stroke....I'm 32 and I'm going to die from a sodding stroke.

Thursday 13 June 2002

I haven't died! And what's more, I'm home from hospital now too. I've been observed, CT-scanned and lumber-punched so much that my lumber now feels more punch-drunk than Frank Bruno at a 'punch-drunk ex-boxers can get drunk on as much punch as they like' party. Amazingly, none of these tests were conclusive, so currently there is no easy explanation for what I experienced, or the numbness I am still experiencing on one side of my body. There is a rare form of migraine that mimics stroke-like symptoms, but these are not something I've ever had, and none of the doctors suggesting it have personally come across it before. All I know for sure is that my head is really fuzzy, my speech is either slurred, slow or both, and for the first time in my life I also seem to have a stutter. If it wasn't for seeing Mandy look so worried all the time, the whole situation would be laughable. I'm trying to make light of it, and stop Mandy from worrying, but I have to admit, it's scared me.

Monday 22 July 2002
I'm feeling lots better now and, frustrating as it is not knowing what's wrong with me, it's also really embarrassing. So many people have now asked me what it is that has caused me all these problems and I have nothing to tell them. I'm sure some of them think that it's stress-related and I'm having some kind of breakdown, but other than not knowing what's wrong with me, I'm not stressed! I've got nothing else to be stressed about!! I enjoy my job, I am very happily married to an amazing lady, and up until these health issues cropped up, I had a full and active social life. Take into account my football too, and the occasional nice holiday, and my life is, or was, pretty perfect. So no, it's not stress. Of that much I am sure. But what is it then? Even if severe migraines explain some of what I have been through, what about the rest of the time? It's been ten months now. It just doesn't make any sense.

Wednesday 21 August 2002
I tried to go back to work a few weeks ago, and initially it felt great. I was only doing a few hours in the afternoons, and nothing too taxing, but it felt really good to be back doing something practical, and interacting with people again. But after the first day, it seemed to get harder and harder. Although, I deliberately avoided working in the mornings, as this is when my head still feels at its foggiest, even the afternoon slots I was working left me increasingly tired. When it came to go to work on the fourth afternoon I was still in bed. I could barely move and my head was really banging. No-one was surprised when I called in sick, and although I assured Jo I would try to go in again the following day, she told me to stay home as she could tell I wasn't right. And she was correct, I've not been able to make it back into work since.

Tuesday 29 October 2002
I had an absolutely amazing day today. Or at least as amazing a day as is possible when a doctor tells you that you have a potentially life changing illness. Let me explain.

A few weeks back Mandy forced me to go and see our GP. This was partly because, even on a good day, I still have the headache and brain fog, but mostly because I've been really down which is totally unlike me. It's understandable I think, given that since my collapse in May all my attempts to return to work have failed dismally. Also, the hospital seems to have lost all interest in me since the numbness in my arm and leg improved, and rather inconsiderately on my part I haven't repeated the whole collapsing thing. But in all seriousness, my health issues have been going on for over a year now and I just felt back at square one, with still no idea of what is wrong with me.

So Mandy and I sat there in front of our GP and, as the frustrations of the last year finally decided to come out, I cried like a baby. Bloody attention seeker! Luckily for me, my GP didn't call me a bloody attention seeker, or say there wasn't anything wrong with me, but instead listened patiently before recommending I see a Dr Martin Lee, whose speciality my GP had only learned of the day previously.

Our subsequent appointment with Martin Lee today was immense. After speaking to him for just a few minutes, he started to describe to me (i.e. not vice versa) what some of my symptoms were, and he accurately pinpointed when they were at their worst. The whole meeting was a revelation as he explained he has a special interest in something called Chronic Fatigue Syndrome (or CFS) which his own daughter had suffered from for many years. He quickly explained that the illness used to be more commonly called ME (or Myalgic Encephalitis), but neither the new nor the old names are particularly helpful given the broad range of symptoms it can encapsulate, and their severity. He felt I must have caught a virus of some description in Florida last September before leading on to ME/CFS.

To be frank, I no longer cared how I got it, or even what it was called. To me, the main thing was that I knew what was wrong with me and I could finally get on with beating it. Martin urged caution, as although ME/CFS patients diagnosed quickly tended to have a better record of full recovery, it had taken over 12 months for my own diagnosis. This meant that I had a long, difficult road ahead, with a possibility that I might not get back to where I was previously. "Not me, Doc" I said, "I'll do anything and everything to get back to normal". Martin reiterated the need for a slow cautious approach, but in my mind I was already thinking timescales.

On the way home I shed a few more tears, but this time they were tears of relief. I also managed to make Mandy laugh for the first time in months - "ME? Blimey, that means I've got Yuppie Flu!" I said, "Mum and Dad will be so proud, we've not had a yuppie in the family before!!"

Tuesday 6 November 2002
So, Myalgic Encephalitis, or Chronic Fatigue Syndrome then. Both names are a bit of a mouthful, so I can see why it's more commonly referred to as ME/CFS. Both crap names if I'm honest, which as Martin explained, makes an already misunderstood illness even more confusing. I mean, fatigue isn't even my main symptom, and from what I have been able to find out, it's the same for most people with this illness. Sure, fatigue is one symptom, but then one of the symptoms of Parkinsons is shaking and that's not referred to as Chronic Shaking Syndrome!

For me, I think I'll stick to the abbreviated versions of the illness and, given that I'm already feeling like it's all about me (i.e. me, myself and I), to keep typing "ME" is going to make me feel even more self-obsessed. So, it's a rubbish name, that sounds like they brainstormed a group of toddlers to come up with it, but out of the two I'll be using "CFS" from here on in I think. Which is just as well as Martin said the wider medical profession no longer accepts the term "ME". Of course, there is also the American version (which also includes the words Immune Dysfunction) but "CFIDS" just sounds like something you might catch from a Bangkok lady boy. Yep, CFS it is. Still crap though.

The good thing is that my recovery, as part of Martin's locally-based support program, starts here. It was the desperate lack of help available to his daughter that stimulated Martin to seek Health Authority approval and funding for it, and I get the impression it's been quite a battle to set the program up. It's clear therefore, that I'm fortunate to be getting access to that level of help, and together with actually knowing what's wrong with me now, it's a massive step forward compared to where I have been. There's plenty to be positive about.

Monday 11 November 2002
I recently attended a medical at the John Radcliffe Hospital in Oxford. You see, after an initial period of sickness on full pay, my salary ceases in favour of a health insurance scheme that my employer has in place. Instead of a salary, this scheme aims to pay a reduced income to an

employee who is long-term ill or disabled, for up to three years. The only issue is that I have to attend a medical first, with a doctor appointed by the insurance company who run the scheme, in order that he can confirm to them that I am indeed unwell and not some skiving charlatan out for an easy life.

Now, I'm a logical person and, logically, given that I clearly tried to continue to work with this illness initially, and since I stopped work I have done everything I possibly can to get back, this medical should have just been a ticking-boxes exercise. However, in the short time I have known about CFS it's become clear that there is no single definitive test to say if someone has it. Combine that with the fact that there appears to be few experts in the field and I was, understandably, pretty concerned about who this doctor would be, and what he would do to me to try to confirm my CFS diagnosis. As it turned out, my concerns were spot on.

Although Mandy drove us, by the time we had travelled to, and navigated around Oxford for the medical, I was already tired. But that was nothing compared to how I felt an hour or so later. Don't get me wrong, I know the doctor had a responsibility to do a thorough job, and aside from some discomfort and a few groans on my part, the physical side of the medical was hard, but tolerable. The real problems started when the doctor moved on to the cognitive side of things, and his approach became progressively more interrogative. He really worked me over - to the point where I really wouldn't have been surprised if he had grabbed me around the throat, shone a light in my face and put on a Herr Flick accent. He even had Mandy in tears at one point I was struggling so much in the face of his onslaught. I guess his aggressive way of constantly interrupting me, and sternly instructing me to read more quickly, or repeat information I was clearly struggling to absorb, was his way of finding out how my cognitive functioning really was. Honestly, a healthy man would just have thumped the bloke. It was only when Mandy got upset that he seemed to realise he was taking it way too far, and sent us on our way.

Anyway, I received a letter in the post today saying that my "claim" had been approved, so although I feel shattered and have the headache from hell, I think it was all worth it. It means I'll continue to be employed and have an income, albeit a significantly reduced one, for up to three years. Hopefully I won't need anywhere near as long as that to get back to work.

Tuesday 14 January 2003

I went and saw a Traditional Chinese Acupuncturist today after my deceased grandfather recommended it via our family medium. What's that? What do you mean you had to read that sentence twice?? Surely everyone has a family medium through which their deceased loved ones offer them medical advice??? Well, okay then, for those out there that have never had Traditional Chinese Acupuncture, messages from the dead or a family medium, let me elaborate.

For some years, my mum and my sisters have all visited a nice lady called Greta who, with the help of her spirit guide and various deceased members of my family, has provided a number of unnervingly accurate nuggets of information. The benefits they gain from this range from reassurance on certain subjects to, if they are honest, simply addressing their curiosity and downright nosiness on others. Anyway, on her most recent visit to see Greta, Mum was told that my Gramps was sorry to see of my health troubles, but that I need to try acupuncture – just look in the telephone directory, he/Greta said, under Chinese medicine. Sod it, I thought, I've tried just about everything else, what have I got to lose? So I looked out the local directory, found that the only Chinese medicine place listed was just a 15-minute walk down the road, and booked an appointment.

Hanqiao (pronounced Han–Chow) is the Chinese doctor I saw today, and after a long discussion about my symptoms and recent health, she explained that she would definitely like to give me some acupuncture. She said it wouldn't hurt, the needles are very small, I might just feel a little prick as she inserts a few in around my head, legs and arms. What she didn't explain was that whilst the needles don't hurt as they go in, a vain pillock who insists on raising his head to check out his reflection as soon as she leaves the room will instantly feel like someone has just wired him up to the National Grid, as a massive jolt shoots through every nerve. When I awoke 30 minutes later, Hanqiao explained that the "chi" effect of the needles often results in sleep. And if "chi" means coma-inducing shock she's spot on.

Seriously though, I was really relaxed, I had a great little kip and my headache felt the best it had in weeks. Hanqiao also waved a smoking stick of herbs called moxa around my head, which was really relaxing and smelt similar to pot (I suspect!). By the end I felt so much better I practically floated home. In fact, so impressed was I with the moxa that when Hanqiao suggested I take some of it home with me (and at £2 a stick momentarily considering buying in bulk to sell on the streets at a huge mark-up) I took two sticks to be going on with. I plan to call it my stash.

So actually, the whole Chinese medicine thing was a really good experience and I'm glad I stayed open-minded about it. Although, truth be known, with everything else I tried having such little effect on my headaches, at this stage I would have been open to buying a jar of fairy kisses from a dodgy-looking bloke driving a van with the words "miracle cures" painted along the side in still-dripping paint. But as I say, a good experience and a useful tip from my long despatched Gramps.

Wednesday 26 February 2003
Met with Martin Lee again today and already it feels like meeting up with an old friend. After so much frustration and not knowing what was wrong with me, Martin is a real godsend. At times he seems like the only person that understands what's happening to me, and what Mandy and I are going through. He's a real football nut too which helps, and I feel incredibly lucky to have him helping me. I just wish I had met him ages ago. While we were there today, I discussed my collapsing episodes with him and he thought these were probably my body's way of telling me I was asking it to do way too much, when the CFS meant it needed rest. Sound logic in hindsight, but then, in my defence, at the time I was being told time and time again, there wasn't anything wrong with me.

Since I first met Martin I have been having regular appointments with Jane, his occupational therapist, who has successfully learned to manage her own CFS. I've been doing every single thing Jane has suggested, and although some things have helped and some haven't, I feel I'm slowly getting to grips with this illness. One thing, called Cognitive Behaviour Therapy, just seems like a lot of mumbo-jumbo to me. But an approach called Pacing, where I structure every day around alternate rest and activity periods, has been a big help.

On the downside, I've discovered that I have exactly the wrong type of personality for getting over this illness. In the past, when I have been unable to do something, I have just worked harder and longer at it until I can. That approach stood me in good stead in football when I was younger, and especially in forging a decent career, but as far as CFS is concerned, that approach leads to what is known as "boom and bust" - with the second of those two adjectives proving painfully accurate on a regular basis. So Martin's prediction of a long and hard recovery is proving spot on. So bless him, seeing how frustrated I am, and how tired Mandy is looking from putting up with me, Martin has suggested we get away for some sun and relaxation, but with just two provisos: no flying, and to nowhere that requires me to have any jabs. Well that cuts it down a bit!

Monday 3 March 2003
We booked a cruise around the Mediterranean today. Yeah I know, I didn't envisage going on a cruise in my early 30s either, but if it allows us to get some guaranteed sun, without having to fly (we sail out of/into Southampton), then so be it. The cost is surprisingly reasonable, and now we've booked the cruise I'm getting more and more intrigued by it. In fact, suddenly every man and his dog seems to be an expert on the subject, with friends old and new saying they have had some brilliant cruises. Someone even suggested we should have tried cruises years ago and then perhaps I wouldn't have caught what I appear to have caught in Florida. Thanks for that!

Chapter 2 – The Maiden Voyage

Saturday 3 May 2003
About 3pm today we boarded the cruise ship Oceana and - wow! We immediately walked into an amazing Atrium at the centre of the ship which looked spectacular – it's about four stories high and, as well as a small welcoming party of P&O staff and a reception area, it houses a central sweeping staircase, floor to ceiling glass elevators, and a waterfall of all things. All in all, a very good first impression.

We didn't hang around though and quickly set off to explore, and find our cabin. The ship just seemed huge. Beautiful, but huge. What was pleasing though, and quite a relief actually, was that wherever we walked it wasn't crowded or noisy, and I think the ship should comfortably handle the 2000 or so passengers on board. It's not that I don't like crowded, noisy gatherings normally, far from it, it's just this whole CFS thing means any type of "busy" is now a real struggle, and has me diving for the exit quicker than a bashful vicar at a lap dance.

We actually found our cabin very easily. The travel agent we booked the cruise through advised us to pick one towards the middle of the ship, or "midships", and, because we needed to book a cheaper inside cabin, to go for a higher floor so it was close to the open decks. This would be handy for when Mandy ordered me to go check out the weather, check the sunbed availability, recheck the weather is still the same as ten minutes previously, etc. As a result we were on Deck A, the highest of the cabin decks and one below the main Sun Deck.

Our suitcases were already in our cabin waiting for us, which was pretty good going as the porter had only removed these from our car about 30 minutes before. And the cabin itself is fine, if a little compact, and has everything we need plus flowers and champagne, courtesy of our travel agent. We even have a cabin steward who popped along to say that, if we needed anything, just to let him know. I thought for a second he was taking the mickey when he said his name was Elvis, but it really was. I behaved myself though, and didn't make any wise-cracks at all, except for curling my lip a wee bit and saying "thank you very much" in a deep southern drawl as he left us.

By now, the excited little boy inside me wanted to get out and explore the rest of the ship, but we first needed to attend the Muster Drill, whereby the crew talk us through the emergency procedures and meeting points for the unlikely event that anything goes wrong. The drill itself was fine, and very professional, and we had no worries at all, but once it was finished, the excited little boy inside me had turned into a very tired little boy; I was pooped. So, with dinner starting at 6.30pm, I thought it best to save the exploring for later and have a nap, as it had been a long day already for a lightweight like me. I think Mand would have loved to explore too, but she said she wanted to unpack, hang up her dresses, and get glammed up for dinner, so all good.

Sunday 4 May 2003
Dinner last night was terrific, even allowing for a slightly disappointing start when we found out we were on a table for four rather than a table for two. Pre-CFS, I would have had a "more the merrier" viewpoint, but we asked for a two because, over the course of the cruise, I will undoubtedly prove hard work. However, Richard and Joyce, our table companions, instantly showed they are warm and understanding people as we were forced to drop in a few details of my illness (I didn't want to scare them off, but I was already forgetting words for the most obvious everyday items). It helps that Joyce is a nurse, and an added bonus is that they are experienced cruisers, so have started to share a few tips with us that we would otherwise not know. For example, having a fish course instead of a soup, or the ability to have two puds!!!

The food and service was excellent during dinner and our two waiters, Glenn and Rafi, explained that they would be taking care of the four of us at the same table every evening. They were efficient, friendly and in Glenn's case, he quickly got the measure of me, as seeing how much I had enjoyed my dessert (I didn't lick the plate, honest) he asked if I would like seconds. "Do large furry mammals defecate in wooded terrain?" said I, or words to that effect, and almost immediately a second serving appeared as if by magic.

After dinner, although there was a very tempting show on at the theatre, I was totally knackered, so Mandy dragged me reluctantly back to the cabin for an early night (not the sexy kind!). When we got there, Elvis had been in to tidy up a bit, straighten towels, and turn down the beds, so combined with the dimmed lighting and a chocolate on each pillow, the cabin looked really welcoming. I was naked, clean-toothed and fast asleep quicker than Mandy could say "hey, there was a chocolate on my pillow a minute ago".

This morning, we awoke to a little bit of movement in the ship, which I'm sure wasn't too bad by regular cruisers' standards, but sufficient to gently rock us awake. We had been told to expect as much as we approached, and crossed, the infamous Bay of Biscay, but hadn't expected it quite this early on. To be fair it was fine when we were laid in bed and, even when we were up and about, it was just a little like walking through a moving train carriage. So we decided to go and get some breakfast and try to acquire our "sea legs".

Unfortunately we made the mistake of going for breakfast in the buffet-style Plaza Restaurant. A mistake because The Plaza is at the very front, and very top, of the ship which, we realised later, was the worst position to be in as, if anything, it exaggerates the ship's movement. I didn't feel too bad, and am not a big breakfast person anyway, but poor old Mand, who always sinks a decent breakfast, was feeling quite nauseous. In fact, due to feeling better the more horizontal she was, she sank so low in her chair that everyone else in the restaurant must have thought she was carrying out some kind of secret surveillance operation. So we swiftly returned to the cabin and Mandy stayed there for much of the day, watching the occasional movie and taking full advantage of the room service menu.

Monday 5 May 2003
Good news. Due to the sea becoming a little calmer, or possibly her acquiring her sea legs, cruise legs or even her "right I'm on bloody holiday so I'm going to get dolled up for dinner if it kills me" legs, Mandy was able to leave the cabin and accompany me to dinner last night. In fact, Mandy felt so much better that we went to the post-dinner show too. And as luck would have it, the show we missed the previous night was being performed again, and came thoroughly recommended by Richard and Joyce. So after another excellent dinner we popped along to the Footlights Theatre.

When we got there, the theatre was pretty big (it seats about 800 I think) and, due to tonight's dress code being one of the cruise's four formal nights (i.e. dicky-bows and dinner jackets for the fellas, just looking gorgeous for the ladies), the place looked like a penguin enclosure at feeding time. Following some advice I had received from a fellow CFS sufferer, we took the longest/quietest route towards the front of the theatre and sat at the back of the front section, about nine or ten rows back – the theory being that you are not too close to the stage so the action and lighting is overwhelming, and you are not far enough back to be under the loudspeakers they tend to hang from the ceiling. We also got there early, and let the place clear at the end, to avoid the worst of any crowding, and it all worked perfectly. The show, "Another Opening, Another Show", was terrific and full of good singers, and scantily-clad dancers performing a selection of West End numbers. What's not to like!

Then, when we awoke this morning, we found the sea to be calm and we both felt fine. A little tired, but fine. So we spent much of the morning exploring the ship and it truly is lovely. It's about three years old, but you wouldn't know it, everything looks brand new. And it's starting to feel smaller now that we are getting our bearings. After a bit, we had a rest and a latte in Tiffany's, one of the open-fronted lounge bars at the top of the Atrium, which was great for a spot of people watching.

Weather-wise, it was a wee bit cloudy this morning but we had some sunny spells this afternoon, so after a swift lunch in The Plaza we took the opportunity to grab a few "rays" on the Promenade Deck. Mandy nipped to the on-board shops a couple of times which is a worry, as on her return, her eyes had acquired a similar look to that girl with the swivelling head in The Exorcist. That normally means she's spotted something expensive and is plotting how best I can surprise her with it. To distract her, I suggested we go to afternoon tea which turned out to be very civilised – waiters in waistcoats and white gloves serving tea, finger sandwiches and a selection of scones and cakes. Far too much food to be honest, given we had already had a decent sized lunch, and dinner was only a couple of hours away but, you know what they say, when in Rome.

Tuesday 6 May 2003
I'm beginning to realise that dinner on a cruise ship is always an occasion. Yes there is the less formal (and more flexible) option of the ship's buffet restaurant, but most passengers seem to instead enjoy the formality of dining at the same table and with the same people each night, and being waited on by the same silver service-style waiters. I have to say we love it, and last night's dinner was no exception. I also got to try mussels for the first time and really enjoyed them. I had always fancied trying them, but had never previously wanted to risk them on a normal meal out in case I didn't like them, or they disagreed with me. But what's good about this cruising lark is that you can try a new dish and, if you don't like it, either change it for something else or

just console yourself in the knowledge that there are about 300 more courses to come. I'm beginning to realise that hungry is one thing we certainly won't be on a cruise.

After dinner we had a couple of drinks with Richard and Joyce in Tiffany's Bar, and I'm glad we did. We still managed a much-needed early night, with tomorrow's first port of call in mind, but Richard and Joyce are proving great company. They really are a nice couple and Richard especially has almost as strong a country-bumpkin accent as I have – it's just his is more Suffolk, and mine is more West Country. Anyway, we had a couple of drinks and a few laughs, and then it was the, all of two-minute, walk up to bed.

And so to this morning, and Gibraltar - our first sail-in and our first port of call. It had been recommended that we get up early to see "The Rock" as we sailed in, and courtesy of my semi-regular insomnia I was up very early. I then learned a very valuable lesson for future sail-ins; namely that a sail-in can happen quite, err, slowly. Consequently, if you are up and about early and your port of destination is just a dot in the distance, you don't necessarily have to turn your video camera on straightaway. Or at all really, for the first 90 minutes or so. If you do, as I did, the sail-in could become more of a snail-in, and you could get very cold, very bored and faced with some major editing requirements on your return home. I was told I would never forget my first sail-in but hey, just in case, I have 110 minutes of video footage to remind me.

Once Oceana was "alongside", we excitedly made our way down to the bottom of the Atrium so we could rejoin terra firma and, 2½ sea days after leaving good old Blighty, these old sea dogs had arrived in, well, Blighty again, I guess, given Gibraltar's British sovereignty for the last 200 years or so. And actually, after not knowing what to expect, other than a large rock and some very streetwise apes, we quite liked it. The walk through the aptly named Main Street was just like walking through a British High Street. A warmer, sunnier High Street admittedly, but it felt very British, albeit with a more relaxed Mediterranean feel to it. It even had red post boxes, and an occasional British "bobbie" on the beat, although they did look rather Hispanic. At one end of Main Street there was a nice town square where Mandy parked me on a bench under a tree, and off she popped for some shopping.

On her return, we did briefly discuss going up the Rock to see the view (apparently you can see Africa on a clear day) and the infamous apes, but I was pretty tired, so we decided to grab the shuttle bus back to the ship for a rest. And it was a good job we did because, when we got to the dock, we saw something that we had been told never happens on a cruise – shock, horror, there was a lengthening queue to get back through security. Joking apart, this was a bit of a worry as, due to the CFS, although walking is okay, I can't stand for long. Anyway, after first opting for chivalry (i.e. refusing to let Mandy queue on her own), and then eventually having no choice but to go and sit on a bench whilst Mandy kept our place, I was in a bit of a mess by the time we got back on the ship. I hate asking for special treatment, and the whole situation is still alien to me, but I felt physically shattered and also humiliated at sitting there in front of all those other passengers, many of them twice my age, who were forced to queue. I will need to take it easy tonight.

Wednesday 7 May 2003
Yesterday's queuing, or more specifically the effect it had on me, was a bit of a wake-up call and shows I can't take my CFS for granted, no matter how well we believe we are managing it. I think I was getting a bit ahead of myself, and letting the otherwise great time we are having on this cruise, make me quite blasé about it. Well, that'll teach me, because one unanticipated eventuality, and it came back to bite me firmly in the bum. But things had been going well up until then, and following a quiet evening in the cabin to recover from yesterday, we plan to have a nice relaxing day at sea today. So this morning I'm off to play five-a-side football on the sports deck. I wish!! Only joking, just want to show Mandy I'm fine today and ensure she relaxes.

I did however just grab a quick drink in the on-board pub, The Yacht & Compass. Mandy was happy sunning herself up on the Sun Deck for a bit, and was so engrossed in her book that I'm not sure she even realised I had gone. I'm pleased to say I had a very pleasant 30 minutes or so sat at the bar next to a Chinese gentleman who was also on his first cruise. Although I'm not sure we understood each other 100% of the time, we had a good chat until it was time for me to return to the boss, at which point I shook my new acquaintance by the hand, and belatedly told him my name. With me being terrible with names anyway, let alone those from other cultures that require extra care with their pronunciation, I readied myself in full on concentration mode to catch his – "And my name is Gary" he said. Go figure!

Thursday 8 May 2003
Mission accomplished yesterday. We just chilled all day and I'm starting to realise that a cruise ship is the perfect place for such inactivity. Apologies if this sounds a little like a Craig David song, but we chilled by the pool, we chilled over a latte, we chilled on the Prom Deck and we made love 'til Wednesday (actually, that last one is from a Craig David song, but I live in hope). Absolutely perfect day, and exactly what we had hoped our cruise would be like.

The show was good last night too, the second of the production shows by the Stadium Theatre Company. Again, it came highly recommended by Richard and Joyce who, in our absence, had been to see it the previous evening. It was good, and at 45 minutes duration just the right length for someone with my dodgy attention span…..oooh look, a balloon!

Today is our second port day and we are at Calvi on the island of Corsica which, courtesy of yesterday's Port Presentation, I know to be most famous for where Napoleon was either born, died or imprisoned (said my attention span was short!). It's a pretty little place and we settled for a short stroll around the fortress and its walls, overlooking a charming little harbour and the bay where the good ship Oceana sat majestically. In fact, that reminds me (yes, okay smart arse, short-term memory is still an issue too), as Calvi is too small for Oceana to berth normally, we were "tendered" into shore from the ship by a series of the ship's little motor boats, or "tenders". It was quite fun actually, and demonstrating that I had not learnt anything at all from needlessly videoing Tuesday's lengthy sail-in, I videoed the entire journey from the window of our tender boat.

One good thing though, we made sure that we avoided any possibility of queuing by going back to the ship on an early tender, and whilst everyone else was still ashore, caught some sun on the Sun Deck all afternoon – it was lovely and quiet on board, like having our own very large yacht. And it enabled us to get plenty of rest and relaxation in time for a really big day tomorrow.

Friday 9 May 2003
Yippee, it's the day we've been waiting for. Partly because it's my mother-in-law's birthday (so need to phone home), but also because today we are in Civitavecchia! No? Never heard of it?? Me neither, but

let me rephrase - today we are in Civitavecchia, just down the road from ROME!! So we're excited. And a little anxious, as with Rome being a 75-minute drive inland, the shortest excursion available is about seven hours long. However, we've been assured ours is a coach-based tour and, although we get the afternoon to ourselves, we can roam (see what I did there) at our own pace, and when we are knackered (okay, when I am knackered) we can just park our bums in a café and watch the world go by. But anyway, got to go now, need to smuggle out a couple of croissants from the Plaza in case we need an urgent mid-roam/Rome snack, and then it's jump on bus time.

Saturday 10 May 2003
What a fantastic day yesterday. A long day, as I anticipated, but some totally amazing sights and we managed to pace it quite well with plenty of rest spells, so not feeling as bad as I feared. But wow, it seemed like every time we went around another Roman corner there was yet another amazing place. If the UK had just one of the sights we saw yesterday, it would be the most visited place in the country, but Rome has dozens of them all over the place. A truly amazing (note to self: don't say amazing for a bit) city and Mandy's new favourite place.

We started off by being coached to the Coliseum, and although the queue to go inside was too long for me to stand in, just walking around the outside of such an iconic place was terrific. We then went to the Forum which was interesting, in part thanks to our excellent Italian guide, although not all of our group chose to listen to her, and one fella's ears only pricked up briefly on the mention of the Vestal Virgins. He quickly lost interest again when he realised these weren't a current offering.

Next we were coached to St Peter's Square and our guide showed us around the inside of the Basilica, which was stunning. She also pointed out the Pope's window that he stands at most Sundays. The crowds were getting a wee bit busy for me at this stage so, as our guide was due to leave us shortly anyway, we said we would meet up with her later at the pre-planned rendezvous point, and went for a much-needed rest. As luck would have it, the towering colonnades that encircle the plaza were quite quiet to one side and had plenty of inbuilt seating, so we sat there for a while watching the Pope's window and guiltily chewing on our contraband croissants. We also saw some of the Swiss soldiers who guard the various entrances to the Vatican, but honestly, in their bright orange and blue jester-like uniforms, short of tickling them to death, they really didn't look like they could fight off a group of rampaging toddlers. They posed for us to take a nice photo though.

The tough decision then was where to go in the remaining few hours before our coach was due to take us back to the ship. Even after our rest I was still pretty pooped, so due to my minimal walking requirement and Mandy finally narrowing down her must-sees to just two, we jumped in a taxi. Firstly to the Spanish Steps, which was adorned with beautiful flowers and not-so-beautiful tourists. Needless to say we didn't climb any more than a few steps, but we happily sat on one, admiring the scene and taking some photos. Indeed, it was when I was taking the crucial "Mandy on Spanish Steps" shot that I think I was relieved of about 150 Euros by a passing pickpocket. Oh well, you live and you learn and it's no biggy; we had more cash on us and transport back to the ship (not to mention travel insurance), so it could have been worse.

Finally, from there we strolled down to where our map said the Trevi Fountain was. Unusually for us, we found it first time and immediately realised two things. One, the Trevi fountain is bigger and more stunning than we had expected. Two, the plaza in which the Trevi is situated is only marginally bigger than the Trevi itself. Consequently, all coin throwing, photo-taking and general appreciation of said monument had to be very carefully timed and/or involve the use of a carefully placed elbow, hip, buttock or, as a last resort, both arms held out pleadingly to one's sides in the (hopefully) universal sign for "Hey, I'm trying to get a piccie here of my missus chucking away perfectly good Euro-zone currency". Anyway, after that it was back to our rendezvous point, and the sleep of a thousand sleeps on the coach back to port. A brilliant day.

Today we are in Livorno which is the main port to access places such as Pisa and Florence. Indeed, many of our fellow passengers are booked on day-long excursions that include visits to both these places. However, having anticipated a certain level of exhaustion following our exertions in Rome, we booked a short, partly coach-based, tour to Florence. And whilst tired, I'm determined to see some of Florence, even if it's just sitting in a café for a bit.

Sunday 11 May 2003
A slightly less active day yesterday, but it still felt like we did and saw a lot. Our excursion was, as promised, partly coach-based with regular

stops, starting with the Ponte Vecchio, a medieval stone bridge lined on each side by shops. Me being me, I videoed and photographed it from every conceivable angle and somehow managed, on fully utilising my zoom facility, to pick out Richard and Joyce about half a mile away on their walking tour. Between you and me, they looked like they were struggling a bit as they were falling behind the rest of the group. For once I might not be the only one at dinner tonight looking like they've just walked the equator.

We also wandered past the cathedral, which I really liked despite all the mad people that our guide pointed out, who had climbed the million or so steps up to the top of the Dome, or Duomo. The guide explained that the view from the top was fantastico – and I would hope so too after all those steps. We opted to settle for the ground floor view, maybe in a different life, hey?

By this time, we were well into the walking part of the tour, so I thought it would be wise to sit and rest for a bit. So, having been taken to an attractive building called the Piazzo Della Signoria by our guide, we told her we would meet up with her later, and found a quiet place to sit in the adjacent square. It would have been nice to have a wander around inside the piazzo, but even after a rest, my legs were telling me not to move far. So we walked 30 feet to the nearest café and, albeit pricey due to its location, drank coffee and relaxed our whole final 90 minutes or so in Florence. And actually it was really nice. We were sat almost directly opposite the statue of Michelangelo's David, and his refreshingly small genitalia, not to mention the window that the disembowelled police inspector is thrown out of in the film Hannibal. Who says I don't appreciate culture.

Tuesday 13 May 2003
Yes, yes, well done Sherlock, I've skipped a day because, due to our Rome/Florence combo, we were both (yes both) shattered. But what I can say is that on Sunday morning we awoke to the beautiful bay of Santa Margherita, which is on the north west coast of Italy, right at the top of the boot. It was another tender port so Oceana was parked well out into the bay, and the sea was so calm that Captain Burgoine barely had need to drop anchor. Santa Margherita itself looked so beautiful that, despite me not feeling well, we nipped ashore briefly to walk around the harbour. It was charming, and, needless to say the tape in my video

camera took another bashing. The small trip ashore also meant that I had got off the ship in every port so far.

Sadly however, we missed Marseille yesterday. Well, when I say "we", I mean Mandy and myself, as Oceana and the majority of her passengers were very much there. We were sort of there too, but stayed on board the whole day lying on a sun-lounger, as I felt like I had gone a few rounds with Giant Haystacks and desperately wanted to be okay for Barcelona tomorrow, our final port. Saying that, my heart very nearly ruled my head when, momentarily, we considered going ashore for a walk and I even took a look, from the Sun Deck, over the side of the ship to check out how far it was to the shuttle bus. But when I realised that the grey coloured carpet running alongside the ship to the shuttle bus wasn't a carpet at all, but actually a long line of our more mature grey-haired fellow cruisers, we gave it up as a bad idea. Shame, that's the first one we've missed.

But a big positive of staying on board, and getting some much-needed rest, was that we were able to enjoy a "full" evening for the first time in a while, i.e. pre-dinner cocktails, then a smashing dinner, followed by another brilliant show by The Stadium Theatre Company. My aim is to add a post-dinner drink to that schedule for the rest of the cruise, but we'll see how things are once we've got Barca under our belts. The show last night was called Moulin, based around, as you will have guessed, songs and dances connected with the Moulin Rouge, all finished off with a dozen or so Stadium Theatre Company dancers can-can'ing their frilly knickers at me. But enough of my troubles, we are now safely berthed in the port of Barcelona, and I've not even been out on deck yet.

Wednesday 14 May 2003
"Barcelona, it was the first time that we met. Barcelona, how could I forget...?" Or at least I think that was how Freddie Mercury phrased it. And he was bang on, a truly lovely, unforgettable city that draws you in right from the start. I always tend to like anywhere in Spain, but Barcelona - which when said correctly in the local dialect (with the "c" pronounced as a hard "th") should see you spit down your shirt slightly - is my new favourite.

After leaving the Oceana straight after breakfast, a five minute shuttle bus ride saw us dropped just along from the bottom of La Rambla, a tree-lined pedestrianised street with shops, craft stalls and, even at 10am, street performers. It was still pretty quiet at the time which meant that many of the shops still hadn't opened (yippee!), and we could just have a peaceful stroll, nipping down the occasional side street or into the famous La Boqueria market. But the highlight of La Rambla for me was Placa Reial, a little square just off to one side. Architecturally it is stunning and, although I'm told it really comes to life at night, it seemed just perfect at that time of the day, with the morning sun poking through a slight cloud cover and the smell of freshly-brewed coffee from the tiny cafés.

As we reached the top of La Rambla it opened up into a big, much busier square with plenty of traffic circling a large, central pedestrian area of fountains and sculptures. I stopped for a rest on a bench whilst Mandy nipped into a large department store (I knew it was going too well). Then on her return, and due partly to the carrier bags of clothing she had now magically acquired, we opted to take one of the hop-on-hop-off tourist buses, to enable us to see maximum Barca for minimal effort. We sat right at the front on the top deck for the best possible view, plugged in our commentary headphones, and pretty much stayed there enjoying our tour for about an hour. It meant that we got to see little bits of a number of places like the Nou Camp Stadium, the Gaudi buildings etc. It gave us a real feel for the place even if it wasn't the more preferable, in-depth, visit to one or two of the sights which was a bit beyond me at this stage of the cruise.

We finally decided to hop off the bus at the Sagrada Familia, Gaudi's cathedral that he started in the late 1800s. It's unfinished due to a combination of funding issues, war and the continual stream of Spanish builders saying "of course we'll be done by Christmas senor", only to siesta their way through most of the 20th century. But what they have done is (mostly) build an awesome, unique building that, judging by the queues to walk up it, people flock to. As for us, we settled for a nice casual walk around the outside taking a number of photos and some video footage (did I mention I have a camcorder?) before jumping in a taxi back to the ship with Chinese Gary and his wife, who just happened to be hailing said means of transport at the same time.

Thursday 15 May 2003
Since we left Barcelona on Tuesday evening we have had two long sea days full of sun, rest, relaxation, and consumed more food than a small third world nation could reasonably expect in a whole year. We even

had something called a Chocoholics' Buffet, which clearly needs no explanation other than to say that every conceivable food, drink and table decoration was made of chocolate – and all on offer, on a help-yourself basis no less, from every single available surface within the Medina Restaurant. From the feeding frenzy that followed you would have thought that Captain Burgoine had announced he was about to abandon us on a desert island, and in readiness everyone was required to consume as many calories of cocoa-based foodstuff as was physically possible. It was heaven. And heaven is a place I may well be residing in soon should my arteries see any more chocolate this cruise.

We've also had a Neptune's Feast which you can get a measure of simply by substituting the word "seafood" for "chocolate" in the previous paragraph. Again, absolutely lovely and beautifully presented. But it's not all been food, food, food. Oh no, now that the port days are over, and obviously we're all spending more time on board, everyone is making up for lost time with their daytime activities and general socialising. Not sure if I missed it during the first few port-free days but when at sea, Oceana's Atrium is a real social hub for everything from shopping to slurping cocktails, to schmoozing with the occasional passing dancer (couldn't help myself, sorry).

Sadly though, as we are now into our last couple of days on board, every meal, drink and game of Shuffleboard (a larger, deck-based Shove Ha'penny-style game) is tinged very slightly with a little sadness. However, whereas normally at this stage of a holiday my thoughts would also start turning towards driving to an airport and a long flight home, on this cruise we have none of that as we are literally dropped off back in Southampton. If only the Bay of Biscay behaves itself tomorrow then it will be a perfectly relaxing end to a brilliant holiday.

Oh and before I forget, yesterday, while sunning ourselves in the Straits of Gibraltar, the voice of Captain Burgoine came over the tannoy to say that we would shortly be passing fellow P&O ship, Aurora, going in the other direction. What followed was a surprisingly spectacular sail-by as both sets of passengers and crew hollered and waved to their counterparts on the other ship. I can't quite put my finger on why exactly, especially as we were in the middle of the sea, and the only two ships for miles around, but I had an immense feeling of pride as I waved to the beautiful Aurora. Good luck to them - if they enjoy themselves half as much as we have, then they'll have a ball.

Friday 16 May 2003
This morning, the Atrium was the setting for a tabletop sale, selling some of the shop's merchandise at a reasonable discount. From what I could see, many of the ladies present had switched into full on combat mode and didn't care what, or who, they had to go through to get a bargain. Being a cowardly, cowardly custard I steered well clear and even Mandy initially appeared to resist the urge to join the melee. Then before I realised what was happening, she had cunningly ushered me into the Yacht & Compass and parked me on a stool next to Chinese Gary, before she then disappeared into the throng. That was okay, rather her than me, and Gary and I are now like old pals.

Over a Pina Colada, Gary started to tell me how he was originally from Shanghai and that he had moved to the UK in the 1970s. I have a Chinese friend at home so I was genuinely interested in what he was saying while I enjoyed my cocktail. Then, mid-Colada, Mandy strolled back through the door clutching not one, but two Guess handbags. "I didn't see those in the sale" I said. Pretending not to hear me, but grinning enough to confirm she had, Mandy then promptly changed the subject by asking Gary how he got his, clearly western, name. That's simple he said, when he first moved to the UK, he adopted the name "Gary" as an anglicised version of his own name, and after his musical hero….Gary Glitter! Do you know, I forgot all about the Guess handbags after that.

As I write we are now halfway across the Bay of Biscay and we're both feeling fine. I'm guessing this is partly due to us now very much having the sea legs we were yet to acquire going in the other direction, but the sea also seems much calmer. So, considering that before the cruise we were a little wary about sea sickness, we've done pretty well. There was that one day across the bay where we struggled a wee bit and Mandy stayed in the cabin for much of the day, but the other 13 days have been fine. I confess I have left the occasional meal early, or nipped back to the cabin for a lie-down, but that's been CFS-related and nothing to do with the sea, so all good.

Saturday 17 May 2003
Last night we had a bittersweet final dinner with Richard and Joyce who have been really entertaining and warm dining companions all cruise. Their understanding of my limitations right from the start of the cruise really put us at ease. The various tips and advice they were able to give us on all things cruising were invaluable too, and I have no doubt that

we will remain friends and cruise together again one day. Before dinner we all met in Magnum's Bar to share the bottle of champagne that our travel agent had kindly organised as a gift, and it felt like we had all been friends for years.

It was sad too saying goodbye to our waiters who were excellent and really enhanced our cruise experience every evening. The only slight issue was with the traditional white 'tip' envelope I gave them on our way out when, for some reason I can't quite fathom, I chose to hand this over in a discrete, clandestine, 'envelope hidden in palm of hand' manner. Not sure where that came from, and the lads didn't seem to mind me coming over all MI5, but we thanked them most sincerely for taking care of us so well for the last fortnight. Then, after farewell drinks in Tiffany's with Richard and Joyce and a few others who had become regular acquaintances over the cruise, we took a slow meander back to our cabin to finish our packing and have an early night.

So, after a decent night's sleep, this morning we made our final breakfast a Full English one before reluctantly returning to our cabin to pick up our remaining belongings, and prepare to go home. Having placed our packed suitcases outside our cabin last night before bed (so they could be taken away to the luggage hold) we had been asked to vacate our cabin by 8am. However, ever helpful Elvis said there was no hurry, and so it was nearer 9am before we had properly vacated. Then, as luck would have it, and as most of our fellow passengers sat around the ship patiently waiting for their own call, our colour of disembarkation card was called over the intercom. So we toddled off down to the bottom of the Atrium.

After a couple of farewells with some of the entertainment team, we were reacquainted with our suitcases and car, and were on the M27 and on the way home by 9.15am. As with most things, P&O have their disembarkation process organised perfectly, which is a shame as I didn't want the cruise to end. But alas, in the end ten members of crew each prised one of my digits from the end of the gangway, whilst Mandy and a security guard simultaneously tugged at my ankles, and suddenly it was all over. But one big positive of arriving home a short time later was that our three cats were all fit and healthy, as were Mum and Dad who cat-sat for us, so I'll settle for that and a few cruising based anecdotes to bore the neighbours with.

So that's cruising then and I have to say I loved it. The whole experience suited us perfectly, and particularly for me, it was great having my bed just two minutes away when I needed it. The quality of the food and the entertainment were real bonuses, as was the sheer number of nice people we met on board. It's true we were amongst a relatively small number of younger (i.e. 40s and under) passengers, and the swimming pool did occasionally resemble a scene from the movie Cocoon, such was the high average age of those on board. But it didn't bother us one iota, we thoroughly enjoyed the company of just about everyone we met. Whatever our age, we all had one big inescapable fact in common – that we were all having one really great holiday at sea. Despite how tired I feel, I sincerely hope we get to do another one.

Chapter 3 – Keeping it up!

Monday 16 June 2003
I went into work today for a meeting with my new boss, Chris. He seems like a really nice bloke and he made it clear from the start that he's heard enough good things about me, that he is in no doubt I'm a "smart cookie" and a valuable part of the team. That was good to hear, as I had been feeling really anxious about whether I would even have a job, since my old boss Jo's talents had seen her move on to pastures new. But Chris said a job is there when I'm ready, and he wants me back in the department just as soon as my health permits.

Ideally, I would like to have been feeling much sharper today, so that I could give Chris at least partial confirmation that I am indeed from the smarter end of the biscuit barrel. However, on return from the cruise last month I made the mistake of aiming to keep up that level of activity, only to find that a) I just couldn't, and b) I'm shattered from trying. So there I was a month on, and almost certainly coming across to my new boss as a mumbling buffoon with the word-finding skills of a three year old. I did rest after the cruise obviously (I had to), but it did me so much good psychologically, I got a bit carried away and tried to replicate those activity levels too soon, I think.

Of course, it wouldn't have been me if I didn't make a dick out of myself while I was there. You see, to ensure a familiar face was at our first meeting, Chris had invited along Sally, one of my friends from our management team, which was lovely and it was good to see her. Trouble was, with Chris and Sally continually stressing the need for me not to come back too soon, the frustration I felt at having been unable to sustain the higher activity levels of the cruise, which could have put a possible return to work on the horizon, just spilled out. I cried. Then Sally cried. And Chris looked anxiously over my shoulder to check the rest of the department weren't gathering like angry monster-hunting villagers because they thought he had just sacked me. Needless to say, I was embarrassed and ashamed and so didn't even hang around to say hello to my old team. As I say, a right dick.

Thursday 3 July 2003
Jane, my occupational therapist, has had me keeping a CFS diary of what I do or, just as relevant, what I don't do each day. It's basically four or five columns to record what I do, for how long, and what my level of

both fatigue and pain is afterwards. My problem is, due to my dodgy memory I forget to fill the thing in for hours at a time. Then, when I do, every other entry is basically "resting". Out of boredom, I tried to come up with other words for resting, but having then also exhausted break, breather, downtime, doze, forty winks, interlude, intermission and interval, I then misplaced my thesaurus. Although when I say misplaced, I have just noticed a half pint of milk on the book shelf, so chances are I've put the thesaurus in the fridge.

In desperation to record something different in my CFS diary I decided to mow the back lawn this afternoon. Now, living in a relatively modern house, and therefore with gardens the size of postage stamps, I find mowing our two tiny little lawns quite manageable on a good day, if I take a rest between lawns. Today isn't a particularly good day but I think it's time well spent, as when the grass gets long, one of our cats (Frisco) tends to think he's a cow and eats so much of it he then throws up all over the house. It was hard work, but this time, to play safe, I took a rest halfway through mowing just the one lawn.

So there you have it, an accomplishment I can be justifiably (?) proud of, which is documented for posterity in my CFS diary. Was it just for the sake of having one line of my diary differ from the relentless monotony of the rest of it? Of course it wasn't, what do you take me for?? No, this time tomorrow I'll now also have higher fatigue and pain scores to write in all day long so, actually, that's one line AND one whole day of my diary differing from the relentless monotony of the rest of it. And so it is that little victories are won.

Tuesday 15 July 2003
Mandy and I had an appointment with Martin Lee this morning and he was genuinely chuffed that we had had such a good time on the cruise. However, he detected straight away that I was not quite as full of sunshine and roses as you would expect from such an experience, and so I shared with him my frustration over not being able to replicate the activity level I had managed on the cruise. Yes, I had really struggled at times and yes, I still needed to get lots of rest on board, but the cruise still represented a higher activity level than I was able to consistently manage at home.

To his credit, Martin talked to me calmly and logically about why this was. Firstly, two weeks, whether it's on a cruise ship or anywhere else, isn't a long period of time. Therefore to use activity levels achieved during such a short period as a gauge to what I could, or in my eyes should, achieve on a consistent basis just isn't reasonable. Secondly, Martin referred me back to the battery analogy he had mentioned in our first meeting, whereby energy levels in CFS patients are similar to the charging and discharging of a battery, i.e. it was only because of all the extra rest I had gotten before the cruise that I was able to "charge" enough energy to enjoy it as fully as I did. Likewise, having used up all this energy, I needed extra rest on my return home to recharge.

So, in short, Martin feels the only reason I was able to do quite as much as I did on the cruise was because I applied the skills and principles I've learnt from him and Jane. That's not to say I can't get there eventually he says, but Martin stressed I need to be patient and take things gradually (at which point I could clearly read Mandy's expression out of the corner of my eye saying Patient? Gradually?? You??? Yeah, right). So from tomorrow I will once again base every day around the principles and Pacing techniques that have got me this far.

Saturday 16 August 2003
We went round to Macca's for a barbeque today and really enjoyed it. I am feeling better now, but aside from my short daily walk I've barely been out of the house recently, and conversationally I know I am really hard work. But Mac kept it to just the four of us today bless him and it was good. Both he and his wife, Michaela, are always a good craic.

Michaela was telling us how it was going with the part-time business she started recently, Posh Girls' Parties, whereby she arranges make-up, dressing up etc. as an alternative style of teenage girls' birthday parties. It's been really good so far, she says, and lots of interest shown in it. In fact the only downside has been the artwork she had done to her car to promote the business, as from a certain (i.e. every) angle, it does look like her car is promoting "Posh Girls' Panties" which, potentially, services a whole other customer base. A good craic today as I say, and with both of them in great form, it was good to forget about Pacing and conserving energy, and just let our hair down for a bit – that is, if consuming one bottle of beer, and a bladder full of fizzy water over a selection of red meats cremated to your liking, counts as letting your hair down.

Actually, not just today, but Macca has been a real godsend right from the start of all this. No matter how bad I've been cognitively (i.e.

speaking utter drivel to him), he's been on the phone as regular as clockwork to check how things are and share some banter. I just wish I wasn't such a muppet most of the time but the phone especially - maybe because it uses only one sense and so needs more concentration than face-to-face conversations - just knackers me out. I have often put the phone down after speaking to him and slapped my head at the absurdity, tedium or just total inarticulateness (is that even a real word? See what I mean??) of what I have just said to the guy. But he's a good mate and understands, I think. And the food he cooked up on the barbie today wasn't half bad either.

Thursday 4 September 2003
I've been varnishing the garden fence this week. Or is the correct term to "paint" a fence? Or does the varnishing or painting depend on the type and colour of what you are sticking on it?? Well, put it this way, I've been applying a wood-coloured resinous liquid to the back fence all week. With a paintbrush. Only it's taking a while. In fact, it's taking ages even though the bleeding thing is only three foot high.

You see, in accordance with the principles of Pacing, I've been doing it 20 minutes at a time, and a maximum of four times per day. That means I get to "paint" about three slats each time and it's killing me. Not killing me in terms of pain as, crucially, I sit on a chair for most of it and I do not have to raise my arms high at all. No, killing me because I hate leaving a job unfinished. It's bad enough taking a rest halfway through mowing the lawn, but leaving the fence unfinished the last couple of days feels even worse, especially when I have to leave the brushes overnight in turps, white spirit or whatever that clear smelly stuff is (you can tell I'm a wizard at DIY, can't you). But hopefully I'll finish it tomorrow.

I did think about getting one of those spray gun things, but I tried one of those years ago and the stupid thing kept clogging up. I'm not great with practical stuff anyway (once an office wallah, always an office wallah), but that thing was such a pain, it put me right off DIY. I always remember Colin, Mandy's builder brother, coming round to help when we first moved into our house and, on seeing my toolbox he laughed so much at my nice shiny screwdrivers and sparkly hammer, it was quite hurtful. After popping out to his van for his own toolbox, he plopped it down right next to my much smaller version whilst saying "that's not a toolbox, THIS is a toolbox!" It was a real Crocodile Dundee moment.

Saturday 6 September 2003
I finished the fence yesterday, hurrah! But my arms, and especially my armpits, hurt like hell. I just wanted to get the damn thing over with, so with the finish line of the final panel in sight, I think I overdid it. So, something that started out as a useful but gentle way of spending another quiet week at home has now meant I'm looking at an uncomfortable, and therefore grumpy weekend. Sorry Mand!

On the plus side, as much as it grated on me leaving it unfinished each night, I was pretty disciplined for most of the week. That meant that I did okay health-wise right up until that last day. So I can do it, it just needs willpower. That and not thinking too much about the pathetically small amount I can actually accomplish. Overall it's a positive though, and I feel better for having ~~painted~~ ~~varnished~~ done the fence. And given that the tin says the finish is good for ten years, it shouldn't need doing again anytime soon. In fact, I've photographed my freshly-done fence next to a copy of today's newspaper and, one day short of doing "what it says on the tin", and I'll be expecting the company concerned to send round a painter to do "what it says on his van", i.e. paint my fence.

Monday 22 September 2003
God I hate insomnia. There's nothing worse than being awake when everyone else is asleep, and time drags so slowly that the blessed release of morning feels like it will never come. It's all part and parcel of the CFS I know, and there are much worse symptoms, but insomnia can be horrible. Sometimes it's getting off to sleep at bed time, sometimes it happens in the middle of the night, and other times it's just very early mornings of say 4 or 5am. Whichever one it is, it generally makes decent sleep unlikely from that point onwards.

The most annoying thing is that, having spent all day failing to raise my cognitive abilities to the level of a marrow, just at the point when no brain activity (i.e. sleep) is required my brain finally decides to wake up. Actually scrub that. Just when sleep is required my brain decides I'm a freaking genius and that I can solve all of the world's problems by just staying awake and constantly running them around in my head. The solutions I come up with for these problems are so brilliant I would surely win multiple Nobel Prizes, if only I wasn't totally incapable of remembering any of them. So, in my attempts to fall back asleep I sometimes mentally count the number of Nobel Prizes I think I would have won.

In all seriousness though, insomnia of any description isn't nice and it's robbing me of the energy I need to progress. In CFS it's very common and is often attributed to a malfunctioning hypothalamus gland which, and don't quote me on this, helps regulate sleep pattern. Short inappropriate bursts of adrenaline can also be part of the equation, so (and quote me even less on this) in CFS patients the normally amiable adrenal and hypothalamus glands act more like feuding siblings who spend most of their lives slamming doors in each other's faces, but do occasionally speak when they get drunk at funerals. Either way, one of the best ways of resolving insomnia is apparently, no matter how knackered you feel, to avoid napping during the day. Which, obviously, if you have a fatigue-related illness and barely slept a wink last night, isn't ideal.

Monday 6 October 2003
I met with my occupational therapist, Jane, again today, during which we reviewed the frankly depressing activity levels that I had recorded in the CFS diary that she had asked me to keep. After a few minutes studying it, she actually did use the word "depressing" herself, but not in the context I expected. Indeed, she felt my activity levels were sensible, given where I am currently, and that I have been pretty disciplined in alternating my rest and activity periods. What she felt was depressing was that so much of my time was clearly spent in the house and on my own. She felt pretty strongly that I needed to have more social contact, albeit carefully structured to avoid CFS-related set-backs.

That surprised me. Although I've tried hard to reintroduce a small social life, I find this uses up a lot of energy which surely I should be using towards getting back to work. I am, after all, receiving an income that I am not earning, so how can it be right for me to effectively use that income and the limited energy I do have, to enjoy myself. However, Jane's view, which makes a lot of sense in retrospect, is that the body also needs a healthy and happy mind to help it heal, and structured sensibly, the social aspect can be just as important as everything we are doing on the physical side.

It is something I have thought about, as my job is very people focused, and so I need to be able to again interact with people, problem free, to do that role. But having worked hard all my adult life, and been well rewarded for it, it just feels wrong to effectively be paid to sit in a bar or café catching up with an old mate or work colleague. I obviously need to get over this guilt I feel at not currently working for my buck. Jane is pretty adamant, so I've promised to make more effort on the social front, as and when I feel able.

Thursday 18 November 2003
I met my old boss Dave for lunch today in a quiet old pub on the edge of town and I barely stumbled over, forgot or misappropriated one word for the whole hour. In fact, Dave was so impressed with how I was doing on all fronts (I'm still sharing my "I painted/varnished/did the fence" story with anyone prepared to listen) he tentatively mentioned a gentle round of golf and asked how my co-ordination is these days. I explained that we don't use the C-word anymore as I find it quite demeaning. But no, my (drops voice to a whisper) co-ordination is not great, I explained, and as much as I really really want to play golf, I would be a danger to myself and others. One day though.

I am making a real effort to have the occasional lunchtime meet-up - as well as Dave and the Curry Night boys, I'm due to meet up with my Uncle Eddie, and old boss Jo, plus Ivan and Phil, another two old mates and colleagues – but boy it's hard. Not so much during the lunch itself, but in the days following I really feel it. However, Jane's very valid point to me is that psychologically it's important to have these lunches, even if it means reducing the length of each one to minimise their impact CFS-wise. As I say, I'm trying.

Friday 28 November 2003
Macca took me down to Salisbury last night to visit our mate Mark, or Yeti as we all know him. It was far from an enjoyable visit to tell the truth, as Yeti is in a full-time care facility, following his heart stopping when playing football. His brain was starved of oxygen for a considerable time and it left him unable to do much for himself beyond breathing. What that means is that you can usually tell when Yeti is awake, and when he is asleep, but it's unlikely he's aware of much of what is going on around him in either state. And to be honest, whenever I visit him I spend much of the time hoping that the Yeti we know and love isn't in there. But, and it's a big but, he does seem to know sometimes when his parents and sister especially are there and so, just on the off chance he can hear me, I think it's important to keep visiting him and boring him rigid, just as I did in happier times.

For me, it's quite a trek down to Salisbury and back, thus the reason Macca was driving, but visiting Yeti is something we are both very keen to do, we think a lot of the boy. In fact, it was Yeti and Macca who jointly organised events on my stag weekend in glorious Blackpool in 1997, and made it one of the best weekends of my life, so for that alone I'm indebted to them both. In Yeti's case he bought not one, but subsequently his second house too, just down the street from Mand and me, and he was my "go-to" guy when I first moved here. I'm not someone who tends to have many close friends and so to sit in that care home, with two mates I think the world of, in such sad circumstances is hard. Glad we went though.

Wednesday 15 December 2003
Note to self - no longer keep Gillette razor in toothbrush holder adjacent to toothbrush as, on selecting incorrect implement, will find razor head is both wider and sharper than that of toothbrush.

Thought to ponder – is it bad to let neighbours believe your wife is physically abusing you rather than admit cut lip is due to you trying to clean teeth with Gillette Mach 3 Razor?

Friday 2 January 2004
I saw Hanqiao today for my fortnightly acupuncture and she wasn't happy with me at all. Basically, although I had been careful, the additional visiting from family and friends over the Christmas period means I'm pretty tired. So tired in fact that she was unable to give me her normal strength of acupuncture, she said, and so would also be giving me Chinese herbs to take at home. I've had these before and, trust me, they are bad news. They do some good I'm sure, and I trust Hanqiao's judgement completely, but they are truly awful.

Having Chinese herbs basically means boiling up a bag of carefully selected herbs twice a day and drinking the liquid produced as a tea. As massive a help as Hanqiao has been to me, with the acupuncture being the one single thing that seems to help my CFS the most, I hate the herbs with a passion. You see, when you boil the herbs the liquid you end up with smells and looks like neat tar, and tastes even worse. If that's not bad enough you, your clothes, your house, your soul all constantly smell like you have just been resurfacing the M4 with skunk-flavoured asphalt. It's horrible and I dread it. Mandy already complains that when I get in the car after my normal acupuncture, the moxa that Hanqiao uses on me makes me smell like a pot-smoking vagrant. Now it's about to get a lot worse, and all I can offer her is "it's only for six weeks, Mand!" I will surely die alone!!

Thursday 22 January 2004

On the advice of my occupational therapist, Jane, I have today been attempting to do some Pilates. No, I didn't know what that was either. In actual fact, Jane had recommended Yoga to try and help me with the increasing muscle pain and stiffness I am getting. But Yoga exercises seem to require good balance, and unless I can hold onto, or lean against something my balance is worse than a one-legged drunk with vertigo. So Jane has suggested Pilates, which I believe is a gentler version of Yoga requiring less balance, less strength and, hopefully, less contortionism.

Luckily, after ten minutes searching on the internet, and dismissing a number of, frankly, "you're having a laugh" exercises, I found a nice gentle Pilates routine which I could do. Sort of. Pilates supposedly strengthens your core, and so assuming a strong core doesn't mean just flopping straight back to the floor, and groaning like a constipated zombie a millisecond into each exercise, I clearly have some work to do. But it's do-able and most of the exercises involve sitting or lying on the floor so, hey, there's not too far to flop, and resulting injuries should be minimal.

I'm so impressed in fact that I've ordered an instructional DVD called Pilates for Beginners, carefully selected so that the lady instructor looks fit, but not so fit that the sight of her in skin-tight lycra isn't too distracting. As any red-blooded, lunchtime telly-watching bloke will tell you, you only have to watch the daily edition of Aerobics Oz Style if it's soft pornography you want. But oh no, I'm far too serious about turning this body of mine into a lean, mean resting machine and to prove it, I'm off to do a bit of Pilates right this minute. Oh hang on, it's lunchtime, maybe I'll just stick the telly on for a bit first.

Sunday 15 February 2004

I'm not sure why, but when I woke up this morning my head felt foggier than it's been in months. I recently tried to increase my activity to nearer that of my cruise again, but stopped over a fortnight ago when the headache worsened. My eyes just didn't want to open this morning and it was a struggle just to put one foot in front of the other in anything approaching a co-ordinated manner. You just never know with this illness, even when you play things very sensibly it can still really bugger you up. It's an anniversary for us today too, as it's 12 years since Mandy and I went out on our first date to see a movie called Bill and Ted's Bogus Adventure. And it's "totally bogus dude" that today I feel about as bad as Keanu Reeves' acting in that film. Mand said not to worry, she would prefer to stay in and have a roast dinner anyway.

On the positive side, I've sent a few emails over the last few days and, if I'm feeling better by the end of the week I'm going to meet Macca, Skelts and another mate Kenty for a lunchtime mineral water on Friday – well, mineral water for me, I'm sure they'll have a proper pint. Really looking forward to it. When we were all working together, circa 1994 to 2002, we all went for a pint every Friday lunchtime and I miss it like hell. We still try and do it a few times a year, when everyone's available and I'm feeling okay health-wise, but we haven't done it for over a year.

Monday 23 February 2004
I went to get some physio on Friday and I really wish I hadn't. You see, to date my CFS has been far worse on the cognitive side of things than the physical. Suffice to say, other than this semi-permanent headache, I might be a mumbling, stumbling, forgetful insomniac, but I've got off pretty lightly as far as the physical symptoms go. However, in recent months, whilst I've been doing well overall, I've had a lot more muscle pain, especially under my arms, lower back and the non-sexy parts (thank you Lord) of my groin. The Pilates helps, but my daily walk, which keeps me sane by getting me out of the house for 30 minutes every day, is proving harder and harder.

So, after a quick chat with my doctor we decided to try a little physio. Not a little physio-*therapist* you understand (midgets do always make me smile, but no - that would have just been unnecessarily picky on my part), but a little physio-*therapy*. The trouble is, although I felt okay during the physio session itself on Friday, I've barely moved from my bed the rest of the weekend as I've been in so much discomfort. Another quick chat with my doctor today and we've decided to leave any further physio sessions for now. To be fair, the (definitely not a midget) physio guy had warned me that this could happen with someone with CFS, but I didn't think it could be this bad. Three days later and I'm still feeling worse each day.

Friday 5 March 2004
Met the lads today for the lunchtime drink I had to cancel in February. They were all in good spirits, given it was a Friday lunchtime at the end of a long, hard working week. Well, I say they were all in good spirits, Kenty was having the usual moan he has whenever we go to a pub that doesn't do a pint and a burger for a fiver, but it was good to see them all and share some banter. With me still struggling a little bit and still having this aversion to crowds and noise, the lads had kindly arranged to meet me in this new trendy music-less bar, and I have to say, aside from not ticking Kenty's boxes for cheap flat beer and mad-cow burgers, it was perfect.

Somehow, many years ago I got this reputation at our regular Friday lunchtimes for always asking "are you up to much at the weekend boys?" It apparently became so predictable that the lads would even secretly make bets on what time I would ask this. But yesterday, it had been so long since we had met like this we had all forgotten. Or at least we had forgotten until I, without even realising I had said it, asked about their weekend plans. Up went a cheer in recognition of my traditional enquiry and, albeit briefly, it really felt like old times. In fact, when Skelts insisted on buying a round of beers to celebrate, I had one too despite previously promising myself I would stick to mineral water to ensure I was healthy at the weekend for Mandy. I was only there an hour, and only one bottle of lager on my part, but it was great to see them all.

Wednesday 31 March 2004
I'm feeling a lot better now. On Jane's advice, I recently started having a ten-minute swim once a week, and whilst I can only manage a very gentle breast stroke, it is relieving the muscle pain and stiffness a bit.

Unfortunately, the CFS means I don't tolerate cold water too well, and the only swimming pool I've been able to find that is warm enough is right across the other side of town. It's okay though, there is a sauna there too which means, even though I'm out for an hour or so in total, I get some (nice warm) rest while I'm there. The combination of my initially lily-white body having a swim, sauna and shower in quick succession does see my skin tone gradually match in with most shades of the modern chic décor of the changing rooms, but I'm loving the exercise element, even if I am being overtaken by gobby six year olds in armbands.

Friday 16 April 2004
With Mandy working full-time and effectively being my carer, not to mention taking care of her mum almost single-handed, I've been trying to take the burden of a few chores off of her of late. One way is to do some of the mid-week cooking. Although when I say "cooking", what I really mean is placing something in the oven, at the temperature dictated to me by its packaging, and then trying to remember to take it out again before it burns. I have two fail-safes to avoid such culinary disasters. Firstly, I have a kitchen timer thing which, as long as I remember to set it, will ring loudly when the designated cooking time has elapsed. Secondly, I always aim to have dinner ready for when Mandy comes home from work. Logically therefore, if the first fail-safe doesn't do the trick, then Mandy arriving home should, at worst, mean dinner is a little well done. It's not a perfect system by any means, as I do also use the kitchen timer thing to ensure I limit any telephone calls to 20 minutes. I just hope the day someone phones me whilst I'm "cooking" doesn't coincide with Mandy getting stuck in traffic. Or if it does, that this book survives the subsequent fire and acts as proof that I didn't burn the house down intentionally.

Another way I have tried to help is by buying our groceries. Not by going to a supermarket you understand - God no, that would be hell with crazy pensioners and manic mums coming at me from all angles – but by using the new online method where you order from home and they deliver it to your door. Mentally, it was quite hard to do to start off with, but now I'm used to it and I can just click on "My Usuals" to quicken the whole process up, it's okay. There were a few teething issues, and them replacing my out of stock Mixed Fruit Soya Yoghurts with Mixed Fruit Flavoured Condoms put me right off puds for a week. But I made do (they were surprisingly tasty) and it generally works quite well. It's a big help.

Thursday 20 May 2004
I'm really bored today. You know when Forrest Gump said "life is like a box of chocolates, you never know what you're gonna gate" (he meant "get" but he definitely said "gate"). Well, if my life is like a box of chocolates then it's a box of Maltesers, because every bleeding chocolate/day is the same. Oh hang on, I love Maltesers. Right, I know - my life is like a box of Celebrations, but the only flavour in there is those really dull Finger of Fudge ones. But does that still work as an example given that you can't actually buy a box of Celebrations with only the

fudge ones in, unless from some kind of factory shop where they sell off all the imperfect ones on the cheap? Right, sorted – if my life is like a box of chocolates, then it's a box of those really boring fudge ones, sold by the Cadbury's factory at a large discount to tight-fisted, misshapen-fudge-loving Brummies. Told you I was bored.

Monday 21 June 2004
Interesting day today. Christine, a lass I used to work with in the late 1980s, and who still works in Mandy's department, came to see me at lunchtime. I had heard via Mandy that Christine had had CFS in the past and, having previously sent home some reading material on the subject, she was keen to come and see me. And I'm really glad she did.

The first thing Christine did was to correct me when I referred to her as having "had" CFS (i.e. in the past tense). Basically, she says she still has CFS and she thinks she probably always will do. The difference is, she has recovered sufficiently, and got a good enough handle on it, that she has been able to return to work and lead a reasonably normal life again. The CFS still flares up occasionally but she has ways to manage this, and so the important thing for me to remember is that there is a chink of light at the end of the tunnel.

Christine went on to share with me some of her experiences and the techniques she uses, and I found it really enlightening. As with other CFS sufferers I have talked to, many of Christine's symptoms are different from my own, but given the wide range of symptoms (and their severity) covered by the CFS umbrella, I'm beginning to think that no two cases are exactly the same. She also urged caution over me placing timescales or targets on my recovery. Like me, Christine has always been very target-driven, but this approach can be the worst one to take where CFS is concerned. She says I'll get better when I get better, and I should just stick to the principles Dr Lee and Jane have taught me.

So Christine's visit really lifted me. Although I had been in contact with other CFS sufferers through internet support groups, I had found that quite depressing due to the clearly poor recovery rate for those that had gone undiagnosed as long as I had. Also, Christine is a career-focused person like me, and we learnt our trade in the same successful, target-driven environment. So if she can recover sufficiently to continue with her career, then surely I can too.

Monday 19 July 2004

I learned something interesting recently. In short, a significant proportion of CFS sufferers have previously had Glandular Fever, and so it's very likely there is some link between the two. Now, I can't remember much about it, other than regular visits to Bath's Royal United Hospital, and not being allowed to play football for a year after I was better, but I did have Glandular Fever as a kid.

My mum says that when I was recovering, the doctor warned that it was likely to come back and cause me problems from time to time. But it never did. Well, not until this CFS anyway, some 25 years later. I guess the link makes sense: CFS does seem a very glandular thing, the obviously very dodgy gland being the adrenal gland which controls energy, adrenalin etc. No logical explanation yet from the scientists as to why this might be, but statistically there is a clear link and so, who knows, maybe I was always going to get this illness, it was just laid dormant in my system waiting to pounce.

Saturday 24 July 2004

I went to a local pub yesterday evening as there were some leaving drinks for some of the lads and ladies I used to manage. Although I'm still not at my best in such situations, Macca knew the people concerned a little also so a) offered to go with me, and b) suggested we go straight there at 5pm when the pub would be at its quietest. Sadly, that meant I didn't get to see all of my old team as some went along much later, but it was really good sitting there, in what turned out to be a music-less pub, catching up with half a dozen old colleagues. There was also plenty of banter which I think included me giving as good as I got. However, one comment that seemed to go beyond normal banter momentarily upset me a little.

James, who's a great lad and someone I really enjoyed working with, basically asked me if I was "swinging the lead" and suggested I was milking the whole CFS thing for as long as I could. I initially took it as a joke and laughed it off as such. But he then immediately followed up by saying that I seemed to have it "pretty cushy", and on his way to work he sees me driving in the opposite direction to the gym. Now, it's not something I had thought about before, and it's not a phrase I would normally use, but I looked him straight in the eye and told him that I would swap places with him in a heartbeat.

I think James was a little surprised by my reaction. It wasn't that I said it with any anger or malice, quite the opposite actually; there was a calmness and matter-of-fact-ness about how it came out. It was almost as if, at that moment, I had belatedly accepted that my recovery from CFS wasn't happening anytime soon, and if anybody thinks for a minute that it's anything less than crap, then feel free to wobble a day in my shoes. Maybe I was over-sensitive (probably) and maybe I'm over-thinking it now (definitely), but part of me wondered if James had just said what everyone else was thinking. The fact is, I looked fine, I sounded fine and, had I seen someone on long-term sick appearing to go to the gym, I may well have thought exactly the same.

But, I'm pleased to say that I did then lighten things up again straight away by joking to James that, as I usually get to the gym at 9.15am and he's due at work at 9am, then clearly his appalling time-keeping hasn't got any better since he worked for me. It also meant that, other than quickly explaining to James that my visits to the gym were purely for a ten-minute swim, we stayed largely clear of the subject of CFS. Which was a relief, as I had wanted to try and forget about it for those couple of hours.

Thursday 12 August 2004
A big day today. It was my nephew's Army "Passing Out" from Arborfield Barracks in Berkshire. Well I say nephew; Gareth is actually my cousin's lad, but he's always been like another nephew to me. He showed loads of determination in first getting accepted into the Army, and then working hard throughout his time at Arborfield, culminating in his proud family attending today's Passing Out Parade. So, as I say, a big day.

It was also a big day for me in that, either side of an hour-long journey, it was clearly going to be a long day. I have got into the habit now of planning any event I go to like a military operation in that our arrival and departure times are carefully planned, and regular rests are scheduled. Ironically however, given this particular event actually was a military operation, other than the start time it was unclear what was actually due to happen and when.

In actual fact the day was pretty seamless. Although there was little opportunity to rest, the main part of the day was us just sat in the stands with big stupid, immensely proud grins on our faces; silently watching the graduating recruits carrying out various drills and marches. The only real issue was the brilliant August sunshine which, if hot for us, was much worse for the recruits themselves, and the Passing Out parade turned out to be unerringly accurate in its title for one or two of them. When the parade finished, all the recruits marched off in formation towards their barracks. They then disappeared behind a perimeter wall at the edge of the parade ground where they all let out this huge cheer and threw their caps up into the air. It looked and sounded brilliant, and was a really touching end to the parade, with many a mum dabbing away her tears.

At that point, I convinced Mandy to stay with the rest of the family, and I nipped back for a rest in the car, which we had parked in a well-shaded area earlier on. Well, I must have fallen asleep, as an hour or so later my Aunty June was knocking on my window to check I was okay. She's lovely, June. Although, by the time I was born, she had already married a Para (my Uncle Ray) and was travelling the world as a military wife, she always ensured she kept strong ties with, and visited regularly, the rest of the family back in Wiltshire. In fact, since I've been ill June has regularly checked on my progress, so much so that I've seen more of her this last couple of years than some of my more immediate family. We had a nice chat sat there, just the two of us, and agreed that he might have been a right little bugger growing up, but Gareth had turned out a really good lad.

After a while, the rest of the family joined us, and we all adjourned to the local Royal British Legion Club with Gareth for a celebratory lunch, where we also raised a glass to Gareth's greatly missed Gran, and my aunt, Rose - who I have no doubt was there in spirit and bursting with pride even more than the rest of us. Sadly, as is normally the case, Mandy and I were the first to (reluctantly) leave, but I was shattered. And the main thing is we had got to see Gareth pass out (without him passing out) and share a truly memorable day.

Sunday 12 September 2004
Macca's wife Michaela phoned one morning last week and told me to turn on the television, as there was someone on there who had had a similar stroke-like collapse to the one I had two years ago. When I turned the TV on, and turned over to City Hospital (a weekday programme based in London), the lady concerned was describing exactly what I myself had experienced. The head pain, the collapse, the

difficulty speaking, even the weakness to one side of her body. Her diagnosis was the same extreme but rare migraine it had been eventually suggested caused my own collapse, even though our migraines appeared to have very different triggers (mine being the CFS).

Even after all this time, I felt massively relieved. You see, I still have a weakness and numbness in one arm and leg which worsens with fatigue, and my speech/cognitive issues are still very much there. That meant that there was always a small part of me that wondered if I did actually have a small stroke, especially as one doctor had told me that not all strokes show up on a scan. Whilst I have no doubt that whatever happened to me was linked to my subsequently-diagnosed CFS, and me foolishly trying to do too much at a time when my body needed rest, it's a relief to see that, in the nicest possible way, there is someone else out there that went through the same thing.

Sunday 19 September 2004
We've had a really lovely day today. Ivan, who's a mate I used to work with, invited us and two other couples over to his house for a barbeque. The setting, the food, the company, even the weather was all great. You see, Ivan (and Cassie and Joe, his wife and young son) have a gorgeous little cottage which, aside from the adjacent farm and one neighbour, is bang in the middle of nowhere. I've been there a few times now and I love it more each time. It has always been mine and Mandy's plan to move to a more rural location, and with the CFS making me more and more noise sensitive, even more so now. It truly is the perfect location, especially for Cassie who teaches at the private school, an old manor house that looks like it's right out of a Jane Austen novel, which you can just about see in the distance beyond a long lush field.

The other couples were mates Phil and Daz, who both worked with Ivan and me a few years back, and their wives Julie and Janine. Thanks to some nicely-timed sunshine and some tasty offerings from head chef Ivan, it was a really pleasant afternoon. I tried to pace myself as best I could, with one eye on our cruise in four weeks' time, and not overdo it. But everyone was chilled and entertaining company, and nobody seemed to mind me "zoning out" occasionally when my mind hit neutral gear, so it was fine. As I say, a lovely day, and now it's four weeks of solid rest and very limited activity, in readiness for our second cruise. I can't wait.

Chapter 4 – Getting Hooked

Wednesday 6 October 2004
Hey, hey, hey we're back on board the majestic Oceana and it's a brave (or foolish) step I know, given how knackered I was after a 14-day cruise last time, but this one is for 16 whole days. I have literally been on countdown since we booked it last year. And in spite of some really tempting itineraries to such places like the Fjords and the Baltic, our constant wish for some sun means we opted for cruising to the Mediterranean again. But we're very happy with the Med thank you very much, especially as our carefully chosen itinerary includes extra sea days (to rest), and stops at such places as Monte Carlo and Naples, as well as our two big favourites from last time, Rome and Barcelona.

We almost had a dodgy start today in that, when we arrived at the Mayflower Cruise Terminal at our appointed time, the queue to check-in was right out the door. I still have real difficulty standing for long, so this could have been a real problem. However, a nice gentleman with a high-visibility fluorescent jacket on recognised I wasn't in perfect health (my pasty white skin and the dark circles around my eyes tend to have that effect) and asked if he could help. He checked my name against a list of some kind (presumably of people with declared medical conditions) and promptly wheelchaired me to the front of the queue. That seemed to be a bit over the top, but it avoided the problems I encountered in queuing in Gibraltar last year so I should be, and am, very grateful.

After check-in, the nice fluorescent man wheeled me, with Mandy tail-gating behind us, through to security too, thus avoiding another queue. I think at this point he realised I was a bit embarrassed by the whole wheelchair thing, so he asked if I wanted to go the rest of the way under my own steam. Walking small distances isn't a problem at all and so, with the worst of the queue now behind us, and me already imagining my fellow passengers shaking their fists in the air behind me, I was up and out of that chair quicker than you could say "here Deirdre, that pale bloke has just jumped the queue". It had helped me out big time, but I think we're going to have to rethink embarkation day on future cruises as this special treatment of me getting to sit comfortably in a wheelchair, while others more elderly (and fairer-sexed) stand in a queue, just doesn't, well, sit comfortably with me. But the good thing was we were into Oceana's stunning Atrium in next to no time and being directed towards the Plaza for a late lunch.

Thursday 7 October 2004
Yesterday, after a stroll around to reacquaint ourselves with the good ship Oceana, and Mandy leaving a Mandy-shaped smudge on the window of the (closed) shop containing the handbags, it was announced that we could access our cabins. After unpacking, and me grabbing a quick nap whilst Mandy seemed to apply more makeup than Coco the Clown, we toddled off to dinner for a really nice surprise.

When we were shown to our table we found we had been given a great table for two in a nice quiet corner. Well actually, size-wise it was a table for four, but it had been laid for just two, centrally-placed, settings. Everyone else must have thought we were royalty it looked so grand. As it turns out, our friends from our first cruise, Richard and Joyce, had written to the restaurant manager explaining my health situation, and he came up trumps for us. I must admit it was a big relief, because with me really struggling some nights on the last cruise due to the CFS, I was worried I could impact detrimentally on the dining experience of any would-be dining companions. So I'm really over the moon that we have our own table, as it means I can go to dinner every night worry-free. I'll also hopefully have more energy for (the more optional) post-dinner socialising on my better nights.

Our first dinner, needless to say, was excellent and definitely on a par with the quality of food we so enjoyed on our last cruise. Our waiters were very good, if a little more reserved than last year's duo, but it was only the first night and I'm sure I'll wear them down. To be honest, we were both pretty tired after a long day so they probably thought the same about us. Anyway, after some tasty scoff, we headed back to the cabin for some rest, stopping briefly on the way out to thank Alan, the restaurant manager, for arranging the table for us, it really will help.

This morning we both feel good which is a bonus considering that, this time last cruise, I was totally knackered, and Mand was feeling dead queasy due to the early effects of "the bay". For me, this is almost certainly due to the additional steps we were able to take this time such as dining alone (and yakking less), and grabbing the extra rest when I can. And Mandy seems to have acquired her sea legs quicker, possibly due to us having breakfast in the cabin this time rather than starting our first day at the front/top of the ship in the Plaza, which I still can't believe us two plonkers did last time. Mandy is also wearing some anti-sickness wristbands, which I hope are helping, as she got a bit touchy about them when I suggested she get a matching headband and stick some Olivia Newton John on the stereo. Either way, we're good and ready for a nice relaxing day at sea.

Friday 8 October 2004
First proper night aboard last night then and we really enjoyed it. The dress code was semi-formal, so I wore a suit and tie and hopefully managed to avoid looking like a sack of spuds next my beautiful wife, who looked stunning. After getting ready nice and early, we headed downstairs to Magnum's Bar for pre-dinner cocktails, which was good, and the drinks waiter even brought out some hors d'oeuvres for us as we relaxed back into a comfy sofa and just people-watched for a while.

It was 6.30pm before we knew it and so we wandered down to the restaurant, via the Atrium, and walked into first sitting dinner which again turned out to be top-notch. Our waiters are gradually starting to warm to us I think, especially our assistant waiter, Ashok, who is doing a great job of keeping the little boy at the next table entertained. Our main waiter is a big lad called Biju (which is pronounced, somewhat ironically for someone built like a brick outhouse, as bijoux) who's excellent, but very serious looking and frowns at me occasionally. But as I say, an excellent waiter, and my strong West Country accent can't be easy for him, so no complaints here.

After dinner we went to the theatre to watch The Stadium Theatre Company doing a show called Downtown Diner. This being our second cruise, I now realise that the Stadium Theatre Company are effectively Oceana's in-house production company that are with us all cruise, so we're really pleased as they were terrific last time. Most of the cast have changed, but it's a similar mix of really talented singers and dancers, including one lass, Dee, who I had a chat with on the last cruise, so nice to see a familiar face. And after that build up, you'll be pleased to hear last night's show was great.

After the show we found ourselves having a couple of drinks watching the ballroom dancers on the Atrium's dance floor who, aside from the two on-board instructors, all appear to be passengers. I think Mandy would love to learn too, and normally I would be happy to accompany her to the sea day classes. But due to me currently having the balance of a newly-born foal, we'll have to park that idea for now. We enjoyed watching the dancers for a while though, and they all obviously have a real passion for it, especially one elderly fella who, in my head, I've christened Mufasa (from the Lion King) on account of his matching animal print waistcoat and shoes, and the most glorious blond mane. Not exactly my dress sense, and those golden locks look of a dubious origin, but fair play Mufasa lad, you can't half shift around that dance floor.

Saturday 9 October 2004
A third consecutive sea day today and I have to say I love them. In fact I think I enjoy the sea days more than the port days. Well okay, not as much as I enjoy stopping at the likes of Barcelona and Rome maybe, but just relaxing on the Promenade Deck in the sun, looking out to miles and miles of sea, takes some beating for me.

Anyway, yesterday's sea day was really sunny and so Mand spent much of the day relaxing up on the Sun Deck reading her book. The considerably less sun-worshippy me did intermittent versions of the same, interspersed with walking a couple of circuits of the Prom Deck, attending a short Port Presentation, and fetching my good lady cups of tea or a snack: i.e. a nice mellow day at sea, which after a few drinks last night, I will be hoping to repeat today, as it's just what I need.

You see, before dinner last night it was the Captain's Welcome Aboard Party in the Atrium. It was also our first formal night so, wanting to a) look our best and b) be on time for our free drink, we were back to the cabin and getting ready from about 4.30pm. This of course meant that I was shaved, showered and shampooed, and even suited and booted, by about 4.35pm. Mandy on the other hand, being of the female gender, took longer. Longer in fact than it took God to create the world, his holiday home, and even lay a tasteful patio for each. I did eventually take my life in my hands and ask Mand how much longer she was going to be, to which she answered "if you don't want me to take these curling tongs to your groin area, why don't you pop off to Tiffany's and wait for me there", which in my mind raised two points – firstly, duh, they are not called short and curlies for nothing missy so why would I need curling tongs down there, and secondly, hello, yes I would very much like to wait in the bar, nice of you to say so while we are still young.

When I got to Tiffany's I sat at the bar next to another fellow sat on his own also looking every part the "husband waiting for all eternity for wife to get ready". And I was spot on: we swapped notes, and as time went by, a round of drinks each, and he introduced himself as Tim. Due to my appalling memory for names, I quickly latched onto the fact that he drinks Tiger Beer and, genius that I am, in my head I immediately pegged him for future reference as Tiger Tim. Yes I know, that system is far from fool-proof, as I could easily recall him later to be a Tiger Tom or Tiger Tony by mistake, but the name Tiger Tim rang a bell, I think possibly due to it being a nickname for the very un-tiger-like Tim Henman. Anyway, Tim's name was consigned to memory and I managed to get it, and his drink order, right for the next hour.

From that point onwards the evening gets a little fuzzy. I vaguely recall both Tim's wife and Mandy joining us at some stage, and also hearing Captain Burgoine doing a toast out in the Atrium, but if I'm honest it's a blur and not helped at all by the fact that we met up with Tim and his wife again after dinner. I was actually alternating weaker alcoholic drinks with mineral water, but my body now seems unable to tolerate even smaller amounts of alcohol, which is a shame. So yes, a gentle day at sea today will be just perfect, and now I intend to go and watch the England versus Wales football game in one of the bars, where I intend to drink fizzy water and fizzy water only.

Monday 11 October 2004
After another lazy sea day yesterday to fully recover from my (pathetically small) excesses of Friday night, we are back in Barcelona today and so, after a buffet breakfast in the Plaza, we were ship-shape and ashore quite early. Last time we were here we really enjoyed walking up La Rambla and so, mindful that I will need as much energy as possible for the cruise highlight of Monte Carlo tomorrow, we decided to "Rambla" again today and just take it easy.

Sadly for me, Mandy is the name and shopping is the game, so after failing to convince her that the "Maximo Reducia" emblazoned across one shop window was the name of a hot new Spanish designer, I left her to it. Mandy doesn't quite have the energy limitations that I have and so, whilst I took the opportunity to soak up some La Rambla atmosphere, enjoy the street performers and grab a relaxing coffee in Placa Reial, Mandy shopped like her life depended on it.

When, and only when, Mandy had scratched her retail itch sufficiently, we popped along to the Olympic Port area (so called because it was developed for the 1992 Olympics) and relaxed on the adjacent beach. Of course, me being me I soon bored of that, and so after checking that the queues to go in the Gaudi's still unfinished Familia Sagrada (bloody builders) were still too long for me, and instead briefly again marvelling at its external beauty, we came back to the ship for lunch.

As a football nut, I would have loved to have gone back ashore this afternoon to do the tour of the Camp Nou, Barcelona FC's stadium, but as I say, it's Monte Carlo tomorrow so best save my energy for that. A lovely morning in a lovely city that we still haven't done justice to, but I have a feeling we will be here often.

Tuesday 12 October 2004
Bad news. Captain Burgoine announced during dinner last night that Monte Carlo harbour is experiencing one of its regular swells and, as such, he felt it was not going to be safe for us to tender boat ashore today. He had therefore arranged for us to call at Cannes instead. Now, ordinarily we would have been dead chuffed to visit Cannes, but coming as it did at the cost of missing the iconic Monte Carlo, we were both really disappointed. But that's cruising I guess, and it's nobody's fault, so we just made the most of Cannes today and we'll do Monte Carlo on another cruise. Also, to be fair it is still possible to visit Monte Carlo today, via the train, but being still relatively new to cruising (and due to my CFS), we're both a little hesitant to travel too far afield from the ship unless it's on a P&O organised excursion.

So anyway, we didn't know much about Cannes other than its reputation for attracting the rich and glamorous, but with my Co-op credit card and a clean pair of Calvin Klein boxer shorts on, I think I pretty much fitted the bill. We had a wander along the palm tree-lined seafront first, which contained a number of very opulent looking shops, hotels and restaurants. In particular, the Carlton Hotel is simply beautiful with its grand palace style of architecture, its marble columned entrance, and its two distinctive domes, some say designed by those French rascals to resemble the breasts of Caroline Otero, the French Rivera's most famous courtesan. A truly glorious building (and a cracking pair of domes) that almost made you feel like a 1950s starlet might suddenly glide out the door surrounded by her fawning entourage.

Obviously Cannes is also famous for its film festival, and as we headed towards Cannes' luxury yacht-filled harbour, it was clear that we had just missed the latest festival. There were a number of large lorries and some temporary fencing around the main venue (the Palais des Festivals) where the festival is held, but to their credit, they were trying to be as discrete as a dozen juggernauts parked outside allowed them to be. I guess in an ideal world you would either visit Cannes during the festival, or when they are not making visible preparations/clearing up in relation to it. But we had a nice couple of hours in Cannes, and whilst it's not Monte Carlo, I would definitely recommend a visit.

Wednesday 13 October 2004
Dinner last night was the best yet. We both had lobster for our fish course that was to die for, and we followed that with perfectly-cooked lamb for main. I then had 1½ portions of one of my favourite puds, Eton Mess, as Mandy was unable to finish the second half of hers. Our waiter Biju, seeing how much I was enjoying finishing Mandy's pud, broke into a grin and offered me a third helping. I reluctantly declined, but it was good of him to offer, and good to see he's warming to us – due partially, I'm sure, to the involuntary but very audible groan I let out the other night, when the captain announced Monte Carlo had been cancelled. I'm not sure if it was just relief on his part that my groaning wasn't a reflection on the food, or that he found me banging my head repeatedly on the table amusing, but I think he's realised there's no airs and graces to us, so he's a bit more relaxed now.

Today we are berthed in Livorno and so, having visited Florence from this port on the last cruise, we had booked a short excursion to Pisa this time which was very good. There was a little bit of a walk from the coach drop off-point, but once we were into the Piazza dei Miracoli (The Square of Miracles) it was charming. It was a little touristy there with a few tat stalls, but we were there quite early (so not totally packed) and the sight of the marble tower, and its adjacent cathedral, just hit you between the eyes as soon as you entered the square. Both were resplendent in the flesh, we really enjoyed wandering in and around them for a bit. As I believe every visitor is required to do by law, we also grabbed the photo of us appearing to hold up the leaning tower with outstretched arms.

After a coffee and a sit-down at one of the tiny cafés in the square we decided to walk over to the smaller building on the opposite side of the cathedral to the tower. We found out that it was called the Baptistery, and once inside, found it to be quite tiny and round with a large font in the middle, and an open-domed roof. The guide we were with then started to sing in a slightly operatic style, and we got to hear these unique sounds bouncing around the roof space, which were very difficult to describe (so I won't try) but totally mesmerising. Whilst few tourists appeared to be taking any notice of the Baptistery, I think it's a must-do. It doesn't take long, a quick in and out, which was just as well as we were due back to the coach, and our lunch back on the ship beckoned.

Saturday 16 October 2004
Hokey dokey then, we've just had a couple of really energy-sapping days, but possibly the two most exciting ones of the cruise. Firstly, on Thursday we returned to Rome, but this time on a "Rome On Your Own" excursion. That basically meant we were coached to and from Rome, but the time in between was 100% our own. Not ideal for me as this meant seven long hours in Rome, so much longer than I can normally manage. But it was the shortest excursion available and we took it easy with lots of rests, and used taxis to get about, which helped. The good thing was that we got to spend a little longer at a few sights that we had to rush, or weren't able to get close to, on last year's coach-based excursion.

So after first spending some time in and around St Peter's Square, we decided to jump onto a horse-drawn carriage after finding one which a) had a beautifully looked after horse, and b) had a driver who looked willing to negotiate down from his normal astronomic prices. After being pick-pocketed in Rome last time, I had decided just to take a credit card and only 60 Euros with me, but Francesco, our driver, agreed to tailor his normal trip slightly in return for a hefty discount. This basically meant a one-way trip to the Forum via most of the main sights in between, plus a stop off at the opticians so that Francesco (or Cheeki Buggerio as I then nicknamed him) could pick up his new sunglasses. But it was most pleasant and a very civilised way to conserve some energy.

The Forum turned out to be a lot quieter this time and we were able to have a nice leisurely stroll in the autumn sunshine, taking our time and seeing much that we missed last time. Sadly, as we got to the Coliseum this wasn't as quiet, and the queues to go inside were once again quite long. No problem, we took some nice photos of the outside (which for me is the most iconic view of it anyway) and we will go inside another time. In any case Mandy wanted to visit the Victor Emmanuel Monument, or the "Wedding Cake" as it's commonly known on account of its perfectly symmetrical marble tiers. I could have kicked myself though, it was only later that we learned that it's possible to take an elevator up to the roof for panoramic 360-degree views over Rome, but even the views we did get to sample were pretty good.

We needed a rest after all that, so we had a long lazy lunch in the wonderful Piazza Navona, eating quite possibly at the very table (or so we told ourselves) that Matt Damon and Jude Law sat at in the movie The Talented Mr Ripley. We liked this piazza last time, and according to Mandy, it's fast becoming "our" piazza in much the same way that Placa Reial has become "our" square in Barcelona. I forget the name of the restaurant, but the pasta we had to eat was excellent and the Chianti they recommended washed it down very nicely. In fact, the waiter said the vino was from a little place just a couple of hours away called Cortona, and it was so good we stayed for another glass.

By that time, we only had two hours to wait until we could rendezvous with our Rome On Your Own group, coincidentally in Piazza Navona, to go back to the coach. So we decided to meander down a few of the side streets leading off of the Navona so that we stayed relatively close to our meeting point, whilst, Rome being Rome, we were still pretty likely to stumble across something spectacular. A Pantheon, a Marcellos Theatre and the Tomb of the Unknown Soldier later we were pooped and fast asleep on a coach bound for Oceana.

The napping continued for a couple of hours when we got back to the cabin actually, which ordinarily would have meant missing dinner. However, anticipating that passengers would be coming back from Rome late and tired, the restaurant team had chosen to offer an Indian Buffet Dinner in the Plaza. That worked perfectly for us as, on Biju's advice, I had pre-booked a table for the 8.30 slot, giving us time to rest and refresh. The buffet-style format also meant dinner was a much quicker affair, and so just an hour later we were all curried out and back in the cabin resting our aching bones, which was pretty crucial in readiness for Naples and our trip to Pompeii.

And so to yesterday. I awoke pretty wearily, but also excited that our stop in Naples (pronounced "Nipples" by our Italian guide) meant that we were able to visit Pompeii, a place that Mandy and I had both studied at school. Having breakfasted continentally in the cabin, to afford us more sleeping time, we soon joined our fellow "Ruins of Pompeii" excursion members, and hit the road for our half day trip.

About 15 minutes into the coach journey we caught our first glimpse of Mount Vesuvius, the huge volcano that dominates the Bay of Nipples. Although it's not done so for 60 years (and I'm sure there are numerous early warning systems in place now) I couldn't help but cast a glance up towards the summit to check for signs of imminent eruption. Whilst no visible signs were apparent, I did detect a worrying rumble or two actually, but quickly identified these to be emanating from those on the coach who had attended last night's Indian Buffet. After that, and me still wondering whether a 60-year gap is a good or a bad thing, we were quickly through the admission gates and up the short slope to enter Pompeii, quicker than you could say "anyone smell sulphur?"

Once inside Pompeii it was clear that to say the town had been excavated was to do 250 years of hard work a complete disservice. The sheer scale and condition of the place is mind-blowing. There are so many buildings, roads and large communal areas that just look, at worst, like they've been unused for a while. Add in its greenery of well-placed lawns, hedges and trees, and you really have to remind yourself that Pompeii is a 2000-year-old ruin. Pompeii in 2004 is in better condition than some parts of Swindon. Having visited Knossos in Crete, in a surprisingly cultured moment of a lads' holiday when I was 17, there is just no comparison – one is a Greek ruin, the other an instantly recognisable Roman city that was frozen in time.

But of course it was only possible for Pompeii to be as beautifully preserved as this because of Vesuvius erupting, and that fact is never more apparent than when you see the casts of those who lived and died there. Not just adults, but alongside them, their children and pets. And these casts are not their bodies, as only slight skeletal fragments remained, but instead spookily-detailed casts of the hollow spaces that were left within the hardened lava. Despite a natural curiosity, and the 2000 year gap since this happened, you can't help but feel the sadness. Overall though, a fascinating trip in a wonderful setting, and the only downside was that Pompeii's brothel, the walls of which are adorned with some pretty racy Roman images I'm told, was closed for some preservation works. Probably just as well, I would have blushed profusely.

Sunday 17 October 2004
Yesterday, we stopped off at a little place called Palau on the Italian island of Sardinia. In fact, Palau itself was so tiny that it seemed most of the ship had booked an excursion to see other parts of the island. We however, had deliberately not booked one, knowing a rest would be badly needed as we recovered from our Rome and Pompeii exertions. Lots of people were very complimentary about what they saw on their various excursions though, so it seems the island, the second biggest in the Med after Sicily, has much more to offer than the short pleasant walk we had around Palau harbour.

As it happens, we didn't do much more today either, as after a lazy morning at sea, we had a sleepy Sunday afternoon stop off in Palma, Mallorca. Much of Palma was closed of course, but it wasn't a problem for us, and it was nice to just take things easy in the sunshine again. As in Palau, we went ashore for a short stroll, and we enjoyed the delightful mixture of Medieval, Italian and Moorish architecture, especially around the area of Palma's sun-kissed cathedral, before returning to the ship for a poolside barbeque.

The "barbie" turned out to be quite a lively affair actually, as a dozen or so kitchen staff manned a sizeable buffet containing all the old BBQ favourites like burgers, hot dogs and ribs. It really was quite a spread, and soon attracted an enthusiastic, hunger-driven queue despite it being (in some cases) literally minutes since breakfast. But I can't blame them, it all looked fantastic, and once that initial midday rush had quietened down a bit, I popped along myself for a burger and some chicken goujons for Mand. Everyone seemed to really enjoy it, so well done to P&O for dropping little variations like this into the normal dining options of the cruise. As much as I love their fine dining, it ain't half nice just to have burger and chips sometimes.

Monday 18 October 2004
A good night last night. It started with pre-dinner cocktails in Magnum's Bar at 6pm, with Tiger Tim and his lovely wife Tiger Tina. Cocktail of the day, the system whereby a different cocktail each day is half price, was Pina Colada, my favourite, and so a couple slipped down very

nicely thank you. Alcohol-wise, they make them fairly weak actually, but that's fine with me – as I say, my pathetic excuse for a body is still struggling to tolerate anything stronger than a wine gum. We shared some laughs and a few stories about our respective exploits in Rome, although poor old Tim was devastated to find he had paid nearly double for their horse and carriage compared to us, hee hee.

Next was dinner, and both Mandy and I really enjoyed it. I had lost my appetite slightly for a few days which is most unlike me, but then Rome especially had hit me a bit. Well last night, despite that burger and chips for lunch, I was really ready for dinner and my choices of mussels, sea bream and a bannoffee dessert were all beyond my already overused list of superlatives. Biju and I also had a bit of fun with the young boy, Charlie, at an adjacent table, who is cruising with his grandparents. He's only about five years old, and there are few children on this cruise to keep him company, but he's been perfectly behaved. I had winked at him a couple of evenings just to make him smile, but last night Biju asked if he could bring him over to our table to say hello. Of course we said yes, and ten minutes later we were all firm friends having some fun.

Tuesday 19 October 2004
Yesterday's stop in the Spanish mainland port of Cartagena was a real surprise, mostly because it didn't feel Spanish at all. It felt very Moorish to me, some of the buildings especially, but also had an obvious Roman influence that gave it a real un-Spanish feel. Chuck in plenty of greenery, some great beaches next to the gloriously blue sea, and it immediately felt a lovely place to walk around. Of course, being Spanish it had that cleanliness and gentle organisation to it that you get in most Spanish resorts, and I don't think we were alone in being pleasantly surprised by the place.

For us, we were soon circumnavigating the city walls, a seldom-enjoyed hobby of mine. Maybe I was a sentry in a previous life, but whether it's York or Rhodes Town, I do like to walk a city wall. And as luck would have it Cartagena has a fine one with good views, and it comes to an end just up the road from our shuttle bus back to the ship, which my legs were very thankful for.

Today we are in Gibraltar, and poor old Mandy has been stitched up like a kipper. You see, at dinner last night we got talking to young Charlie's granddad who we had already realised is a bit of a joker. So when

Mandy was talking about her planned purchases in Gib, we were both extremely dubious when Charlie's granddad suggested there was a Selfridges here. Not put off by the extremely doubtful looks on our faces, he proceeded to draw a map on a napkin as to where Selfridges was. Now, as soon as we were out of ear shot, Mand and I basically said that the poor old fella was going loopy if he thought there was a Selfridges in Gibraltar. But did that stop us looking for it this morning? Did it hell as like! And even with the very small consolation that we actually found said establishment just yards from the route we would have taken anyway, we still felt very foolish indeed on discovering a small electrical appliance store called…..wait for it…..Sell Fridges! Duh!!

Still, on a positive note, the experience seemed to curtail Mandy's retail-related enthusiasm and we were back to the ship nice and early, with two bottles of duty free under my arm, and up top sunbathing well before our 1pm departure time. It's a nice place, Gib, and although we didn't make it up the rock this time either, "it's a nice place to just stretch your legs and save a few quid stocking up on your lippy" as one lady put it. The fridges were pretty reasonable too.

Wednesday 20 October 2004
After shamefully missing the lunchtime sailaway party yesterday, as a result of me falling asleep on my sun-lounger (only closed my eyes for a second), we grabbed a late lunch in the Liguarian Restaurant where they were having an Oriental Buffet. Very nice it was too, and Tiger Tim would have been proud of me as I washed it all down with a Tiger Beer.

What made it extra special was that as we got inside the restaurant (just before the doors closed at 2pm), Biju, our man-mountain of a dinner waiter, started jumping up and down on tip-toes on the other side of the restaurant, waving a napkin and calling our names. Basically, Biju was waiting at the table we sit at every night for dinner, and far from wanting to nip off early for a well-deserved rest, he wanted to serve us our lunch there, too. We both found this quite touching, especially as we could barely get a smile out of him at the beginning of the cruise. Needless to say, we enjoyed his company and some gorgeous oriental food but, given the waiters rely on a couple of hours of afternoon rest due to their late nights and early mornings, we didn't hang around too long.

In the evening, after making Charlie's granddad's day at dinner by confessing that we had checked out Selfridges/Sell Fridges (he laughed so much he nearly choked on his Tiramisu!), we popped off to Tiffany's for a drink. The Tigers, Tim and Tina, joined us after they first went to the show. Mand and I gave the show a miss as it was a classical vocalist tonight, and whilst Tina had clearly been impressed, Tim compared the gentleman's vocals to asphyxiating various household pets, so take from that what you will. You can't please everyone I guess, and it just goes to show what a job P&O have on their hands catering for all tastes.

Friday 22 October 2004
It was our last day yesterday, and the sea proved to be quite choppy over the second half of the Bay of Biscay, which made Mandy feel a little off colour. This meant that she spent much of the day in the cabin, watching a mix of the movies available on the in-cabin TV, and a few DVD's on the portable DVD player we had brought with us from home. She also made full use of both the room-service menu and the dedicated one man waitering service (i.e. me) delivering direct from The Plaza's excellent buffet. That was fine actually, it meant I could get Mandy a little treat now and again to make her last (cabin-bound) day a little more fun, and personally I don't mind the ship movement much at all. In fact it's good for me when it's a little choppy as it makes everyone else walk around as slow and wobbly as me.

Although I spent much of the day in the cabin with her, Mandy insisted I get out and about for a bit so I thought right, I'll sit out on the Prom Deck for a while. It was so draughty out there that I must have looked a real sight with my coat zipped right up to the collar, and my chin hunkering down to meet it. But hey, it was sun and sea air that I was unlikely to get much more of for a while, so I wasn't bothered what I looked like. It was quite refreshing in a bracing kind of way. But if I wasn't worried about what I looked like then, the total opposite was true later on, as I discovered the effects of a nautical phenomenon called "windburn" – or in other words, the acceleration of sunburn to oddly specific parts of one's body or face due to the effects of the wind. I basically burnt no other part of my body except two large circles around and under each eye, and I now looked like something from Andy Warhol's experimental 'Magenta Panda' period.

Consequently, it was with a slightly heavy heart that I self-consciously went to our final dinner last night with my miraculously-recovered wife (note to self, if she feels queasy on the next cruise, just induce 20 minutes of hysterical non-stop laughter by showing her freakishly odd facial sunburn). I would describe the reaction in the dining room to be mixed - everything from pointing (little Charlie bless him), to a strangely santa-like ho ho ho (Alan the restaurant manager), to the simultaneous bending at the waist with hands on knees to support the sheer strength of the laughing policeman-like glee of our two waiters (Biju and Ashok). I remained unmoved throughout, even when Charlie's granddad likened my beige/brown ensemble, and reddish face and eyes, to a matchstick wearing pink sunglasses.

After dinner we went straight in to see the final Stadium Theatre Company show, which I'm pleased to say was on a par with all the other excellent shows they performed this cruise. They got a standing ovation from most of the audience at the end, which was good to see and just recognition of a job well done. And then, with an even heavier heart than the one I had going into dinner, we were off to bed for an early night. Many passengers, I should explain, had intentions of partying well into the night, and in a different life I would have happily joined them, but alas I have tested my limitations too much already this cruise so, it's Mr Sensible bidding you all good night.

Saturday 23 October 2004

Okay, all back at home now after a seamless disembarkation this morning and a nice drive home. Our parents and our three cats are all in fine health, so that is the best end to a cruise we could possibly have. Also, we now have two cruises under our belt so that must make us regulars I suppose, and I think we are truly hooked. If anything, this time was much easier for me, health-wise, knowing how things operate on a cruise. It helped too that we had a quiet table for two for dinner each night, and whilst we missed the company of Richard and Joyce from our last cruise, I certainly found I had more energy this time around. So all good and another fantastic break.

Chapter 5 - Am I going to lose my Job?

Sunday 14 November 2004

Two old mates came to see me last week which was great as we had lost touch a bit and I hadn't seen them for a few years. They are only 20 or so miles down the road and so, when I first moved here, we did initially make a real effort to meet up and go out on a Friday night. But as often happens in life, gradually contact became less and less frequent and then, what I now suspect was the CFS started to affect me, and I just found it hard going out with them even occasionally. That meant that when the CFS really did take hold, and eventually got diagnosed, I felt too embarrassed to phone and tell them, especially as telling other blokes I have CFS felt, well, pathetic. Obviously, these days it's widely-recognised as a serious debilitating illness, but the old "Yuppy Flu" stigma still remains and so, rightly or wrongly, it can feel uncomfortable telling other people that's what I have.

As it turns out, they would have been delighted to know I had CFS, as when they did find out I was ill, via the rumour mill of our home town, the consensus was that I had MS! Bless them, when I explained that someone somewhere must have got a letter mixed up, as I have ME, the lads seemed quite disappointed. Not that they know much about either MS or ME, just that they presumably saw MS as a very serious illness, and were concerned for me. So that then led to a lengthy explanation of what I did have, what had happened, and when. At which point they looked even more disappointed, and I felt every bit as pathetic as I thought I would had I phoned them in the first place. But it was good to see them, and know they are well and happy.

Monday 29 November 2004

I saw my boss Chris again today, and having met with him a few times now, with no clear improvement in my health, he had some answers for me on the concerns I have about my ongoing employment. Basically, I have now been off work for two-and-a-half years, and so whilst I never thought for a second I would ever be ill for this long, it means I now have just 12 months left before my employer's health insurance ceases to pay me an income. At that point my employer will make a decision over my ongoing employment with them. It's something that has been increasingly worrying me, and so Chris had offered to look into it and come back and level with me.

Chris explained that the situation, assuming I can't get back to work beforehand, is basically an either/or of two very specific scenarios. The scary option is that in the event that I am considered to be permanently disabled from doing my job, I will be retired (in my thirties no less) on an ill-health pension. The really scary option is that if I'm not considered permanently disabled from doing my job, then my employment will be terminated under a process called "capability" (in effect due my incapability to do the job). As I have enjoyed working for the same company since I was 18, I dread both options, but in purely financial terms, an ill-health pension would at least give me an income, whereas the latter option is effectively the sack. I still have those 12 months to get better, but any progress I'm making is just so slow and, sadly, there appears to be no sign of a miracle cure.

I have to be honest it's worrying me, and I have to keep reminding myself that the anxiety I'm feeling is partly due to the CFS. I used to be very good at handling stuff like this, but these days it does affect me more as my brain just seems to work differently. Fortunately, Macca phoned this afternoon, which helped me get my thinking straight on the matter, and then took my mind off it completely. We had pencilled in to go and visit Yeti tomorrow, and after discussing whether I'm still up to it, we decided we would still go if I'm feeling okay tomorrow. Thinking about Yeti also gives me a timely kick up the arse not to be so totally self-obsessed, and worry so much, when things could be so much worse. And, if there are any miracle cures at all to be had out there, then you can have mine Yeti, we all miss you buddy.

Wednesday 1 December 2004
Macca and I did go down to see Yeti last night and whilst again it was not an enjoyable experience, I felt better for going. There's still no change in the lad, and it now seems very unlikely there will be. I just hope that the very brief periods of semi-consciousness he has, such as when his mum kisses him goodbye at the end of a visit, are the only times he's really there. Such a shame, it really is, and I just hope that the cardiologist who told him that it was absolutely fine for him to start playing football again (Yeti's heart stopped five minutes into his second training session) has learnt a huge lesson over this, and he's a damn sight more cautious with his advice in future.

One good thing from those trips to see Yeti, at least for me, is that I get to bore Macca rigid on the journey there and back. He's a good sounding-board actually, and due to my recent worries over my job and income, it was well timed. I felt loads better for talking about it. The problem is, even when I'm feeling quite sharp, my fuzzled brain seems to act like a bad DJ at a wedding, spilling out any old rubbish with little, if any, connection to what went before. I'm not sure how, but for some reason we got onto speaking about kids, possibly because Macca was updating me on events with his three boys. We then moved on to Mandy and me, and whether we would have a family. In short, it got a bit heavy even for me.

You see, I love kids and have always enjoyed spending time with my nieces and nephews particularly. Before I was ill, I was even involved with football training under-11's, which was great. However, as we only got married in our late twenties and had no immediate or burning desire to have kids, Mandy and I said we would think about having a family when we were 35. Trouble is, my health issues started to show around the time I was 32 and now, three years on, we don't think it would be fair to bring a child into our situation. It's possible it could work, and my current position could even lend itself to me being a house-husband in the future, but the more I accept that my CFS could be here long-term, the more impossible it seems.

And as if to confirm that I am thinking along the right lines, Macca finally got a word in edge ways to tell me, in all seriousness, that he's always had us pegged as "cat people" anyway! Charming!! I'm guessing Mand and I are a long, long way down the list of people who would take care of their boys in the event that him and Michaela are both tragically asphyxiated in some kind of kinky sex game, but it's only now I realise this is because he thinks his boys would, in our care, end up licking their own arses. He could have a point I guess.

Tuesday 7 December 2004
Had a strange old experience today with a Homeopathic doctor in Bristol. It came about at Martin's suggestion, and due to my constant need to be trying something new to get well. And I do mean constant need. I just find that if I am trying a new treatment or approach, or learning something new about CFS, then in my head at least I'm moving forward. The problem is, two years in and I've pretty much exhausted the treatment and support that is available. I think even Martin would normally have withdrawn from the picture by now, but he's continuing to see me thankfully, albeit less regularly than before.

So anyway, following Martin's suggestion to give Homeopathy a go, this morning I found myself in front of a nice lady doctor who asked me some very strange questions. Now, I am very open minded about alternative medicine, particularly due to how much Traditional Chinese Acupuncture has helped me, but I found this session not just strange, but exhausting too.

Initially the Homeopathy doctor questioned me about my dreams when I am asleep. She was interested in what they are about, and how often I have them. Now, I'm always keen to provide as much information as possible (many would say too much information), but I rarely remember my dreams, so I said so. Not to be put off, the doctor then proceeded to grill me so hard about <u>any</u> dream I have had, that eventually I wearily recounted a dream involving Claudia Winkleman, a Liverpool football shirt, and a large can of squirty cream. I know, I know, it's obvious to me now it's not the sort of dream she was interested in, but she wore me down and, like a water-boarded Michael Ball, I sang loud and strong in the hope of a release from the questioning.

Next she wanted me to describe my headaches to her, and so using the same "aching", "throbbing" and "shooting" descriptions I've repeated ad infinitum to doctors for the last three years, I thought I was in for a much easier time. Wrong. She asked me the same question in subtly different ways again and again, until through sheer frustration and exhaustion I very nearly answered her latest "Yes, but how does it FEEEEEL?" with "Well, it FEEEELS a lot worse since I came in here!" I tried to remember that she was only there to help me, and eventually she seemed happy when, in a moment of inspiration, desperation, or possibly exasperation, I described the feeling in my head as being like a pea being pushed through a slightly smaller straw. She seemed happy with that, made some notes, and soon afterwards explained my Homeopathic medicine would be sent to me shortly.

When I walked back into the waiting room my dad, who had kindly driven me to Bristol, likened the look I had to someone who had just returned from the Somme, the six-mile stare and all. I was shattered. Oh well, if Homeopathy helps then it will all have been worth it.

Wednesday 22 December 2004
Yesterday I met Phil and Ivan, two old mates and colleagues, for lunch and I tried a new approach. Actually, that sounds a lot more drastic than

it was: I didn't sit there and ignore them for an hour or anything, just to try and conserve energy. No, all I did differently was instead of walking 15 minutes each way, I drove there and walked back. See I told you, it's hardly earth-shattering stuff. I generally limit my driving to ten minutes or so duration, because of the concentration it requires, but this journey was well within that ten-minute window, even allowing for traffic. And even though I needed to walk home afterwards due to all the talking (Mandy picked the car up on her way home), today when the delayed fatigue usually hits me more, I'm feeling better than after previous lunches. So, on the days when I feel sharp enough to drive, it gives me a good option.

Meeting up with Phil and Ivan is always good as they rarely seem to change at all. That feels good to me, as my brain gets fooled into thinking the last three years haven't happened at all, and for an all-too-short a spell, CFS, and being unable to work, is completely forgotten about. Ivan still moans about Sky television (and its monopoly of UK sport coverage), and Phil still dresses entirely in clothing from Next, so it really did feel like nothing had changed. Or at least it did, until they started showing me photos on their phones of offspring that had literally doubled in size. That meant two things: firstly, those three years have happened after all, and secondly, I seriously need to get a new phone because mine can do little beyond, well, phone.

Friday 31 December 2004
Well it's New Year's Eve and, party animal that I am, I've been looking on the internet at what to spend all the "what do you buy the man that does nothing" money I got for Christmas. As I am now painfully aware how much people are starting to point at me whenever they catch sight of my old Nokia mobile phone, I thought I should check out how things have moved on. They've got expensive, that's how things have moved on, and based on the fact I spend 23½ hours per day within these four walls (i.e. not very mobile), it seems crazy to spend a fortune on a new one. Plus, I'm as tight as a camel's bum in a sandstorm, so maybe I'll offer to buy one of Skelts' old phones, as he seems to change them with his underwear.

Anyway, it's New Year's Eve as I say, and thanks to Mand, and Jools Holland, this place will soon be rocking. That is if you take into account that due to my semi-regular balance issues, our house always feels like it's rocking a wee bit because, I can assure you, the music volume will be at a very sensible level. Oh no, none of that partying business here thanks very much, it's just me, the missus and the cats. Oh and the largest, most varied two-person buffet you have ever seen, thanks to Mand making it her mission to ensure a great new year, even if we can't go out. Again. But that's okay, we're quite happy here with Jools.

Wednesday 26 January 2005
I've been thinking a lot about my job and what I can do to avoid losing it. Part of me wonders if I should just try going back anyway, and just see how it goes. But what could I do, and how would my employer facilitate my need for regular rests? If I could just find a way of making it work I would jump at the chance. I know that all the signs, and everything that I have learnt about CFS, suggests the exact opposite currently, but maybe it's just worth trying. What's the worst that could happen?

The trouble is, if I went back to work and the worst really did happen, as would seem inevitable in my current state of health, then I would be back at square one, barely able to get out of bed. I would also put Mandy through all that stress and difficulty again, and I can't do that to her. Besides, I would need both my doctor and my employer to agree to my return to work, and that isn't going to happen until I'm better than I am currently, and consistently so.

I'm kidding myself really. At this point in time, despite the Pacing helping me improve things considerably, I'm a million miles away from being able to work. Realistically, even if I could work from home my health is still so inconsistent that I couldn't guarantee to meet a deadline, or even the accuracy of the work that I do. Working from home is the likeliest possibility, and something I've thought about before, as at least I wouldn't be using up energy travelling, so hopefully it's something to consider in the not too distant future.

Friday 28 January 2005
Yesterday I sat down to watch a movie on DVD. It was called Insomnia and starred Al Pacino. It was good. Or at least it was until I fell asleep.

Today I sent an email to the Oxford English Dictionary, suggesting they add "When an insomniac falls asleep whilst watching the movie Insomnia" after the entry for "Irony".

Tuesday 15 February 2005
It's once again the anniversary of when Mandy and I first went out. Our first date was originally due to be on Valentine's Day but, having initially said yes, Mandy then decided that particular day might be a bit too "heavy" for a first date. So we went out on the 15th instead, and I will be forever grateful, as it means each year I get to avoid taking Mandy out on an overpriced, overcrowded and over-marketed 14th February (bah humbug), in favour of a nice quiet (and cheaper!) anniversary meal 24 hours later.

My plan was to do something different this year, as obviously we've not done much in the way of celebration for a few years. So, based on a TV programme we've been watching about John Burton Race's new restaurant, The New Angel, I thought it would be a nice treat to take her there. But I now know it's in Dartmouth, about a two-and-a-half hour car journey from here, and I struggle, even as a passenger, with anything more than an hour. A train could be do-able but with multiple changes and taxis, the journey time doubles. Staying overnight is a possibility but again, the journey time, and the delayed fatigue of CFS could mean I am very ill and a long way from my own bed.

So instead, Mandy drove us to Marlborough for a couple of hours and we lunched at an old favourite, Coles. It was very nice, Mandy said she loved it, and the food was excellent as normal, but I couldn't help but feel a little disappointed that I couldn't take her to Dartmouth. There will be other times when I can, I hope. Either there or - Mandy being a Rick Stein fan - a trip to Padstow, which is a place that has proved equally tricky to get to these last few years. One day Mand.

Thursday 24 March 2005
I had another new boss come and visit me today as Chris has emigrated to Australia (I told you I was hard work!). My new manager, Steve, seems a nice fella who, after listening to me drone on for an hour about how determined I am to get back to work, seems keen to help. He even agreed to have a think about any work I could possibly do at home for him, which would be good. I have suggested this in the past, but the nature of the business means pretty much all the work is deadline-driven stuff, that isn't really able to be done 100% off-site by some numpty with the cognitive ability of a plum.

Of course my anxiety over whether I will still have a job at all come November is still very prevalent, and so Steve would have gone away in no doubt that this situation is a) on my mind, and b) not helping. Having been at the same company so long, and having worked my arse off to gradually climb the ladder career-wise, it really would be a big blow to lose my job. And the nearer we get, the more I'm conscious of the fact that this might not just be my job that is ending, but of course my income too. I'm sure the stress I'm feeling over the situation is exaggerated by my CFS, but I have to find a way of putting it to the back of my mind and focus on getting better.

Saturday 30 April 2005
Well I'm dead chuffed with myself as I attended one of the lads' regular "Curry Nights" last night which, having missed out on many since my health issues started, I had been looking forward to for weeks. I had already tested the (mineral) water a wee bit by joining the lads early on for an Evian or two at one of the more recent Curry Nights, but last night I was there at the curry – surely the essential part of any Curry Night. Not much to get excited about you might think, but our Curry Nights are something that started circa 1994, and have formed a firm and regular appearance in my life ever since. So to me, it's not just leaving these four walls and forgetting about everything for a while, but it also represents normality.

So, what is Curry Night? Well, you need to concentrate here or you will miss the brilliance that is Curry Night - first and foremost, to attend Curry Night you need to have been one of the original forming members, namely Macca, Kenty, Skelts, Bruce, and myself. Next, Curry Night takes place periodically on a Friday, unfeasibly soon after (or preferably earlier than) the clock strikes 5pm to mark the end of the working week. The objective at that point is just to consume a sizeable, but not unreasonable amount of alcoholic beverage in preparation for the curry element of the evening later on. When, and only when, the amount of alcohol consumed by attendees has sufficiently impaired their normal dietary/dining-related judgement, and the mental capacity of said attendees is still at a level where the objective of moving onto the curry still registers, then the final crucial stage can commence.

The curry part of the evening, as is hopefully obvious, involves the eating of a curry. But it is so much more than that. Indeed, the exact order for the five regular attendees is five Chicken Madras curries, five pilau rice, five naan bread and five pints of Cobra beer. Each attendee is then tasked with consuming their meal, not ridiculously so, but faster than the other attendees present, with the objective of winning the mystical Yellow Jersey – mystical in that, unlike the one in the Tour De France, our Yellow Jersey has never actually existed (never will) and that, other than for bragging rights by the winner, the imaginary jersey simply qualifies the holder to choose the location of the subsequent Curry Night.

So, turning back to last night specifically, Mandy dropped me off just after 5pm to meet the rest of the lads at our usual bar. That was good, as at that time it was quiet and it also ensured I was on very familiar ground in the company of people who know me, which helped a lot, and we were soon having a real craic. Then about 7.30pm, as the place started to fill up and the music volume was knocked up a couple of hundred octaves, Mandy came and picked me up. But was my evening finished? Oh no, this crazy dude was planning to hit the town again later, and party like it was 1999.

Okay, so in 1999 I wasn't in the habit of going home for a mid-evening rest. Neither did it involve sitting by the phone waiting for my, by now heavily inebriated, mates to phone me and a) drunkenly chuck abuse down the phone at me, questioning everything from my masculinity to the colour of the shirt I was wearing, and b) tell me it's quietened down now, so come and join them for the curry. But that's exactly what happened, and so at about 11.30pm Mand dropped me at the curry house of choice. The lads were of course all ten sheets to the wind by then, and proceeded to dribble and giggle through their curries so much, that I for the first time ever won the Yellow Jersey. None of them will remember that obviously, and due to my CFS-affected stomach being adverse to anything the least bit spicy, my Madras won't be quite as easily forgotten, but I am well and truly chuffed to have been there. A good night.

Tuesday 17 May 2005
Mum and Dad popped in today and I was horrible to them. The problem is they have always tended to pop in unannounced, which pre-CFS, wasn't a problem, but, these days I need to ensure a rest period beforehand. I've explained this to them, and how I plan out my day to alternate rest and activity periods, but they keep turning up just as I've had my daily walk - probably the most tired part of my day. At that

point, although I always try not to walk so far as to feel overly tired, I need to rest both physically and mentally. If I don't, I get tired, and therefore grumpy, pretty quickly.

So when Mum and Dad turned up I was a little vexed that they hadn't warned me. When they then asked me the same questions I felt I had answered numerous times before, I was more than a little grumpy. When they left, understandably miffed, I then felt more than a little guilty. So guilty I couldn't stop thinking about it. Which means that, mentally, I didn't then get any rest at all, which made me feel even grumpier. I do love them, and they have been a massive help these last few years, but I just wish they could give me a bit of notice of when they plan to pop in. I will then, hopefully, be all sweetness and light and not come across like a pre-menstrual bear with toothache. I guess it just shows that my family are having to adjust to the new me every bit as much as I am.

Sunday 12 June 2005
It was Gareth's 18th birthday party last night, and as great an occasion as it was, and a milestone very well celebrated, it was also a little bittersweet. You see, very soon after Gareth's passing-out in August, it was discovered that my aunt, June, had cancer and June being June, she made damn sure she was at last night's party. As it happens, June was on fine form and put me totally to shame energy-wise. As normal, she wanted to know how every individual branch of the family was doing, and how big all the kids were getting.

I, on the other hand, was struggling to keep up, so Mandy kindly kept our side of the conversation going, which is easily done with June as she is so easy to talk to. In my defence, I hadn't been feeling good all week, so wouldn't normally have gone along to the party, but I wanted to see June and not disappoint Gareth. And despite not being at my best, I'm glad we went, even if it was just for an hour or two. It really was good to see June and also Gareth walking around with the widest of grins on his face. Luckily, home was only five minutes away, so although I pushed my luck energy-wise, I was home and resting pretty soon afterwards.

Tuesday 26 July 2005
I've had a couple of chats with my Homeopathy doctor over the last few months. The good news is that there has been no repeat of me travelling all the way to Bristol to be grilled about what it is exactly a football-

shirted Claudia Winkleman and I would get up to with an unending supply of squirty cream. The bad news is that even though we have reviewed, on the phone, how I am doing with the Homoeopathic medication, and the doctor tweaking it as necessary, it's not having the slightest affect.

I've discussed it with Martin too, and I think I'm going to stop it unless I see some change soon. Admittedly, I have been rather anxious of late, which may not have helped, but at the end of the day, if it isn't working, you need to know when to stop and try something else.

Saturday 30 July 2005
Mandy and I went to the Mela today and it was brilliant. It's an annual event that's held in the town gardens, just up the road from us, to celebrate Asian culture. There's everything from Asian music to stalls offering henna tattoos and Asian crafts. But the best bit, and the main reason we go if I'm honest, is the food. Just about every Indian restaurant in town, and many more from elsewhere, cook the most amazing food on-site in these gigantic pans. It smells fantastic and tastes even better.

The Mela gets more and more popular every year, and is fast becoming one of the largest free events in the whole country. Consequently, to avoid the crowds and noise I still really struggle with, Mandy and I get there very early, walk around the food stalls whilst they are still getting ready to open, and then, at the midday opening time immediately buy the food we most like the look of. We then wander off to our favourite little corner of the gardens to eat our curry and numerous accompaniments, with a small bottle of wine. It really is good and one of the highlights of our year. When the Mela first started two years ago, and I was really struggling with the CFS, we would just pick up a terrific curry and take it straight home. However, as I got stronger and we realised just what a perfect location the town gardens are, for both us and the Mela, we started to make a concerted effort to spend a little time there every year. Of course, me being me, we've normally left within the hour, before the real crowds arrive or the music starts, but those 60 minutes are, to borrow a word from my childhood, ace!

Today, as we sat there mid-curry, and shielded from all but the very tallest of fellow attendees by a wall of shrubs and flowers, we suddenly had an elephant walk by, ridden by an Indian Princess. It was quite surreal, even at an Asian festival, and it was only the sheer combined height of said mammal and Princess, that allowed us to see them from our location, but they looked amazing. For all we know, they might be at the Mela every year (as I say, we come and go quite early), but as they wandered by to the sound of gentle Indian music, and the Princess all dressed up in her finery and makeup, Mand and I just stared up at them open-mouthed (which couldn't have looked pretty at that stage of the curry). The way the Princess swayed her hands and arms in time with the music was mesmerising. Or at least it was until the little girl next to us decided it was time to address the elephant in the park with "Mummy, why's Sunita from next door riding a metal elephant?" I karate-chopped my poppadums and went back to my curry.

Friday 12 August 2005
We went to June's funeral in Colchester last week and so it's obviously been a really sad time. In the end, after seeming so strong at Gareth's party, June's passing just seemed to happen really quickly. It was hard seeing my dad so upset, let alone my Uncle Ray and my cousin Tracey, who were devastated. And it's only small consolation I know, but there was standing room only available at June's funeral, it was so packed. I think that, and the cavalcade of taxis and private hire vehicles that followed June's coffin all the way to the chapel (June and Ray ran their own private hire company for many years), just goes to show how much she was loved by everyone that knew her.

As well as obviously being a very emotional day, it was also a very long day. Bless him, despite my dad grieving over the loss of his sister at the age of just 59, he insisted on driving me there and back the same day, knowing that the delayed fatigue of my CFS is usually at its worst the following day. And with Mandy never having been a very confident driver, and never having driven on a motorway, it was a big help. Travelling that far is really hard now and the day really took it out of me, but I was honoured to be there to say goodbye to a truly lovely lady. Rest in peace June, we'll miss you.

Saturday 20 August 2005
Phil, my brother who is a mechanic, came and picked up our car today as the engine management light keeps coming on. His workshop, to where I should be taking the car, is only about 20 miles away from here, but I wasn't feeling so good so he came and got it. He said he and his wife Karen would take the opportunity to do some shopping in the area

whilst they were here, but I think he was just trying to make me feel less like the pain in the arse I surely am. He'll pop the car back Monday evening which again is great for us, and a real help, but hardly ideal for Phil at the end of a 12-hour day.

To be fair, I did try and get it sorted out locally so as not to bother Phil, or at least not have the headache of getting the car down to him when it could be just a trivial fault. But not only did the local garage fail to resolve the issue, they miraculously discovered a whole range of other stuff that supposedly needs doing instead. So if I can I'm going to stick with Phil from here on in, as although those 20 miles can be harder than they sound, I would much rather take the car down to him every time, knowing that he will do it properly, than get ripped off. Fortunately the car doesn't need much in the way of maintenance as we only do about 3000 miles per year now, so hopefully Phil doesn't need to provide a pick-up and drop-off service too often. It's really good of him and Karen to help us out.

Friday 14 October 2005
I had verbal confirmation this week that my employment will cease next month and I will instead be paid an ill-health pension from my employer's pension scheme. This should feel like good news given that the only alternative, had I not been deemed permanently disabled from doing my job, would have been termination of employment with no income at all. But other than the huge relief of knowing I still have an income, I just feel sadness.

From the age of 18 I really did work incredibly hard at my job, and, despite being amongst colleagues who were often more talented and, in pretty much every case, better qualified than me, I built a decent career. Financial Services isn't an area I ever envisaged working in to be honest, but with the Head Office of one the largest such firms in the country just down the M4, and the 18-year old me feeling increasingly claustrophobic in the small accountants that I joined from school, it seemed like a good step. And I loved it right from the off. Not necessarily the work back then (although I did, for the large part, enjoy it), but more the people side of things. The company felt massive, it was full of like-minded people of a similar age who liked to play hard, as well as work hard. It was also a performance-driven environment which strongly encouraged career progression for those prepared to work for it. It suited me down to the ground.

What I really loved about the place was that it was so big, and so multi-faceted, that you could even change onto a completely different career path, but still stay within the same organisation. That meant that after some initial entry-level administrative roles I gradually moved into more specialist and technical positions, before latterly moving into management. If I had enjoyed my previous roles, then I absolutely loved the managerial side of things, and it immediately seemed the perfect fit for me. I can actually remember thinking, in around 1999 or 2000, this is it, life is good, everything is great, if I could stop time now I would.

But time didn't stop. And whilst life and work continued to get even better for a good time after that, what I didn't know was that things would change so drastically. I had envisaged working for my employer until I retire – as does Mandy, who's now been there 18 years – and it just seems like a bad joke that my retirement has come so prematurely and in such frustrating circumstances, when I still hoped to do so much more. But now it's all just gone and it's not even my fault. It's not my fault I became ill, it's not my fault it took so long to be diagnosed, and it's not my fault that, despite trying everything available, I haven't been able to get better. At the risk of sounding like a petulant child, it's not bloody fair. I know I should just be grateful that I will be getting the pension, especially when many with this same illness aren't anywhere near as fortunate, but what I really want is something I know is not possible – my life back!

Chapter 6 – The Pensioner in Amsterdam

Tuesday 18 October 2005
I've been gradually telling our families and a few close friends about my ill health retirement. It's not something I really want to do just yet, as in many ways I feel like a complete failure that it has come to this. However, I felt I needed to speak to Mandy's family especially, given that I had, after all, promised to take care of her until death do us part, and at least the ill-health pension now provides us with some financial security. And what was pleasing actually was that Mand's mum, and every one of her three brothers, all said the same thing: that they have never had any doubt that Mandy will be absolutely fine with me, whatever happens.

Actually, both our families have been really supportive throughout this. There are some that we see more of than others, and undoubtedly a couple of wider family members who believe the solution to my illness is to "just pull yourself together", but mostly they've been really supportive. To a person they are clearly saddened to see us in this situation, given how active and full our life used to be, but they have been there for us - in varying degrees admittedly, but they are there if we need them, I think. Mum and Dad, retired as they are, have even moved back from the Isle of Wight, in part, I suspect, so they can help taxi me around to doctor and acupuncture appointments. So, as sad as I feel currently there is plenty to be thankful for.

Thursday 20 October 2005
I'm starting to feel more positive about things now, mostly because I've realised just how fortunate I am to still have an income. Most in my situation don't have the luxury of moping around with a face like a smacked arse because they have been pensioned off. For many there is no pension, but instead a constant fight for state benefits; i.e. the exact position I would be in had I not been lucky enough to be working for a good company with a decent pension scheme since I was 18.

Also, since word spread about my "retirement" I have had a few of my old bosses and colleagues get in touch to suggest that, just as soon as I can get well, there is a job waiting for me with them. That was so good to hear and a real shot in the arm. Hopefully it means that my working life is far from over, and I may still be able to recommence my career in the future. And logically, if anyone is prepared to take a chance on me given my appalling sickness record of the last few years, and the prognosis of how limited I may be in future, it's my old employer, where people know what I am all about. I'm not expecting to fit back into my old role, or even get back full-time necessarily, but there's a realistic hope of a job, and I need that. I have even found myself fantasising about getting a job back there as one of the internal postmen like Macca's dad, Brian, is doing in his semi-retirement. In fact, if I didn't need it to sort the post, I would give my right arm for just that.

On the downside, my discussions with my (ex) employer's Pension department have not been as encouraging. I simply asked what happens to my pension if I return to work with the company in the future. Would it, for example, return to the position I was in as a normal employee, as I hope it would, in order that I could instead receive it from age 60. But the easy, and pretty much only answer is that this situation has never arisen, as nobody awarded an ill-health pension has ever been well enough to return to work with them. To be fair, the lady I spoke to was really nice, and tried her best to offer a hypothetical answer, but the message was clear – it's never happened, it's never likely to happen, we haven't really thought about the situation if it was to happen. But that's okay, I can be the first.

Now, there was another reason I was starting to feel a bit happier. What was it? Oh yeah, to forget the stress of the last few months we're off on a mini-cruise – four days on the good ship Artemis, no less. In many ways, perfect timing.

Friday 21 October 2005
Do you know, whenever I get on a cruise ship the stresses and strains of life just seem to fall away. I'm not sure Mandy would totally agree, as she always seems to have one eye on what I am doing or saying (or in her words "where you're stumbling and who you're upsetting!"), but for me, the "tizz" I had got myself into, worrying about such tiny little things as a job, income and the meaning of life, just disappeared when we boarded Artemis today. And so with knickers untwisted, I am looking forward to what looks to be a great weekend away. Even the Muster Drill we had earlier turned out to be enjoyable, and that's a first!

It's a strange old experience, the Muster Drill, in that despite every single person present being in 100% agreement with its importance, no-one actually wants to be there. Or at least that's how it always seems, as everyone, both crew and passengers, gather together for the drill with faces like a wet weekend in Rhyl. Why is that? For us passengers at least, it signifies the start of our holiday, after all. But no, we all sit there looking as miserable as sin, barely acknowledging our fellow passengers even though, minutes before over a buffet lunch we were all happily chatting away to the same complete strangers as if they were long-lost lovers. Sure, once the drill starts we need to be quiet and pay attention, but even in the 20 minutes before it starts (i.e. the 20 minutes after the official start time, when everyone finally turns up and takes a seat) barely a grunt is exchanged for fear of someone actually smiling. And then when the drill finally starts, the crew member with the shrillest voice they could find, using the screechiest microphone they could find, repeatedly says "don't put your lifejacket on yet" to those people putting their lifejackets on.

But in this instance our Muster Drill was an absolute pleasure, due mostly to Brian and Gill, the couple who joined us at a quiet corner table of our designated Muster Point. You see, they didn't look miserable at all. In fact, totally contrary to normal Muster etiquette, they said hello and sat down to chat with us. And as it turns out, despite their lovely south Welsh accents they live quite close to us, just down the M4 in Newbury. Furthermore, Brian makes a living as a sports journalist, the job I had wanted to do when I was growing up. In short, perfect company, and we chatted so much that before we knew it everyone had been mustered, drilled and told off for putting their lifejackets on too soon. Like me, Brian is a huge football fan, so before we went our separate ways we loosely arranged to watch a game or two together later in the weekend. Oh yeah, and the girls got on quite well too.

Saturday 22 October 2005

Just before lunchtime today, those of us on board, and a large number of locals, watched aghast as the majestic Artemis squeezed through canals and locks only marginally wider than herself, to arrive in Amsterdam unscathed. A day and a half here includes an overnight stay that should give us a real insight into one of Europe's most talked-about cities. Also, by getting here early afternoon it meant Brian and I first got to watch the lunchtime football match together in the Horizon Bar.

Following the football and a quick lunch, Mandy and I hit terra firma, and after finding a queue as long as the river Amstel waiting to get into Anne Frank's house, we instead opted for a meander along some of the quieter canals. It quickly became clear that not just a few, but all of Amsterdam's canals were lined by the same picturesque combination of thin, tall trees and thin, tall houses. Some of the latter were so thin, and leaning so much, that it's amazing they have remained standing for centuries. In fact, by focusing on the canals and houses rather than the large number of parked cars crowding its otherwise beautiful cobbled streets, we quickly took to the place. And what's refreshing is that practically all these houses remain lived in by real people. Whereas elsewhere in Europe, the lower floors of such buildings would have been sold off to house a McDonalds or a travel agents, here (aside from the parked cars) Amsterdam's streets remain relatively unchanged, full of character and very much lived in.

After popping back to the ship for a rest, a scrub up and an early buffet dinner, we joined some of our fellow passengers on a pre-booked evening excursion aboard one of Amsterdam's canal boats. Only this was a little different as it involved cheese and wine and promised an unrivalled view of Amsterdam by night. We were joined at our table on the boat by a nice couple, the male half of which looked incredibly like Adrian Chiles off the telly, and had the same Brummie accent to boot. But he denied it straight away claiming "Oi git that all the toime". I said "it's no wonder, you luke right lioke him" and promptly helped him tuck into the wine.

The highlight of the boat ride came almost immediately as we approached this huge illuminated Chinese restaurant, built on top of a large barge in the style of one of those tiered Chinese temples. Had I known that was to be the highlight I would have taken more photos, or even drank more of the wine that not-Adrian-Chiles was knocking back like his life depended on it. But we weren't to know, and to be fair the boat ride was pleasant enough, it was just a lot of the time we were looking straight at canal walls or the bumpers of parked cars. But all was not lost; the boat ride had at least conserved some energy, so we intended to explore a little by foot before bedtime.

Now, at night Amsterdam takes on a whole different feel, especially around the red light district. Even during the day there had been ladies in the occasional window presenting their scantily-clad wares to the world. But after dusk their numbers increase tenfold and, as much as you try to convince yourself that it's harmless fun, at the end of the day it's prostitution. Rightly or wrongly, it's very much part of the tourist scene to have a walk around these parts, and thus, part of our plan (okay, my plan) was to take a gander too. So after a couple of drinks in one of those cafés where you don't need to buy drugs as you end up breathing in someone else's anyway, we went off to window-shop.

The ladies of the night are of course clearly used to the curious glances of the tourists, and instantly distinguish between a potential client and those who just come to gawp (the presence of a significantly less-curious wife must be a clue), but it didn't stop one or two giving me a wink. I was strangely chuffed by this and briefly thought about winking back, but no, my brain decided a childish giggle and blushing were the appropriate responses in that situation. I opted to hurry on past like a naughty schoolboy.

I guess due in part to Amsterdam itself looking so nice, I found in my head I was still trying to inject a little romance into the red light area, but I soon realised I was being ridiculous. No problem, I told myself, it's the way of the world, and hey, if it's romance I want there are always the sex shops! Alas, I was overruled and swiftly ushered back to the ship by a wife whose own ideas on romance, I'm pleased to say, are a million miles away from seedy little shops selling large phallic-like paraphernalia. It's probably just as well: I spotted one or two gadgets apparently guaranteeing "Maximum Pleasure" - and, as someone whose sexual goals are more realistically aimed at seeing his partner hit a state of mild amusement, I'm not sure I like the sound of the competition.

Sunday 23 October 2005
This morning we had another short excursion booked which took us on a, mostly coach based, tour of the countryside around Amsterdam. It was exactly the sort of nice gentle trip we needed. To be honest, we knew I wouldn't be able to resist witnessing Amsterdam's nightlife at least a little bit last night, and so by default I was going to be very tired today. But we also knew we had a full day in Amsterdam, and didn't want to waste that. So we booked today's excursion as a way of seeing and doing stuff without too much effort. Oh yeah, and in the excursion booklet they promised me a windmill. In fact, due to me being a little bit fuzzy and, it has to be said, rural Holland looking very flat and samey, I can't really remember much except the windmill. So, let me tell you about the windmill.

The windmill was brilliant. It looked like a windmill, it worked like a windmill, and strangely, given I didn't have a clue how one would smell, it even smelled like a windmill. It was a bit shorter and stockier than I had expected, but then my only point of reference to date was the windmill owned by one Windy Miller in 1970s children's TV programme Trumpton, so I'm hardly an expert. Although I am a bit of an expert now having concentrated so hard during the demonstration part of the tour that my head hurt. But it was lovely, as were the family who owned and worked it, and the numerous art and craft products they sold as a sideline. I felt so warm and fuzzy from the experience that I bought some clogs, even though I know for a fact Mandy will never let me wear them on our wooden floors at home. I didn't care; I was stood in a windmill, wearing my clogs, and insisting that everyone call me Windy for the rest of the morning. And even not-Adrian-Chiles, chipping in to question if this was down to my baked bean intake at breakfast, was going to ruin it for me.

After that it was back to the ship, and having concluded that I was just too knackered to go back ashore for Anne Frank's house, I planned a lazy afternoon in front of the football with my new mate Brian. The game actually turned out to be quite dull, but Brian kept me entertained with journalistic snippets of inside information on certain players, which was fascinating. Also, it turns out Brian was heavily involved in the investigation, and resulting story, on the Lester Piggott scandal in the 1980s. Not my sport at all, horse racing, but I remember it all happening, and that side of Brian's job is quite intriguing. It wouldn't be for me though, I would just like to go along and report on football games. And if they could work it so I could have evenings and weekends off too, that would be perfect.

Monday 24 October 2005
Today we are in Zeebrugge, and once again anticipating I would be knackered, we had booked a nice gentle trip. Our excursion of choice this morning was "Bruges by Coach and Canal", a title which should ensure both our major requirements are met, namely a) Bruges, and b) by coach and canal. And as it turned out, it was an inspired choice, not only to avoid the walking my legs were now incapable of, but also because of the rain – it persisted down. Indeed, it was so cold and wet, I momentarily thought our guide was taking the mick when she told us that, in Flemish, Bruges is pronounced "Brrrrugh". And it was very bloody "Brrrrugh" I can tell you.

Our coach took us from the port of Zeebrugge (meaning, literally, Bruges on Sea) on a 20-minute journey into central Bruges. Well, fairly central Bruges anyway, as much of the real centre of Bruges is off-limits to motor vehicles. But it was just a short stroll to join our canal boat, and we were soon looking aghast at the absolutely stunning sights Bruges has to offer. Whilst this was the second city in as many days that claimed to be the Venice of the North, for my money Bruges has by far the greater claim, based simply on so much of it seeming to be accessible by canal only. Whereas Amsterdam's canals were always lined not just by roads, but by row after row of parked cars, the canals of Bruges have only fleeting contact with either. What that means is that from the perspective of a canal boat, we had the most glorious views of Bruges' beautiful canal-side buildings, with their autumnal trees and plants apparently sprouting straight from their walls. Actually, many of those hotels, pubs and houses are so canal-side that their own walls are also the walls of the canal in which they sit. Absolutely stunning, and Bruges is only enhanced I think by seeing it in all its autumnal beauty.

After the boat trip we had the opportunity to explore by foot, and whilst in our case distance was limited, we easily found a number of lovely cobbled streets and beautiful little market squares. Bruges is pretty compact, so as much as I loved the boat ride, for people of greater mobility I think walking is a good way to explore. As for us, in the little square where we were due to rendezvous with our guide, we found a great little chocolate shop (or chocolatiers) called Dumon, in which the generous lady owner insisted we sample just about everything. We left with chocolates and waffles a-plenty, all of which had been made that very day. A memorable final day of our mini-cruise.

Wednesday 26 October 2005
We got home okay yesterday and have been resting and reflecting on our first mini-cruise which, I have to say, was a really nice break. Artemis is a great little ship, and despite her being quite old, I would have no qualms going on her again, she was like a mini-Oceana. Her smaller size was quite refreshing actually, and meant that, where on a bigger ship you might bump into some people a couple of times over the duration of a cruise, on Artemis you ran into them a couple of times a day.

In terms of it being just a four-day (long weekend) cruise, it worked well. Until now I had looked on cruising as two weeks to somewhere warm and sunny, but this trip opened my eyes. For me, it was much harder going than the previous cruises due to the lack of sea (i.e. rest) days, but for most people I think it's a great way to have a short break away and see not just one, but two iconic cities. Mandy said she didn't have long enough to truly switch off, like she does on the two week cruises, but that she thoroughly enjoyed herself.

Before disembarking we grabbed some breakfast in the Conservatory, Artemis' buffet restaurant, and who should join us at our table for four but Brian and Gill. It was a really good way to end the weekend as we had got on really well with them, and with us living quite close to each other they were keen to meet up again sometime soon. That's always nice to hear, as I know how incredibly hard work I can be, but Gill wasted no time in writing down their contact details for us. We'll definitely meet up.

Friday 25 November 2005
Someone asked me today why it is that I have been advised against flying, and I realised I didn't exactly know. Obviously flying, even for a healthy person, can be both tiring and dehydrating, so having a fatigue-related illness with a symptom of pretty much constant headache, it seems a sensible thing for me to avoid. But what about one of the shorter flights? Would that be okay, or does the air pressure play a part too?? I guess I should ask Martin next time I see him.

However, I don't miss flying. On long-haul flights I always seemed to be the one who got sat next to the morbidly obese passenger or a screaming child. Or on one particularly memorable journey, a morbidly obese screaming child! It's never seemed the easiest or most relaxing form of transport, and it sounds like it's only got worse since 9/11. Check-in times are so much earlier now, and even hand-baggage seems like it's becoming a thing of the past. The way it's going, you'll soon have to turn up a day early, strip to your undies and provide a list of all previous sexual partners before you are permitted to board. No, I don't miss flying, and even though (non-fly) cruising can be a little restrictive as to where you can go, especially if limited to an annual two-week holiday, I can see it being our vacation of choice even when I'm well.

Wednesday 7 December 2005
For a few weeks now I have been attending the Pain Management Clinic at the local hospital as, with Hanqiao having returned to China for a

spell, Martin had suggested the NHS clinic could provide some interim acupuncture for me. In practice however, it's proved a frustrating experience. I've now seen Sharon, the pain-management lady, for a few sessions, and acupuncture has been strangely absent. In fact the only pain-management offered was a seven-day loan of a "tens machine" to provide the kind of pain relief that apparently only comes by having your thumb repeatedly pricked.

In her defence, Sharon wants to address my CFS as this is the "source of the pain", and I understand her logic in wanting to do so. But that's not why I was referred there. Whilst I'm always keen to try anything new that could get me better and back to work, what I primarily go there for is to replace the one aspect of my management system that is temporarily absent – the acupuncture. The process Sharon is taking me through isn't even new: it's the exact same one I went through with my occupational therapist, only harder. In fact, given each session means a long trip to and from the hospital on the other side of town, and then a lot of talking and analysing, I've been returning home feeling significantly worse than before I went. What's the point of that?

To make matters worse, Sharon wasn't too happy today, as even though it was for a good reason, I was late. It was because I was being the Good Samaritan on the road to Marlborough. You see, I got Mandy to drop me off about half a mile from the hospital this morning as my head-fog was so bad I felt like a zombie, and needed to try and clear the cobwebs. Well, the weather was foggy too - a cold crispy morning with very limited visibility, which gave things a really surreal feel. As I turned a corner things got even more surreal, as through the fog I could see the figure of a lady laid on the ground up ahead. The lady in the fog (ooh, 'ark at me going all Stephen King!) turned out to be an off-duty nurse, who was in some distress having come off her bike due to the ice. I picked her up, I picked her bike up, and after she assured me that a 400-yard ambulance ride wasn't necessary, I slowly walked her (and her bike) the rest of the way to the hospital, cradling her very painful arm all the way to A&E, where I was assured they would take good care of her.

The trouble was, even though I had by now phoned ahead to the pain clinic to say I was going to be late, it was a good 30 minutes into my appointment time when I eventually saw Sharon. What was worse, I'm not convinced she even believed my story of the nurse in the mist (perhaps I should have left out the bit about the howling werewolves).

So our final session was brief, and like the weather, it felt a little frosty. I do hope I imagined that last bit as I do like Sharon, and as I always try to, I picked up a few useful tips from her. But the fact is today's shorter session means I feel so much better than after all the other ones. So, that's progress!

Anyway, after I left my session with Sharon, I stopped off at A&E to ask "how's that nurse I brought in?" (I nearly added "single-handedly" but we were at borderline superhero status already and it's not like me to milk it). They explained that she was a little shook up, and currently having an X-ray on a suspected fractured wrist, but basically fine. So all good, and after momentarily popping into a telephone box to switch my pants back to beneath my tights, I shot off to meet my uncle, Eddie, for my lift home.

Friday 9 December 2005
A bonus of my shorter session at the pain clinic was that I was able to go out today to celebrate my niece Hannah's 18th birthday. She had kindly arranged her birthday meal for a very early evening slot to make it easier (i.e. quieter) for me. Even so, when Hannah invited us my initial reaction was that it was too far to go; I would be knackered before I even got there. But I need to try and get out more, so whilst the restaurant was further than was ideal, I wanted to give it a go, particularly given Hannah's special occasion. And it worked really well. It meant lots of extra rest beforehand, and at least the next week or so to recover, but I did okay and feel pretty chuffed I was able to make it. I have always made the effort to be there for my nieces' and nephews' birthdays, but I'd missed one or two in recent years due to my health. So it's good to be part of Hannah's birthday celebration, even if she is now at an age where, apparently, being tickled relentlessly by your uncle is inappropriate all of a sudden.

Actually, during my sessions with Sharon, she reiterated a point that Jane, my occupational therapist, made about the need to have at least some form of social life. Sharon said that it's crucial to get out of the house and enjoy myself occasionally, and that I should look on a social event as a building block towards a return to work, not an obstacle to it. I do enjoy meeting up with mates and family, I just tend to wait for others to ask first, as it feels wrong somehow for me to suggest going out when I'm still not well enough to go out to work.

Monday 19 December 2005
Due to a combination of my birthday, and it also being the perfect opportunity to share a little pre-Christmas cheer, we had some friends over for dinner at the weekend. However, despite feeling okay in all other respects, cognitively I really struggled, and so, conversationally I was really hard work. And the only thing that's worse than feeling like you are hard work, is when you can actually see it on the faces of your guests. God that's depressing.

Sunday 25 December 2005
We had our three parents round for Christmas Dinner today and it all went fine. They all said they thoroughly enjoyed themselves and left with much larger bellies than the ones they came with. It really is the best meal of the year in my eyes, and Mandy once again did us (and hopefully the rest of the rugby team she was presumably cooking for) proud.

Amazingly, I felt so much sharper today too, which is just typical. Last weekend I could barely string a sentence together, or when I did, it would be on nothing more enthralling than my neighbour jet-washing his drive. However, today, when ironically we had guests who would have been very happy with that exact line of conversation, I was entertainment personified. Sadly, I fear it's too late to save our social life, and any dinner invites we now get will be token, sympathy-based, gestures akin to giving an elderly neighbour a lift to the shops.

Tuesday 27 December 2005
Our youngest cat, Cosette, died today. She was only seven years old and we can't quite believe it. We are both distraught, she was a lovely little thing. So sad. And it was all so sudden, she seemed absolutely fine until yesterday morning. Mandy is beside herself, I have never seen her so upset. It's a real shock. One minute we were having a great Christmas and then yesterday morning it just all changed completely.

When I first woke up, it seemed all three cats had just slept on our bed with us as normal. But Cosette wasn't good at all, almost non-responsive. She was conscious but just hunched up and wouldn't move. I lifted her up and placed her next to some food and water, but she just remained in the same hunched position. Something was clearly very wrong. We immediately took her into the emergency vets who identified she was having renal failure, and painted quite a bleak picture. The vet admitted her and put her on some fluids straight away. Well, obviously Boxing Day was neither here nor there for us, we just sat by the phone all day. We phoned up a couple of times for updates and they said she was stable and comfortable, but that she was still very ill.

At about 9pm we phoned up for the last time and asked if we could possibly come along and say goodnight to her. They said okay, and we literally couldn't get there fast enough. As soon as we walked into see her, Cosette meowed at us and came right to the front of the little indoor kennel-thing to say hello. She still had a drip taped to her leg, but looked so much better than when we had last seen her, and her eyes were sparkling. We opened the little door and stroked her constantly for about 20 minutes. Mandy was itching to pick her up and give her a cuddle, but as I say, Cosette was still attached to a drip, so we settled for the strokes. It was so hard to leave her there for the night, but we felt loads better for having seen her and we hoped it was reassurance for her too. On the way out, I noticed that the only other cat in the kennels was one called Dennis. That had to be a good omen didn't it?

At 7am this morning the bedside phone rang, and I immediately knew it was the emergency vets with bad news. I'm sure Mandy knew too, but as the vet told me, I tried to keep the emotion out of my voice, and my words neutral, so Mandy didn't know for definite until I could tell her myself at the end of the call. The vet must have thought I was a hard unfeeling git as all I said was "ok", "I see" and "thank you". But at least it meant I was personally able to explain to Mandy that Cosette had slipped away last night, curled up in a ball as she (always) slept. We cried so much laid there on our bed together that our other two cats, Frisco and Maui, who heartbreakingly had already been downstairs calling for Cosette, came up to see what the commotion was. She could be a right little madam, and ruled the roost as far as those two boys were concerned, but they were going to miss her too. A crying shame.

Later in the day we popped along to the vets to say our final sad farewell to Cosette, and to keep a small piece of her fur as a keepsake. Lots more tears of course, and even some from the young nurse there too, which surprised me, but then Cosette always stole everyone's heart. As hard as it was, it was comforting to say goodbye to her - she had been a big part of our lives, and we will be forever grateful for the time we had with her. We really loved that little cat.

Thursday 12 January 2006
I seem to be stuck in a real rut. Well okay, I seem to have been stuck in a CFS-related rut for some years now, but what I mean is that, even with the illness I'm usually a positive bloke. I always try to see the best of a bad situation. But I'm missing that part of me at the moment, and aside from the very brief respite of that four-day cruise, it's been missing for a while. It's been a rough old few months admittedly, and losing my job hit me surprisingly hard, given I haven't actually worked for over three years. Cosette dying so suddenly was a shock to the system too. She spent all day, every day, at home here with me, and I really miss her.

Normally I can bounce back from such events quickly, but not this time. And I feel angry all the time too. Often, irrationally so. I feel angry about my situation, the loss of my employment, and how the lifestyle I had has changed beyond all recognition. Anger at those things is understandable, I guess. But, at the moment, it's even hard to hear mates telling me about their mountain-biking exploits, or them going away for a spontaneous weekend. And that's not like me at all. Yes, it used to be me doing such things. But anger? Jealousy?? Is that what I'm feeling??? If so, I need to shake it off because it's destructive and not doing me any good at all.

Saturday 14 January 2006
Today I read back through some of the information I have collated over the years about CFS. I just thought if I could remind myself what causes certain feelings, I might just be able to shake off this black cloud. I also had a chat with the ME Association who I have found it helpful to talk to on occasion. It proved very useful, and I was reminded of a couple of points that I had just dismissed in the past, as I felt they would never apply to me.

Firstly, quite aside from the physical pain and cognitive issues of CFS, there is the potential impact of emotional trauma. That basically means that as well as the more obvious symptoms, CFS can also result in psychological problems. The despair and anger everyone can experience at one time or other are emotions which in CFS can be extreme, due to the sudden and drastic changes to lifestyle caused by the illness. So when heightened further by the typical CFS symptoms like sleep disturbance and hormonal imbalance, it seems my own emotional maelstrom is quite reasonable. I just need to ensure it remains a temporary, or occasional thing and doesn't become a permanent fixture in my life.

So I'm not nuts, and as importantly (because people were starting to wonder), I am not depressed. Sure, my situation is depressing and it gets me down sometimes, but that's not the same as being depressed. I do not, for example, have suicidal thoughts. Also, whilst CFS can prevent me from doing either, I do not wish to withdraw from social contact, or feel I do not want to exercise. Things, I am informed, that are strong indicators of clinical depression, but in my case, things that I very much want to do more of. I just can't.

In addition, on the odd occasion when I am not solely focused on recovering from CFS, I appreciate just how fortunate I am. Things could be so much worse. That awareness hopefully confirms that I retain rational and proportional feelings in respect of my illness. So, as I say, that was a useful exercise today. It doesn't stop me feeling miserable, or worse, angry, but it does at least remind me why it is affecting me just so much currently. And hopefully, understanding the whys and wherefores is a start towards feeling happier.

Saturday 8 April 2006
A successful, if all too-brief, trip out last night. It was a party to celebrate my sister, Linda's, recent wedding abroad, and although I wasn't at my best, Mandy and I got along there for a bit, which was the main thing. Many of the wider family were there too, so it was also good to catch up with them. In fact, given it was a) a party, and b) involved a reasonable drive there and back – both things I continue to have great difficulty with – I'm pleased with how I did. And it was nice to be there on Linda's special day. Wish we could have stayed longer though.

Wednesday 12 April 2006
I keep reading about new miracle cures for CFS. Scratch below the surface however, and you find there are just as many people who felt worse after trying these new treatments, than there were those who were apparently cured. The two things these new treatments all seem to have in common are:

a) They all seem to be a variation on the Cognitive Behaviour Therapy theme that most people with CFS have already found to be unhelpful.

b) None of them are offered, or even approved, by the NHS, so they cost a small fortune.

Don't get me wrong: for a long time now I've been at the stage where I will consider pretty much anything if it means a chance of getting healthy. However, the sheer number of these "new" treatments that crop up make me wary, and every single time I've sought an opinion on one, those better qualified than me have advised waiting for solid, verifiable results data first. Of course, that doesn't stop every friend, relative and their dog popping the latest "miracle cure" article from the newspaper through my letter box, but they mean well and I'm grateful they are thinking of me.

The whole subject of a cure (or lack of it) is another thing which I currently find quite frustrating, especially when I seem to have exhausted everything normally recommended for CFS. Hanqiao continues to give me acupuncture, which helps a lot, and in the absence of a new approach I continue with the Pacing. But as much as I like and understand the logic of Pacing – i.e. whether it's physical, mental or emotional, my energy is finite and so needs to be paced - it's tough constantly staying within my energy limit, as it means missing out on so much.

Sunday 16 April 2006
I woke up this morning and I really felt happy for the first time in a while. In fact, having just read back, it's the first time I have really felt happy in a long while. I'm not sure why things should suddenly feel so much brighter, but I think it's helped that there are three positive things all coming together at the same time.

Firstly, being Easter, Mandy has a long weekend at home, and four consecutive days together is doing me the world of good - it is hard spending so much time alone. Also, two old friends, and former colleagues, phoned this last week to reiterate that there is still a job for me with them when I'm well. And finally, in just a few weeks' time, we are cruising to Venice and back, and I have to say, as dark as things got at times these last few months, that cruise has been something good to just focus on and work towards.

Health-wise, I still remain some distance from where I want to be - and need to be - in order to get back to work. But hey, today feels like it has so much more promise than the days that proceeded it, so for now I will happily settle for that and enjoy our Easter.

Chapter 7 – An Adriatic Adventure

Thursday 25 May 2006
And so today we joined P&O's spanking new ship, Arcadia. Well okay, it's a year old, but it's new to us and I'm sure if I ask Mandy nicely, spanking could reluctantly enter the equation at some point. But seriously, as regular cruisers (ooh, 'ark at me!) P&O tempted us with such frequent updates throughout the building of Arcadia that we already felt like we knew her well, even before we boarded. A retractable roof over the main pool and an immense three-tier theatre are just two of the highlights on offer. Arcadia is also adults-only which, although kids have not been a problem at all on our cruises to date, selfishly I'm intrigued by it. But the most exciting thing of all for both Mandy and me is that we cruise to Venice!!!

Friday 26 May 2006
Yesterday, having boarded, napped, explored and listened to the excellent sailaway band situated on the dockside, we were showered, shaved and shipshape well in time for our dinner at 6.45pm. Joining us at a nicely-positioned table for four were our friends from our first cruise, Richard and Joyce, who couldn't resist the combination of a new ship and a cruise to Venice, either. It'll be nice to spend some time with them again, and with me still very much a lightweight health-wise, good to have a couple of understanding mates around.

After dinner we all went to see the show, which we were looking forward to even more than normal following a promise from the cruise director, Neil, that the Arcadia Theatre Company are "truly spectacular". It was only a short introductory show last night, and initially it looked like a very similar set up to the Stadium Theatre Company we had so enjoyed on our previous cruises. But it soon became clear that amongst the usual mixture of excellent singers and dancers were acrobats, circus performers and specialist ballet and ballroom dancers. Tomorrow they are back doing a full show for us entitled The Songs of Andrew Lloyd Webber (I wonder what that one is about?), so looking forward to that.

As for last night, after the show we just had a slow meander along the two main communal passenger decks that run the length of the ship and appear to make up Arcadia's main social hub. I would love to have stayed up for a couple of drinks actually, but once again the long embarkation day had got the better of me, and my bed was a-calling. Still, we are cruising to Venice and back, so we've got plenty of time.

Sunday 28 May 2006
Well, that's a couple of really relaxing sea days under our belts, and very nice they were too. The Bay of Biscay not only behaved itself, but we've had enough warm sunshine to see Arcadia's retractable roof (over the Neptune Pool) opened already. We even managed to do the mid-afternoon quiz from the comfort of our sun-loungers, and thanks to Mandy having just finished reading an "OK" magazine with half of the answers in, we came joint first. We won a Pedometer. Or Paedo-Meter, as the elderly lady who finished joint first with us pronounced it.

Of course, on Friday night we had the Captain's Welcome Aboard Dinner, with everyone looking resplendent in their formal wear. Sadly, we missed the captain's speech and the traditional glass of bubbly, but the four of us instead raised a glass to a wonderful cruise at dinner. And a mighty fine dinner it was too - I had Hot Asparagus Mousse, Lobster Thermador for a fish course, and then Pot Roast Venison for main. I couldn't decide between the desserts so, having foolishly asked our waiter, Mohammed, for his opinion, he brought me both the Hot Chocolate Fondant and the Trio of Miniature Lemon Desserts. That very nearly brought a tear to my eye, but then one of those lemon puds did taste a little sharp.

The Andrew Lloyd Webber-themed show afterwards wasn't half bad either, and as you would expect, all his most popular numbers were included. There were a couple of Miss Saigon numbers in there too, as two of the singers, husband and wife Nick and Cezarah, have both appeared in the West End show, and one song in particular they sang brilliantly. The whole company contributed to a terrific show actually, with the young Ukrainian ballroom couple performing a dance that Mandy described as "magical".

After a couple of early nights, I'm pleased to say we had a few drinks in the Spinnaker Bar last night. The most popular watering hole of an evening seems to be up in the Crow's Nest on the top deck, but we were happy where we were, so stayed in the Spinnaker for the rest of the evening. At one point we were joined by one of the Entertainment Team, I think called Matt, who explained that he had just been "Oriana'd". Faced with four confused faces, he explained that whenever P&O have a new ship there is a tendency for some of the older cruisers to regularly repeat the mantra "it's not like Oriana", in reference to another of P&O's, clearly much-loved, ships. In fact, so ingrained in some passengers psyche is this view, that last year one passenger said this to Matt even before they had boarded Arcadia for her maiden voyage. I can see we are going to have to try Oriana for ourselves in order that we can adopt this phrase too.

Monday 29 May 2006
Yesterday we were in sleepy Cadiz (well it was Sunday) and it was a really mellow kind of day. Much of Cadiz was closed obviously, but we did our normal routine of going ashore and having a short wander. Almost immediately we found this long thin park that ran parallel to the seafront, so we parked our bums on a bench and soaked up some early morning sunshine, whilst watching a couple of small cats playing. It reminded us how much we are missing our two back home. Then after about ten minutes of watching them frolic around in the undergrowth, all of a sudden their ears pricked up, they stopped momentarily as if analysing whatever is was they were hearing, and then they sprinted off, at full pelt, towards the far end of the park. When we continued our stroll, we eventually caught up with them sat underneath a large tree gazing upwards at dozens of parakeets singing their early morning chorus. The two cats were drooling, bless them, but the parakeets had clearly played this game before, as not one came anywhere near.

Next we had a walk around the old town, which included lots of pretty old buildings and tiny little alleyways, in amongst what remained of the old town walls. Apparently the name Cadiz originates from an ancient word for "wall" and you can see why; the town walls are still very prominent. It's just a shame they are not in better nick, but then Cadiz is said to be the oldest city in Western Europe, so it isn't doing bad. And as if to demonstrate that point, we stumbled across a really striking, gothic-style, plaza which confirmed, if we didn't already know, that we were definitely in Spain. It was called Plaza Mina, and it contained a statue of someone called Jose MacPherson who, in my mind at least, was better known locally as Jock.

By this time the sun was really beating down, but everywhere we went in Cadiz was cooled by a nice gentle breeze. I think this must be because Cadiz is situated on a thin lollipop-shaped piece of land, so it is almost completely surrounded by the sea. Even so, as cool as it was, we are still talking southern Spain here, and with my English Rose complexion to consider, I needed to be careful to avoid lobster-like colouring come dinner time. It's okay for Mandy, she immediately turns brown as soon as her feet touch foreign soil, but then that could partly be an optical illusion due to dragging around a hubby the colour of dim sum alongside her.

Coincidentally, and nothing at all to do with the Spanish Navy being in town (strumpet!), Mandy's hair was hung seductively over one shoulder, and had acquired a flower, to look very much the Spanish senorita. Sadly for Mand, we didn't see one sailor and her hair frizzed so much that by lunchtime it had quadrupled in size. Oops. I, on the other hand, seem to be experiencing the phenomenon known as "aircon throat", whereby over the course of the cruise your throat becomes drier and drier due to the on-board air conditioning (especially if you're sleeping in an inside/windowless cabin). It's something that I have experienced at the very end of a cruise before, and this time it could equally be due to overzealous sunbathing in a chilly wind (guilty as charged, m'lord), but I hope it goes away. I don't really want to spend the rest of the cruise sounding like Darth Vadar with laryngitis.

Wednesday 31 May 2006
Today is the last of three consecutive sea days, and with the emphasis very much on rest and relaxation in readiness for Dubrovnik and Venice, I have little to report that won't bore you to tears. That said, we've seen a couple of really good shows and had a great laugh at a wine-tasting class that was well worth the small cover charge, even if it did give me a bit of a thick head. And so, with Arcadia currently sailing along the bottom of Italy's boot, I'll quickly recap those events.

Firstly, the wine-tasting was good fun. I had wondered beforehand if the class would be full of wine buffs, with palates far better qualified than my "anything red and half price" approach to wine drinking had afforded me. I was also wary my ignorant palate may not be able to pick up a wine's subtle hint of cherries, chocolate, or indeed any of the other ingredients of a Black Forest Gateau, but hey, worst case scenario, I guessed I could just wing it, and blame my malfunctioning taste buds on aircon throat. The main thing was we intended to enjoy some nice wines and learn something.

Mand and I were actually running five minutes late for the class as a result of a lasagne jack-knifing on blouse incident (don't ask). So when we arrived, the only two seats left together were at a table with an elderly gentleman who, judging by the colour of his nose, was very much a wine lover. In fact, if he hadn't been beforehand, he must have been a wine lover by the time we joined him, as much of the wine and most of the crackers and bread supplied for our sharing had already been consumed. Not bad at all given the class actually hadn't started yet. Fortunately, the lecturer realised that this gentleman had been a little over-enthusiastic, and with a knowing smile in our direction, replenished both wine and nibbles. Bless him, ten minutes into what proved to be a very interesting class, the elderly gentleman was fast asleep and snoring so loudly the lecturer was having to raise her voice so that the rest of the group could hear her. But she was still able to get her points across well, and everyone seemed to enjoy it. I enjoyed it so much, I needed a lie down afterwards.

In terms of the shows, the Arcadia Theatre Company has performed two terrific shows over the last few nights. The first one, The Knights of Rock and Roll, included covers of songs by artists honoured by the Queen, from Bob Geldof (and the Boomtown Rats) to Shirley Bassey. Quite a range covered there as you can imagine, but all delivered really well vocally. And if that show was good, last night's Best of the West End was even better. The singers belted out classics from Chicago and Mamma Mia, and some of the dancing and interaction from dancers – everything from acrobatics to full-on energy-sapping high speed group dances - had them all visibly gasping for breath. The whole show was great.

Thursday 1 June 2006
Well, today we were in the Croatian port of Dubrovnik, and whilst everything outside of the town walls fell well short of write-home-ability, step through the small, arched, medieval town gate and you walk into a whole other world. It really is a "through the wardrobe" moment as you enter one side of the town gate in 2006, and emerge the other side, a second later, in medieval Europe. You see, Dubrovnik's old town is surrounded by a remarkably conserved (and fully walkable) city wall, which means access to the old town is only possible through one of the two town gates.

Sadly, it was drizzling constantly this morning and it felt quite cold as a result. It also meant that the old town's marble-like paving was quite slippery if you weren't careful. But we adapted to both factors fairly instantly and enjoyed an umbrella-sheltered stroll through all that this place has to offer, namely medieval churches, palaces, plazas and fountains – and a whole range of sympathetically placed shops and restaurants selling everything from t-shirts to ice cream and burgers to paella. We quickly found ourselves in a picturesque little harbour with the beautiful Adriatic lapping at its steps. Due I think to a combination of the rain and it still being reasonably early, it was just Mand and I there, and not a tourist or tourist boat in sight. The harbour looked amazing, like a scene from a painting. But things were about to take an unlikely turn.

As we walked to the far end of the harbour wall to try and get some nice photos looking back at the old town, we heard a tiny meow. Then, just as we thought we had imagined it, we heard another one. We thought this was strange as it was quite remote that far along the harbour: it was just inches from the sea and cats don't tend to go near water, particularly the salty type. But as the meowing grew more insistent I spotted some rubble in the corner where the walkway met the city wall. I lifted a piece of wood and there was this tiny ginger kitten, about eight weeks old I reckon, soaked to the skin, and its eyes and nose all gunky. It was shivering from the cold, so I picked it up and held it to my chest to warm it up. It instantly stopped meowing and just huddled against me. We stayed there with it for ten minutes until it was warm and then, telling ourselves its mother must be close, carefully placed it back where I found it and went on our touristy way.

The only trouble was there was no sign of the mother, and the rubble the kitten was sheltering under didn't for one minute look like it was a place a mother would leave its young, even briefly. So 20 minutes later, having walked the remainder of the old town without managing to shake the image of that little kitten from our minds, we returned to the same spot hoping to see that the kitten's mother had come back. She hadn't. What's more the kitten was once again cold and wet, and now sneezing too. So, picking him up once again and placing him inside my coat, we walked to the nearest café. But they didn't want to know. All I wanted was some milk, or a pointer in the direction of the nearest vets, but no, they looked at the kitten like it was vermin. In the end we had to walk back to the town gate and ask a taxi driver to take us to a vet.

Once at the vets, the taxi driver kindly translated our predicament to the lady vet, and our wish to pay her to give the cat some medication and food. The vet was great; immediately injected the little fella with antibiotics, and fed him enough food for three kittens. She then said that she didn't think the kitten had eaten in days, so most likely the mother had abandoned it. But no problem, she knew of a good home so, if we were happy to, she would take him there rather than us return him to the old town. Ordinarily I would have been a little suspicious that maybe she was just saying that (to the soppy British tourists) so she could make a few quid, but not only was our bill next to nothing, she also wouldn't accept anything for the food. She wanted us to name him, so Mandy, as we said our goodbyes to our furry friend, decided he was a Luka in honour of the Croatian hunk she fancies the pants off in the TV programme ER. Oh and if you're wondering why I started referring to the kitten as a "him" halfway through - a) I don't have a clue, but b) I was right.

After that the taxi driver took us back to the ship, a journey he tried to provide us with for free. We were having none of that obviously, and as luck would have it, we had just enough local Kuna currency left (after paying the vet) to pay him and give him a reasonable "this currency is no good to us now so you might as well have it all" argument. That said, I took the shuttle bus back into town on my own later in the afternoon just to check the mummy cat hadn't returned, and don't tell Mandy, but I walked a small bit of the town wall too. The kitten's mother was still nowhere to be seen, but the walk on the wall was great, especially when the sun came out. It does get a little tight and steep in places, but there are some great views and photo opportunities.

Friday 2 June 2006
And so to yesterday and, the highlight of the cruise, Venice. No, it didn't smell; no, it wasn't packed solid with tourists; and no, we weren't continually accosted by locals trying to sell us tours left, right and centre. It wasn't the middle of summer obviously, when possibly all those things may apply, but we can only judge by what we saw – i.e. that Venice was everything we had hoped it would be and more, and even the one downside, the little carts selling tourist tat, were few and far between.

We got off the ship straight after breakfast and took the free shuttle bus into Pizzale Roma, which sounds grander than it is, but is basically a modern pizzale where the combined train, bus and vaporetto station is located. A vaporetto is a water-bus, but the best most scenic bus we are ever likely to go on, in that they shoot up and down Venice's larger canals all day and evening. We bought a 24-hour ticket and took the very next vaporetto up the Grand Canal to the Rialto Bridge as we had been warned that this was likely to be the most crowded of the sights later in the day, due to the funnelling affect Venice's famous bridge has on the increasing crowds. And I'm pleased to say it was still quiet when we got there. It was also, as promised, a beautiful 16th century bridge, with little shops cleverly incorporated into its structure. But best of all, given its position on a bend halfway along the Grand Canal, the Rialto provided a terrific view on both sides. Mandy went photo crazy.

As we were walking away from the Rialto, we passed a Gondola station (I'd put money on the Venetians having a far more romantic sounding name for it, but in my ignorance, I'm going to stick with "station") where I foolishly tried to spot a price list. Seeing my curiosity, one of the Gondoliers (see, just when you think I'm an uneducated oik, I hit you with "Gondoliers") came over to me and offered his services for 60 Euros. Well at that price, surprising as it might be to you who have me fairly accurately tagged as a tight wad, I was tempted. When he also then replied to my "maybe later" line with a sound logical argument about later not being anywhere near as good because the canals get much busier, he'd hooked me. I had already decided in my mind that, short of a pricing policy taken from Daylight Robbery for Beginners, I was going to take Mandy on a Gondola today. And whilst 10am was a little earlier than anticipated (I was also going to use the Gondola as a mid-Venice rest), I decided quiet was good in a place renowned for anything but.

And it was quiet, we barely saw any other traffic on the smaller canals. Even Venice's High Street, the Grand Canal, was quiet enough for our driver, Fabio, to manoeuvre our Gondola into the middle for a few minutes so he could use our camera to take a photo of us, in our Gondola, in front of the Rialto – a photo which is surely just a week away from pride of place in our living room. But to be fair, the entire Gondola ride was great; the sky was blue, the sun was out and we saw so many stunning bridges, buildings and canals, I couldn't begin to list them all here. It was lovely and so quiet that it felt like much of the time we had Venice all to ourselves to just soak up and take as many photos as our hearts desired. Indeed, Mandy's heart-to-desire ratio must have been positively overflowing, as she filled up a whole memory card on the camera. Luckily, I had anticipated as much and had brought a spare.

After leaving Fabio, we just decided to wander down some of the endless number of alleyways leading away from the Grand Canal and, almost instantly, we came across numerous signs indicating the way to St Mark's Square. After some initial concern that some of these signs just vaguely pointed in the direction of anything up to four similar sized alleyways, all vaguely going in a similar direction, we decided just to go with the flow even if "the flow" (i.e. other tourists) were randomly taking all four alleyways. As it turned out, all the indicated alleyways tended to go in the same direction and, whichever one we opted for, it did seem to join up again with the others later on. In short, there are probably a dozen different ways of getting from any point A to any point B, but, as long as you follow the signs, other tourists, or both, you will get there - and usually via some wonderful little canal, or bridge, that you would otherwise have completely missed.

And so it was that, ten minutes after leaving the Rialto, we literally stumbled (clumsy bugger) into the utter mayhem of St Mark's Square. Well I say utter mayhem, St Mark's Square is vast so it handles a few hundred tourists quite well, but what I mean is the hordes we had so far avoided were now starting to gather here in droves. So we kept to the quieter spots and were still able to enjoy the architectural wonder that is the Doge's Palace and St Mark's Basilica, and we even managed to look up to the Clock Tower at just the right time to see two ancient Moors smack hell out of the bell. It was increasingly crowded here however, and so before long we exited the square via the two big lion-topped columns that dominate that end of St Mark's. Fat chance of a rest though, it was now starting to busy up everywhere so, after a gawp at the Bridge of Sighs (named after 17th century CFS sufferers who have just walked all the way from the Rialto to St Mark's), we jumped on a vaporetto back to the ship.

Luckily, for those of us hoping to catch St Mark's on the quiet side, Arcadia was in Venice until midnight. As a result, with a sleepy afternoon on the Sun Deck to recharge, and a slightly quicker than normal dinner under our belts, Mandy and I joined Richard and Joyce for a second, evening, sortie ashore about 8pm. By that time, St Mark's was deserted, and had taken on much more of a relaxed feel. We now had the space and energy to fully enjoy the square, and loudly exclaim

"Quanto?" at the price of a drink in the posh cafés that line the piazza, before opting for the same drink, for half the price, around the corner. Seriously though, for me at least, the St Mark's area was far more enjoyable by night, and the fact Arcadia was in Venice all day and all evening was a real bonus. Our final act was to wave Arrivederci to Venice from the Sun Deck for a chilly, but visually stunning midnight sailaway.

Sunday 4 June 2006
A much-needed sea day yesterday and after the best, but most energy-sapping, two ports of the cruise, I was more than happy just to kick back and rest as we travelled back down the Adriatic Sea. For Mandy, that meant hitting the Sun Deck with her book and my ipod, to soak up some sunshine. And I, once again having my usual case of ants in my pants, and the tanning ability of an albino mole, joined her, on and off, to do likewise. But my wish to progress my skin tone beyond varicose blue just wasn't enough to keep me there for long, so I regularly went off to stretch my legs, grab a drink or a snack for Mandy, or just pop to the excellent Café Vivo for a coffee and some cake. In fact, Café Vivo is fast becoming a favourite haunt of mine as the young Filipino girls who work there are good fun, the selection of little cakes you get with your coffee or tea are delicious, and it's situated out of the way in a nice quiet area of the ship, next to the Cyber Study (or computer room).

One thing I've noticed when I'm on my own is that other cruisers are even more likely to strike up a conversation. That's good for the most part, as even when I'm really tired, I can manage a few lines on auto-pilot, and you meet some nice people that way. I can certainly see why cruising is so popular for single travellers. But, as in all walks of life, just occasionally on a cruise you come across someone who can talk the hind legs off a whole barn full of donkeys, and see it as their sole mission in life to share their knowledge with everyone, whether they are passengers, crew or even the captain. The trouble is such knowledge can be them just repeating tales from cruising folklore that everyone has heard a dozen times before, such as the mythical fight in the laundry room that seemingly happens on every cruise, but which nobody appears to have personally witnessed.

Also, a line I'm growing very familiar with is the legendary "so how many times have you cruised?" question. I usually don't mind it actually, as most people say it as a genuine enquiry or a conversation starter. However, there are always a few passengers who only ask that question because they are itching to tell you how many hundred cruises they have done, and wish to then talk you through each one at length. If that's the case, I just pretend it's my first cruise and then continually interrupt their never-ending narrative with stupid questions like "do the crew sleep on board?" or constantly refer to the ship's "pointy end".

But as I've said before, I do like the days at sea, and especially the interaction with the others on board. It's nice to get to know people, whether they be passengers or crew, and I think they add as much to the cruise experience as the ports and the fine dining. I just wish I had a bit more energy when doing so. Actually, scrub that: if I did have the energy to do so, the whole hind leg/donkey thing would almost certainly become as applicable to me as it would anyone else. Arcadia, you've had a narrow escape.

Monday 5 June 2006
Today we have been on the Greek island of Zakinthos. Having tendered ashore for the first time this cruise, once on dry land we were treated to a stunning view of Arcadia back through some palm trees that line the shore here. I'm not generally known for my photography (Mandy is the David Bailey of the family), but I managed to capture a real beauty of a shot with Arcadia nestling perfectly between two such trees. And, Zakinthos town carried on in pretty much the same photogenic theme from there on.

It was the first time I had been to a Greek Island since the lads' holidays of my youth, but I'm glad to say I saw nothing resembling the neon bars and clubs I remember from those days, and certainly witnessed no goldfish bowls of alcoholic concoction being sold to spotty teenagers. It was just a lovely clean Greek town, baking in sunshine, and lush with so much greenery and so many flowers that it looked more like Hawaii. You certainly wouldn't have thought they had experienced earthquakes on Zakinthos as recently as April. Zakinthos town isn't big by any means, so most passengers gave it a miss and excursioned to other parts of the island. But it was plenty large enough for us after all the walking of the last few days, and a really pleasant stop off.

Tuesday 6 June 2006
If Zakinthos town was small, then the fishing village of Naxos Giardini on Sicily is tiny. Of course, these days a fishing village in the

Mediterranean equates to a harbour full of yachts and leisure boats, with just the occasional fishing vessel barely visible through the glare of fibreglass hulls and veneered decks of its neighbours. But they are there, and reportedly still make a decent living in the busy stretch of water between Sicily and mainland Italy, called the Straits of Messina.

For us, a small quiet port is never an issue, which is just as well, as other than the harbour and a few tiny shops and cafés, there is little here. Once again, Arcadia's excursions desk must have been very busy, as many passengers took one of the options the excursion team had ensured was available to them. And again, for us, we were very happy walking the seafront and admiring a few boats, before seeking out a nice-looking café to grab a drink.

The café we chose was very well located overlooking the harbour and two other couples, who I recognised from the ship, were already seated and mid-beverage. That left just one remaining outside table with a sea view, so we grabbed it even though it was a table for six. Well, no sooner had we ordered a couple of coffees from the waiter, but five suited gentlemen pulled up in an expensive-looking Mercedes, and marched into the café. They immediately looked straight at our table and I got the distinct impression we weren't just sat at a table, we were sat at their table. The most authoritive-looking of the five seemed quite unconcerned, but the other four started gesticulating at the waiter who became quite agitated.

Now at this point, one of the couples that were sat next to us at a table for two, finished their coffees and made to leave. I therefore indicated to the waiter that we would instead take their table, so as to free up our bigger one for the five gents. So problem sorted, and the authoritive-looking man even gave me a very slight nod on his way past, which I think was meant as gratitude but somehow came across as a little more menacing. It was only then that I remembered we were in Sicily and so, somewhat belatedly, judging by the way Mandy was urgently raising her eye brows and widening her eyes at me, it occurred to me that this bloke could be some kind of Mob boss. If he was, then Mandy was quite right to supplement her whole scary eyes routine with a subtle nod towards the exit soon afterwards as, by leaving quietly, I may have narrowly avoided being fitted with concrete wellies and sent to swim with the fishes. Judging by the dirty looks he was still getting when we left, the waiter may not have been so lucky.

Thursday 8 June 2006
After a short walk around a surprisingly busy Palma yesterday morning, Mandy and I came back on board for lunch in the Orchid Restaurant, which is described as offering "Asian fusion" food. It has a small cover charge, but the location alone is worth that as it is situated, along with the Orchid Bar, right at the top of the ship on Deck 11, and provides the most amazing views. Although we've been in Arcadia's fun external glass lifts a number of times this cruise, this was the first time we had taken one to the top. And it was worth the trip as both the restaurant and the bar were a real find. Although open every evening, we hadn't been to the Orchid Restaurant so far on the cruise because Richard and Joyce aren't keen on Asian food, and we didn't want to desert them for a dinner. But as the Orchid had decided to open for lunch yesterday too, we intended to make the most of it.

As soon as we walked in, we were made to feel really welcome, due in part to the waitresses being the same young Filipino girls I had got to know from Café Vivo. Three young, very attractive girls instantly came towards us, and pretty much in unison chirped "Hello, Meeester Deneeece", and all with broad smiles on their faces. Mand smiled back and looked as delighted as me with the welcome, but the second they left, she kicked me under the table and said "and how the hell do those girls know you then?" Fortunately, the truth is a story easily told, and so I just explained that whilst Mandy had spent hours on end sunning herself on the Sun Deck, her poor pale husband had wandered the decks alone, seeking good coffee and tasty snacks to take back to his beloved prostrate wife. And, just like the yummy lunch she was about to have, she swallowed the lot.

Actually, describing the lunch as "yummy" just doesn't go far enough: it was fan-bloody-tastic and the best meal of the cruise so far. Between us we ate Slow Cooked Honey Glazed Pork Ribs, Crab and Shrimp Cakes, Garlic Fried Jumbo Prawns on Sesame Toasts, Beef Teriyaki with Maple Black Pepper Glaze, and so much other just absolutely lovely stuff that they chuck in to make your meal a gastronomic delight, that it was, well, a gastronomic delight. It was so good, that over the course of the meal Mandy turned a full 360-degrees re my budding relationship with the Filipino girls, and was now contemplating how we could entice them home to cook for us. We ate so much that, come dinner time, we were still glowing (i.e. bloated and windy) from the experience, and really didn't need to eat anything more.

But eat more we did, because as tough a job as eating all this gorgeous food is, someone has got to do it. And to be fair, the chefs and waiters in our usual Meridian Restaurant provided us with another fine dinner, which we enjoyed thoroughly. I think that may be partly due to the fact that we only have a few evenings left on board, and that we realise we will soon be faced with being back home and cooking for ourselves. But it had been a good day all round, and from my point of view, it just doesn't get any better.

The day did get even better though, as we went along to the show entitled Le Cirque Arcadia. The performers from the Arcadia Theatre Company were swinging, jumping and dropping from all angles. The singers were still there of course, but the emphasis of this show was very much on the other performers, whose full abilities we had only seen glimpses of in the earlier shows. One minute there was gravity-defying acrobatics, and the next, the most stunning physical artistry that surely required more strength than these modestly-sized performers could ever possess. Then, making full use of Arcadia's three-storey theatre, there were girls flying through the air above our heads, with barely a silk sheet stopping them from ending in our laps. Even the ballroom dance couple, who logic suggests might have little place in a circus-themed show, upped their game still further with a mesmerising number of their own. The whole thing was breathtaking, and a terrific end to a great day.

Friday 9 June 2006
I was pretty foggy yesterday morning, and Mandy said I was doing and saying everything in slow motion. I was shattered. Which was a downer for two reasons. Firstly, we were in our final port of Malaga, and I was in no condition to go ashore. Secondly, having done so well this cruise vis-à-vis my normal doing and saying stupid stuff, I made a right dick of myself at breakfast. But on the bright side, there's a good chance I will never see the couple from breakfast again. And, as Malaga is reportedly Europe's most southern mainland city, we were guaranteed some good weather to just laze around all day in the sun.

Anyway, having slow-motioned my way out of bed yesterday, it was too late to have breakfast anywhere else but in the Belvedere's buffet restaurant. Fortunately we found a much-needed quiet table in a corner, but we were then immediately joined by another couple, the male half of which I recognised as being the ship's classical pianist. Mandy, bless her, did most of the talking, as she often does when I'm feeling foggy. But not wanting to appear rude, I then decided to join in briefly, and ask a question that made it clear I thought the couple were man and wife. But she wasn't his wife. She was his mother. His, once I looked again, quite elderly mother. The pianist fella was mortified and it showed. All I could do was try to apologise. But I'm not sure he heard me in the deafening silence that ensued my faux pas, so I spent the rest of breakfast with my head buried in my muesli, hoping to be dragged under by a strong currant. Plonker.

But as I say, we were in sunny Malaga yesterday so there was plenty to be happy about, even if I was knackered and unable to do much more than lie on a lounger sunning my (now) sizeable tummy. And that's pretty much all we did as, interspersed with regular intervals for food (obviously!) and refreshments (ditto!!), we just relaxed all day. I did feel sorry for Mand as she was looking forward to Malaga, but she refused to go ashore without me and instead took regular glances over the side of the ship at what she was missing. I think she was actually on the lookout for Antonio Banderas who, her Hello magazine tells her (so it must be true), is a regular visitor to his home town. No sign of him however, which means yours truly will be forced to slip on his black leather Zorro outfit as penance when we get home.

Saturday 10 June 2006
Last night, in celebration of Richard and Joyce's wedding anniversary, the four of us went to Arcadian Rhodes, the select dining venue on board run under the guidance of celebrity chef Gary Rhodes. At first glance the menu didn't look that exciting, as dishes were just entitled "Chicken" or "Sole" for example. But reading the description underneath revealed that something like "Beef" was actually "fillet of beef with glazed calves sweetbreads and buttered crayfish tails", or that "Pork" was in fact "crispy pork squares with three sauces". It was all quite enticing to be honest, and right from the start promised to be a real treat.

When we first walked in it was clear that a lot of effort had been put into the décor, seating arrangements and service to create an atmosphere that made you feel really special. From the manager, to the waiters, to the sommelier, we received warm and informative attention without it once getting anywhere approaching stuffy or invasive. After making our menu choices, we were brought just-baked bread rolls and, later, a complementary tomato soup in a tiny little tea cup which, somehow, was the colour and texture of cream, but tasted both divine and, crucially for a tomato soup, tomato-y. The freshly-baked bread rolls weren't bad either, topped with a little rock salt, and so nice they brought us seconds. The other courses we had, either side of a gorgeous complementary sorbet, were even better, and despite the unlikely food combinations of some of the dishes, they all tasted fantastic.

Then, in terms of our desserts, the sounds made around our table were such that, had we been at home, our neighbours would undoubtedly have thought we were hosting an orgy. Selfishly, my complete attention was on my Jaffa Cake Pudding, which successfully replicated the flavours of a Jaffa Cake biscuit, albeit in the heavenly form of a deliciously squidgy and layered pud.

And so it was, after coffee and chocolates and a culinary experience that had lasted nearly three hours, that all four of us sat contentedly around our table and just stared at each other. When we finally regained the power of speech, it was to ask ourselves how we were able to enjoy all that, Michelin Star quality no less, for a cover charge of just £15 each. Shore-side, we would surely have been looking at an absolute minimum of £100 per head. We've been to the occasional Michelin Star restaurant over the years, but I have to say that meal in Arcadian Rhodes last night was the best I can remember, ever. A really good night and the perfect way to celebrate Richard and Joyce's anniversary.

Sunday 11 June 2006
Yesterday was the last day of the cruise, and I'm pleased to say the sun was out and the sea was calm. That meant that we could doze away the excesses of the previous evening, laid on a sun bed at the aft of the ship overlooking the wake. Of course, it being our last day, we ensured breakfast, lunch and afternoon tea were not only attended by us, but enthusiastically so – i.e. I ate too much, and Mandy just looked on in what I told myself was awe, but was instead almost certainly embarrassment. But it was nice to spoil ourselves for one last day, and in my case, I was at least able to slightly redress my increasing weight issue with my regular, pre-dinner, sauna.

In actual fact, the sauna has become part of my daily routine on a cruise and I find it really relaxing. All the ships seem to have one as part of their, free-to-use, gym, but amazingly, it seems really underused, which is perfect for me as I can get a good, conversation-free, rest before dinner. Also, the sauna eases the muscle stiffness and fatigue I get from the CFS, and sweats out all that sun block gunk from my pores, so that I'm feeling and looking loads better even before the shower, shave and sharp dressing parts of the process. Of course, occasionally I'll have company in the sauna but, pre-dinner, that will usually be one of the crew or a performer, who doesn't want to talk much either. That's not to say I am not charm personified if they do want a chat, as Megan the Australian dancer found the other day (couldn't believe my luck), but normally it's just an opportunity to chill.

Anyway, after a final goodbye dinner with Joyce and Richard in the Meridian Restaurant, and us all saying our farewells to our two excellent and very busy waiters, Mohammed and Gopal, we went to one last show. The plan had been to just have a couple of drinks in the Orchid Bar before bed, but my new dancer friend, Megan, had recommended the show, so we popped along. In actual fact, "Flashback" was a slight anti-climax after the high of the Cirque Arcadia show, but its flash back to a number of 1960s, 70s and 80s hits was still good, and an opportunity to give the Arcadia Theatre Company one final standing ovation. Sadly, the curtain was coming down on our cruise too, and with a long disembarkation day on the horizon, we retired to an early night.

Chapter 8 - This time I'm going to do it!

Friday 23 June 2006
Okay, this time it's going to work. So far, I have failed at all attempts to consistently hit anything approaching a normal level of activity, as no matter how gradually I have built up to it, I have been unable to stay there for more than a few weeks. This time it is going to be different. This time I plan to stick so rigidly to the Pacing techniques, and gradually increase my activity plan in such small increments, that it has to work. I will be sensible and take things steady, but I'm determined to get there. I have exhausted the recommended support and treatment options available to me, so it's now down to me to use the tools and knowledge I have learnt to try and get myself better.

So having just spent a month at "Base Level", which is the very low level of activity I need to operate at every day to avoid (or recover from) a bad spell, I feel okay. I will now gradually increase my activity until I get back to what I call my "Sustainable Level", which is the level of activity I have managed to operate at for much of the last two years, and which avoids the extreme peaks and troughs of my illness. Then of course there is my "Target Level", which is that level of activity that, realistically, I need to attain consistently before I can return to at least some form of employment. Whilst it's crucial that the actual timeline of this process is determined by how I am doing, and that I also need to remember to temporarily reduce activity level along the way when needed, I'm determined to do it.

Wednesday 19 July 2006
Things are mostly going okay with the Pacing, but I'm deliberately taking things carefully and increasing my activity level slowly. In fact, I'm still gradually building myself up to my Sustainable Level to give me the best possible chance of successfully exceeding that point later on. However, I went to see my GP about a small but annoying inner ear spasm that I'm getting, and which is really uncomfortable. I'm pretty sure it's either linked to the frequent muscle spasms (known as "fasciculations") or tinnitus, which I get all the time, and are common CFS symptoms which I can normally handle. I was just hoping my GP could suggest something to help the inner ear spasm specifically, as it's fairly constant at the moment and driving me mad. It's a bit like having a slightly painful, annoying itch you just can't reach. But in your inner ear!

Due to the fasciculation element, my GP convinced me to first go back and see Dr Dym, the neurologist, to rule out any other, non-CFS, cause. But I suspect Dr Dym will be about as pleased to see me as I will be to see him. It's not that I attach any blame to him for not diagnosing my CFS or anything - it wasn't his area of expertise, and particularly in 2001 it was an illness the medical field as a whole still seemed largely in the dark about - but I think we both found the previous failure to identify the cause of my problems a huge frustration. However, my GP has been very supportive, and I trust his judgement, so off to Dr Dym it is.

Thursday 27 July 2006
Well, I have been to see Dr Dym, and it was a little strange to say the least. He clearly remembered me, and seemed genuinely sorry to see that I was still ill. But right from the start he looked and talked to me as if he didn't know what to make of me, almost as if my CFS meant that I was some kind of strange creature, the like of which he had never seen before. After explaining to him about the spasm sensation I was experiencing in my ear, he first angled his head sideways in an analytical manner, and then he leant back in his chair rubbing his chin. After a few seconds contemplation, and still from his seated position about six feet away from me, he smirked and said "Well, I can't see it spasming at the moment". It was then my turn to be quiet for a few seconds as, with the penny finally dropping inside my head, I just looked at him dumbfounded – this man thinks I'm a fruit-cake who's imagining some sort of crazy trembling ear syndrome!?!

Now, at this point I'm sure that my face must have betrayed my true feelings, and my delivery must surely have come across a little like "no, you plonker". But, as politely as I could muster, I explained that I wasn't talking about a bloody party trick here, I have no issues whatsoever with the external, visible part of my ear, it is the inner ear that is the problem. In response he smirked again and moved swiftly on to the scans I had had done earlier. But by now my mind was elsewhere - did Dr Dym even believe I was ill? Or was it the CFS he didn't believe in?? I wish now I had asked him such questions there and then, but it had been a long day, I was struggling to concentrate, and I just wanted to go home.

The rest of our appointment was a bit of a blur, but the outcome, as I know from the letter Dr Dym sent to my GP, was as I thought it would be: i.e. that my scans were all relatively normal and there is no suggestion of anything more sinister going on. It was a box-ticking exercise and the right boxes had been ticked. But the whole experience had left me feeling really down. Sure, I had come across scepticism about CFS before (as all CFS sufferers do given the nature of the illness), but this time it really got me down. It's possible of course that I misunderstood him, but even in his letter to my GP Dr Dym explained that he had ruled out "a neurological cause again", even though, confusingly, other doctors (and the World Health Organisation) say that CFS is a neurological illness. Maybe I'm being over sensitive, but now I wish I had just kept quiet about this spasm thing, and just learned to live with it as I have done with numerous other symptoms.

Friday 4 August 2006
I'm thinking a bit more positively about things now. At the end of the day it doesn't matter what Dr Dym does or doesn't think about me or CFS, he was involved purely to check out the cause of that one symptom. This he did, and so after a few days reduced activity to recover, and concluding that this inner ear spasm thing is just another symptom to manage as best I can, I got straight back into the Pacing. The experience did make me wonder about the position I would be in today had my CFS been diagnosed and addressed earlier than it was, but what's done is done, and ifs and maybes are absolutely no use to me. It's important to focus on moving forward, and for now that means the Pacing.

Actually, the Pacing has been going so well that Mandy and I decided to take Mum and Dad out for a treat yesterday evening, to say thanks for looking after the cats during our last cruise. Well I say evening, but after taking into account my now regular CFS-related requirement of going somewhere close by when it's quiet, we were actually sat down and eating at a local pub by 5pm. The food wasn't great if I'm honest, fairly standard "Tex Mex" stuff, but Mum and Dad said they enjoyed it, so that's the main thing.

It's funny you know, having spent most of my adult life finding that my social venues of choice were popular "happening" places, full of like-minded noisy people having a good time, the new me is the exact opposite. Now, whether it's a drink with the boys or a meal out with Mandy, I opt for the quietest places at their quietest times. The CFS means busy or noisy can be exhausting, and even so-called background music, if too loud, can make it difficult, especially if travelling to get there has already tired me out.

It's Mand I feel sorry for, as it means pretty much all her special meals for birthdays, anniversaries, or simply a weekend treat, tend to take place at home or in near-empty restaurants. To her credit, she never complains and says she's just as happy eating at home as long as it's with me. Fortunately she's one hell of a cook and will always try and come up with something special at the weekend, but it's not ideal after she's been working hard all week. It's one of the reasons the cruises work so well for us I think, as she really gets to switch off for a while knowing that, if things get too much, my bed is close by.

Sunday 23 September 2006
I'm really chuffed with how things are going with the Pacing. I've not done anything too strenuous, but my daily walks are back up to a consistent half an hour per day. I'm also having a ten-minute swim once a week, sending a few emails and having the occasional decent-length phone call. In short, I'm back to what I call my Sustainable Level, and having built up to it slower than before, I'm feeling okay and my CFS symptoms seem under control. It's not all been plain sailing, as following a rough couple of days last month, I had to miss most of the annual Fantasy Football auction I try to attend every year. Also, my uncle's Stag Day took place last weekend, and I had to miss all but the final hour or so. But it meant that I didn't undo all my good work, and what's more, it ensured I was in good nick to attend his wedding yesterday.

Yes, Uncle Eddie tied the knot yesterday at the ripe old age of 68. Having lost his first wife, my Aunty Rose, to cancer about ten years ago, he's been on his own for a while, but he met Margaret at the local bowls club a year or so back, and they really seem happy together. They got married at the same local church where Mandy and I had got married in 1997, and (drops voice to a whisper) shamefully hadn't been back to since. It was a lovely ceremony, and great to see many of the family we hadn't seen for a while.

In fact the whole occasion was terrific, even after one small surreal moment when, at the end of the ceremony, my Uncle Ray tried to lead a round of applause. Everyone had just started to join in the applause when the very serious-looking priest overseeing the nuptials pulled a very stern face and started shaking his head from side to side to signify we should stop. The applause didn't so much cease as suffer an agonisingly slow death, as one by one, all of us gradually spotted the priest's shaking head, slowed our clapping whilst we interpreted his dissatisfaction, before finally stopping. One fella, either slow on the uptake, or out of eye-line with the disgruntled clergy, carried on a final solo effort for a good four or five claps of decreasing pace. It was fine, and everyone smiled at each other in a bemused fashion whilst the happy couple signed the register, so no harm done, just a little surreal as I say.

The reception was held at a nice local hotel within walking distance of the church. Mandy however was keen to keep our car handy in case I had any problems later on. But with a few well-timed rests, and popping home for a couple of hours in the middle, not only did we attend most of the afternoon reception but a bit of the evening one too, so I was really pleased. Although it was only an approximate timescale, in my head I had Eddie's wedding down as the point from where I would increase my activity levels again. I wanted to first ensure I was well enough to attend it obviously, and now with everything having gone so well, I intend gradually increasing my activity towards my Target Level. I'll just get some extra rest first due to yesterday's event.

Monday 16 October 2006
As a way of taking another small step towards my Target Level, I have been trying to meet up with someone every two or three days for a chat, coffee or even a short lunch, as this requires a reasonable amount of mental effort that goes beyond what I have been able to consistently achieve to date. On a cruise of course you interact with people all the time without even thinking about it, but crucially, that is usually for a few minutes at a time. These meet-ups on the other hand are longer, and cognitively more testing, even if the meet-up concerned is just popping to a neighbour's house for a coffee. When I am operating at my Sustainable Level, I would limit these to one, or occasionally two, a week, so it's a definite increase.

One of these meet-ups was Mandy and me popping up the road to Eddie and Margaret's to see their wedding photos. They were very fortunate with the weather that day, so combined with everyone dressed in their finery and with big wide smiles a-plenty, the photos were excellent. We promptly ordered a few for ourselves. What didn't look quite so good was the video footage, as short of picking up the television, turning it 90 degrees and placing it on its side, you couldn't watch it without getting a crook in your neck. You see, Eddie had lent my video camera to a family friend to do the honours but, much as you might do with a photographic camera, he had turned the camera sideways to get tall and narrow footage, rather than the shorter and wider view it was designed to provide. The result being that much of the footage was permanently stuck in a sideways view. As Homer Simpson might say, "Doh". But I can't talk, as I actually saw him doing this on the day and thought absolutely nothing of it, so I clearly wasn't that sharp either. Fingers crossed they can get someone more technically minded to sort it out for them.

Tuesday 7 November 2006
Just as things were going so well, I've suffered a pretty major relapse. I was only thinking to myself the other day that I need to be careful as I was approaching the point where I normally get setbacks. What's really frustrating is that although I had been pretty active by my normal standards, I had been really careful to only increase my activity level in small increments. It's so damn frustrating. But it's a familiar story. It seems whenever I try and exceed my Sustainable Level for anything more than a few weeks, the exact same thing happens. And then I'm back at square one and feeling so down and sorry for myself, I wonder why the hell I keep trying. TO GET BACK TO WORK! That's why!! It's just hard. Really hard. And it gets harder every relapse.

Tuesday 21 November 2006
I had to cancel lunch with a couple of lads I used to work with today as I'm really struggling. It's a shame, as having had to cancel these frequently in recent years, I've done well over the last 12 months or so, even if it meant just sticking my head in to say hello for ten minutes, or inviting them here instead. God knows, the number of friends and colleagues I am still in contact with has reduced drastically over the years. I don't blame them: they rarely see or hear from me, and when they do, I'm really hard work. It's me too, even on my better days I've probably not picked up the phone or sent them an email, but I've lost my confidence a bit, and let's face it, my end of the conversation tends to be the same old "not done much, rested lots". Hardly a barrel of laughs. So instead of meeting the lads for lunch, I ended up reflecting on how the whole relapse thing had occurred.

I think the first sign was about three weeks ago when we had a kitchen design lady come to the house. We've needed a new kitchen for a while but, with being ill, I just haven't been able to face thinking about it, let alone contemplating a couple of blokes banging hell out of the house for a week when they fit it. Straight from the start of the meeting with this lady, I was really struggling to follow what she was saying, and whenever any text or pictures were placed in front of me, they made little sense. By now I'm used to losing my focus regularly (and have started to unknowingly make automatic "uh huh" or "oh right" type noises that give people the impression that I am still following them), but this time my concentration didn't even get started. She might as well have been speaking Latvian. Needless to say the meeting ended prematurely, and Mandy will be waiting a little longer for her new kitchen.

Up until then I had been doing well overall and feeling relatively okay physically, but I took this hiccup in the cognitive side of things as a sign I was doing too much, and reduced my activity immediately. However, whilst my headache had been manageable, a few days later it started to slowly worsen each day. Therefore, although they had occurred in reverse order to anytime previously, the definite worsening of the two earliest and most prominent symptoms of my CFS (severe headache and cognitive dysfunction) acted as definite warning signs. The trouble was, despite that immediate reduction in my activity level, I still wasn't able to avoid the full relapse, which kicked in over the subsequent days.

So here I am, three weeks on and still waiting to turn the corner towards feeling better. My head is banging, and as normal, painkillers are taking only the slightest edge off it. I'm incredibly noise-sensitive, with every banging car door or screeching fan belt in our quiet little street, going right through me. And the blinding autumnal sun is so low in the sky it seems to find a way to seek me out through every window. Even the bloody birds have got it in for me with their singing seemingly extra screechy. My swollen glands are something I normally live with fairly easily, but these last few weeks it's been horrible. It hurts to even think about moving. I had forgotten how bad all this feels. Sometimes just being exhausted is exhausting.

Wednesday 10 January 2007

When I saw Hanqiao today for my fortnightly acupuncture appointment, we discussed how I was still struggling after the relapse in November. I explained how, for example, I had tried to join the lads for a quick lunchtime drink just before Christmas but that I had to leave within two minutes. We analysed the reasons for that, and how things like close-proximity noise and movement were now a bigger problem than before, and how this was starting to become a real obstacle. We concluded however that, as strange as those particular symptoms are to fathom, the single root cause is still the CFS. As such, Hanqiao is still positive that Chinese medicine can help me; it was perhaps just time to try something different, like "cupping". And like now. As in "get your shirt off and lie face down on my couch" type now.

Thankfully, it quickly became clear that the Chinese version of cupping is totally different from the cupping my testicles experienced at the shockingly cold hands of the lady doctor during my medical in 2001. This was because Hanqiao now brought in seven or eight little jars – or, and I'm going out on a limb here, "cups". She then proceeded to light a small flame inside each of the jars - sorry cups – and place them upside-down on my back. She explained that, as with my normal acupuncture needles, it was important to be very specific with their placement and not just lump them on willy-nilly (I know! Who knew the phrase "willy-nilly" existed in ancient Chinese medicine?).

Now, the good news is that the flames inside extinguish quickly, and before the cups are placed on you, as logically all of the oxygen inside gets used up. This then creates a vacuum effect that results in each jar, or "cup", sucking so hard on your skin that it feels like you're getting love bites from seven or eight extremely affectionate leeches. In actual fact it's okay (you just feel a slight tightening of the skin), and what this does is stimulate certain pressure points on your body, in a similar logic I guess to how the acupuncture needles work. And, as with the needles, I found it really relaxing and instantly fell asleep.

Where cupping very much differs from the needles however, is in how you look afterwards. When I was a lad at school, I remember the class pillock cutting a tennis ball in half and pressing one half against his forehead until it effectively stuck, very tightly, to him. He really struggled to get it off, and when he did it left this perfect, very angry, red circle which stayed there for a week. If you multiply this by eight you'll imagine what my back was like after the cupping. It looked like someone had been using me for target practice. But in all seriousness it's absolutely fine, with little if any discomfort, and hopefully its benefits will far outweigh this very minor inconvenience.

Tuesday 20 March 2007
Well I'm not sure if it is down to the cupping or not, but I'm pleased to say I'm finally feeling back to my old self – i.e. my old self as in old CFS self, rather than my old, old self as in old pre-CFS self. Clear? No?? Okay, let me try and quantify what being back to my old CFS self means.

The main point is that for the last couple of weeks I've been back operating largely problem-free at a level where living, and living with me, is tolerable. Cognitively I'm a little foggy, but I'm okay for short spells of reading, talking etc. I still only leave the house for a short walk most days, but that half an hour that I allow for the walk itself, and sometimes sitting on a bench halfway, is just brilliant. I time myself as I walk along the canal path close to our house, and then when my watch beeps, I turn around and come back again. It's 30 minutes out of the house and I love it. It also breaks up those long lonely days at home quite nicely.

My recovery thus far also now permits me the occasional foray outside my own post code, which is quite therapeutic in itself. So far that's only really meant meeting up briefly for a drink of hot water (party on!?!) with my old bosses, Dave and Jo, and reintroducing my weekly ten-minute swim, but it's all good stuff, and life already feels so much brighter. In fact, at times I have to remind myself not to do too much too soon, as I find I am already forgetting just how hard the last few months have been. But whether it's the haggard-looking man who now looks back at me in the mirror, or having to answer fellow swimmers' enquiries about the angry cup-sized circles on my back (with an explanation that my wife is a sexual deviant), there are still a few reminders.

Sunday 8 April 2007
We had our three parents over for Easter Sunday lunch today and it was really hard work. A strange way to describe a meal with one's parents I know, but much as I love her, my mum could talk for England. My dad's not exactly quiet, but with Mum it's constant, and for me, exhausting. It might help if she were to occasionally talk about someone I knew, but no, my poor overworked, underperforming brain has to mentally map out the family tree of the neighbour's daughter's postman's son's dog, to even loosely follow what she is saying.

My trouble is that although I'm continuing to do a lot better of late, cognitively I still get so tired. And therefore irritable. And therefore grumpy. And so at some point I will inevitably say something like "Mum, do I know these people, have I ever known these people, am I ever likely to know these people? Because if not, can we please, for the love of God, try and talk about someone that has at least a tenuous link to those of us around this table". And then I feel guilty. And therefore bad. And therefore miserable.

The daft thing is I look forward to such lunches and today was no exception, it was lovely to have everyone around our table, and they do all seem to have a good time. Which is just as well as we have our three surviving parents around for one of Mandy's legendary roasts pretty much every Christmas Day, Birthday, Mother's Day, Father's Day and Easter Sunday. But - and it's a big but - it is really hard sometimes. Poor Mandy plans these events for weeks in advance, to make them special for our parents. She then slaves over a hot stove for hours, patiently listens to the same family stories she has heard many times before, and still has the energy and grace to be the perfect host. Her husband on the other hand is just a miserable, intolerant old goat. Did I mention that I will surely die alone?

Sunday 22 April 2007
I'm pleased to say that things are continuing to slowly progress CFS-wise, but now I have a predicament. We are due on a seven-day cruise in a few weeks' time, so I would normally be reducing my activity now, in order to "charge up" the extra energy I'm likely to need. However I'm only just back to a decent activity level after the relapse, and I fear that to reduce things too much now would do more harm than good. It's a fine line. Do too much, and risk getting fatigued and ill. Do too little, and my body will get out of practice and decondition, especially given how inactive I have already been quite recently. So what I have decided to do is to try and keep my activity at a fairly reasonable level this time, in the run-up to the cruise, even if this results in me being able to do less on the cruise itself.

It's a one-week cruise rather than one of the longer two-week ones, so hopefully it should be okay. We very nearly cancelled it a few months back, but having booked it over a year ago, it's been something good to look forward to for a while now. It was certainly something I focused on when I felt low, and with me causing her even more concern than normal, I'm pretty sure Mandy did too.

So, whilst energy-wise it means being very sensible over the next three weeks, we did have a final pre-cruise treat yesterday when we met up with Brian and Gill, who we met on the Artemis cruise. Brian has been in regular contact through my rough spell, via both emails and phone calls, and we wanted to ensure we met up with them pre-cruise just in case I suffer another setback. In fact, Brian's phone calls provided a regular source of entertainment through the winter as he would invariably phone up, put on a different voice, and pretend to be someone else. Only trouble being, I know for a fact that neither Rafa Benitez or Alex Ferguson, or a single one of Brian's personas come to that, have a strong Welsh accent in real life. But he always brought a smile to my face, which was much appreciated, even if it was his attempts to impersonate that were funny rather than the impersonations themselves.

Brian and Gill were also good enough to travel down to us yesterday and meet us at a great little pub just a few miles down the road, which helped a lot. Given the upcoming cruise and our new found love of all things cruising, we had a good old chat over some good food, about stuff that would have had our non-cruising friends looking at their watches, I'm sure. But I guess it's a sign of how much CFS has changed things and not always for the worse – I certainly don't think we would have discovered cruising if it wasn't for me being ill, and that's something we absolutely love, and absolutely love talking about.

Sunday 6 May 2007
We eventually boarded Oceana late today after a longer-than-normal journey down, and a lengthy wait in the embarkation lounge. Although we left home early, all the extra traffic heading to the coast on a Bank Holiday weekend just made it very slow going, which then resulted in all us passengers arriving a) later, and b) together. Foolishly I hadn't pre-arranged any "assisted boarding", so we found a quieter corner of the embarkation lounge and tried to get some rest whilst waiting to be called. In actual fact the wait was probably only just over an hour, but with it being so busy, and coming after a much harder-than-normal journey down, it felt like much, much longer.

Once on board, and walking once again into Oceana's stunning Atrium, I instantly felt a lot better. Still tired, but just lifted somehow, and judging by the broad smile on her face, Mandy felt the same way. Given we had boarded a lot later than normal, and with me no doubt looking a little weary, our "welcome aboard" lady advised that our cabin was already available so we headed straight there. I couldn't sleep of course, as there was far too much going through my head, but the cabin was quiet and uncrowded, and it gave my senses a rest at least. And we have seven whole days aboard the beautiful Oceana now, so plenty of time to make up for a slow start.

The cabin is fine by the way (although I note my request for my inside cabin to have a balcony has once again fallen on deaf ears), and according to the little sign in our cabin, our cabin steward this cruise is "Jesus" – full credit to P&O, they really do pull out all the stops don't they? Anyway, Mandy should have unpacked by now, so I've got an "oh, you've finished, I was just coming to help" line to deliver with a sad face combo. Toodle Pip.

Tuesday 8 May 2007
After a relaxing and restful sea day yesterday, we were chomping at the bit first thing this morning as we arrived in Hamburg. We got off the ship quite early to explore, and found Hamburg wasn't what we expected at all. But in a good way. Knowing Hamburg to be one of the busiest ports in Europe, I think I was expecting it to be a grim industrialised city which, courtesy of watching Auf Weidersehen Pet on the telly in the 80s, I guess I also imagined much of (non-Bavarian) Germany to be. But it is a nice place with bright open streets, a blend of old and new buildings, and large leafy areas and lakes.

We initially had a meander around Hamburg's centre which was very clean, modern, and at that time of day, pretty quiet. So quiet in fact that we managed to walk through the infamous Reeperbahn almost without realising it. I imagine it takes on a whole other life at night time, but at 10am the only clues were an occasional beer lorry on restocking duty, and a few stern-looking night-worker types walking around with the air of those who haven't slept yet. There was one sex shop that was tentatively opening its shutters, but it felt way too early for gawping at inflatable sex dolls even if they did offer enhanced "Arsch" and "Titten" – and if all German can be translated that easily then I think we'll get by.

Further evidence that I could unknowingly sprechen sie deutsche came in the shape of the large park we had been advised to check out, as we realised it is actually called Planten un Blomen Park. And even from the relatively small portion of its 47 acres that we covered, it was clear that there was planting and blooming a-plenty. Given this place is bang in the middle of the city centre, its size and beauty took us by surprise, as it's packed full of greenery, brownery, and even waterfall-ery. It felt like we had been transported to somewhere much more rural than Hamburg city centre. After a while it started to drizzle, but luckily for us, at exactly that point we stumbled across one of the many surprising little features that the park has to offer. It was the Japanese Gardens and Tea Rooms, housed in this pretty-looking glasshouse, and the perfect place to take shelter and a breather.

Leaving the park, and with the rain having stopped, we took the short walk to the Alster lakes of which there are two – the Inner Alster and the Outer Alster. I understand that these were created when a dam was built on the River Alster, but they look totally natural. By now the city itself was very much hustle and bustle, but similar to the park, the lakes provided an oasis of calm, wham bam in the middle of Germany's second largest metropolis. My wobbly legs told me to jump on one of the regular boat tours on offer, where we were subsequently informed, entertained and generally made to feel very welcome by our Kevin Keegan-loving guide. Keegan was voted European Footballer of the Year whilst playing here 30 years ago, and by all accounts loved the place. And judging by the amazing houses and hotels we saw on our trip around the lakes, I suspect that his was the one and only time that anyone called Kev resided in one.

So yes, Hamburg is a real surprise, and a really great looking city which I would be very happy to return to. And even though I can distinctly remember our languages teacher at school saying pretty much "It's Spanish if you're a thicko, and German for the bright sparks" (and me being very much the former), the language wasn't an issue at all. Yes okay, as usual pretty much everyone spoke English, but all joking apart, some German words translate so literally, they seem to have come straight from a 1970s sitcom. Even the Town Hall is called the "Rathaus" (pronounced Rat-House), which clearly doesn't say much about the integrity of their local councillors. It's architecturally beautiful by the way, the Town Hall, and by far the best looking building in Hamburg, complete with a 300-foot high tower if you like that sort of thing.

Wednesday 9 May 2007

Although Oceana was alongside in Hamburg until 8am this morning, I'm afraid we didn't quite make it back ashore last night, which is a real shame as we had "bought a ticket to ride" the Beatles excursion. But I was tired and my head was really banging, so it would undoubtedly have proved "a hard day's night". So it turns out that our trip ashore "yesterday" morning was "hello, goodbye" Hamburg, but on the plus side, today I'm "feeling fine", courtesy of some rest and taking enough pain killers to finally take the edge off the headache, so all good.

We departed Hamburg as planned this morning, but the weather had turned a little nasty overnight. So nasty in fact that our pilot, who was on board to navigate us safely down the River Elbe back to the North Sea, was not able to disembark to the usual transit boat, and will now stay with us until we port. The sea didn't feel that bad to us actually, and part of me wonders whether he just fancied some sex, drugs and rocking and rolling all the way to Amsterdam with us, but it's definitely a little choppy out there, so let's give him the benefit of the doubt.

Mandy and I, as I say, were finding the movement okay this morning, so we breakfasted in the Peninsular Restaurant, as I quite fancied their usual poached eggs on wholemeal toast offering. We were soon joined at our table by two youngish couples who, due to a combination of the choppy sea, and them clearly having taken full advantage of Hamburg's nightlife, were a little, um, fragile. They were tired and hung-over. And in one case, likely to keel over at any second. What followed was like the worst-ever episode of Come Dine with Me – one of them nearly fell asleep in his cornflakes, two of them had a full blown row, and the final one left in one hell of a hurry to go and throw up. It was so Come Dine with Me that had we returned to our cabin to find them rifling through our drawers, I wouldn't have been the least bit surprised.

Thursday 10 May 2007

In Amsterdam today, and we were up and off the ship nice and early so that we could avoid the long queues at Anne Frank's house that prevented us from seeing it last time. And it worked. At 9.30am there wasn't so much a queue, as a steady trickle of people wandering in and through the house, so that was okay, I could manage that. We walked straight in, paid 15 Euros total admission for the pair of us, and joined the trickle.

Having studied her diary at school, both Mandy and I found Anne Frank's house really interesting, but also quite moving - even more so when you are reminded that after nearly three years hiding there, Anne and her family were just a few weeks away from liberation when the Nazi's found them and condemned them to death in concentration camps. Anne's father, Otto, survived his own internment and returned to the house after the war, but I can't even begin to imagine how he found the will to go on.

As I say, an amazing place to visit and an absolute must-see in my opinion. Whilst the front part of the house is pretty ordinary, the back (or annex) is emotionally gripping. It's not furnished as such – the Nazi's emptied it and Otto Frank's wish was that it should stay unfurnished after the war – but, from the moveable bookcase that was built to cover the entrance, to the coverings on the windows, you get a real sense of the hiding place that it once was. Quite a harrowing visit if I'm honest, but captivating even for someone like me who isn't a museum buff at all. Glad we went.

Friday 11 May 2007
You might have noticed that this cruise I am making fewer references to the more social side of things, like pre/post-dinner drinks or the shows. That's primarily because I'm still not feeling as strong health-wise. It's not that I'm in danger of another relapse, and in actual fact I am being very careful to avoid just that, I think it's more that I am still getting back to where I was, activity-wise, before things went south last year. We're still having a good time though, and have thoroughly enjoyed both Hamburg and Amsterdam, even if we have failed to go back ashore for either of our two overnight stops in two of the party capitals of Europe. Maybe in another life hey?

But what we did do, in addition to Anne Frank's house, was have a nice walk around Amsterdam, in between some heavy spring showers. We even stumbled across the Flower Market which looked and smelled amazing, and contrary to popular opinion, didn't just sell Tulips! It mostly sold Tulips!! Also, last night we shared the mid-ships elevator with a couple in their 30s who had clearly just come from one of Amsterdam's infamous cafés. They were as high as kites bless them, and giving off such a strong scent of wacky baccy that I briefly thought we might get stoned ourselves just by travelling a few floors with them. Who says I don't know how to party?

Saturday 12 May 2007

Due to torrential rain, and me needing another quiet day to recharge, I'm afraid our second day in Amsterdam yesterday was spent entirely on board Oceana. But that's no hardship by any stretch of the imagination, and we had a nice quiet day, alternating between food and relaxation, with the ship largely to ourselves. The extra rest meant we also got to see our first Stadium Theatre Company show of the cruise last night which was good, especially as we had missed the others. It's all a bit fuzzy (due to tiredness not alcohol!) so I'm struggling to remember specific numbers, but it was called The Seven Deadly Sins and was very good.

After the show it was back to the cabin for another early night in readiness for our final stop in Bruges, or Zeebrugge to be exact. It's a little bit of a journey into Bruges itself, so not sure exactly what we will do, but if I feel okay in the morning we will definitely go ashore. We loved Bruges last time, so ideally would like to go there again, even if just for a short stroll.

Sunday 13 May 2007

Well sadly we are back at home today. But everything came together very nicely for the final day of our cruise in Bruges yesterday, including our first bit of sunshine on an otherwise showery cruise. Our plan was to take the free shuttle bus into Blankenberge and then, if I was feeling okay, take the short train ride into Bruges itself. Plan B was to stay in Blankenberge and just have a wander, but as pleasant a town as it looked, it would have been disappointing in comparison. So I was chuffed I felt able to chuff-chuff onto Bruges, albeit on the slowest train I have ever been on. It was a short, straightforward journey however, so we were at Bruges Station (about ten minutes from Bruge's traffic-free centre) in next to no time.

That said, I was feeling it a bit when we got to the centre so, particularly as it was so sunny, we opted to do one of our favourite resting/touristy combo's - a horse-drawn carriage ride. And after selecting the carriage and driver with the best looked-after horse, on we jumped. Okay, in my case, not so much "jumped" as groaned and pulled my way into the carriage (while Mandy, a hand to each buttock, pushed), but the key point was that I got in, and I was very much looking forward to a sunny ride around beautiful Bruges. Which is exactly what we got for the next 40 minutes.

Although, we had joined quite a thorough excursion the last time we were here, we still discovered some pretty new places on our carriage ride. One place in particular which we either didn't see last time (seems unlikely) or that when we did my brain just zoned out for a bit (seems more likely), was the Market Square. There was only a small market on yesterday, but it's a beautiful old square which, basking in the spring sunshine, and with its medieval belfry and striking bell tower (are all bell towers striking?), really finished our carriage ride off nicely.

One place I definitely did remember from our last time here was Dumon, the chocolatier. So once our carriage-driver had taken a quick photo of Mandy and me with his horse and carriage, we went straight there. As you would expect, Bruges has a mouth-watering number of shops selling chocolates, but so generous and friendly was Madame Dumon last time, and her chocolates so good, that we were never going to go anywhere else. The trouble was, this time, we got so carried away buying chocolates for family and friends, we forgot we still had to lump them all back on the train. But we managed it, and despite getting the munchies halfway back, most of the chocolates even made it to the ship with us.

Monday 14 May 2007
So a slightly less active cruise this time, but still one we are both glad we went on. I think, after a difficult six months or so, that we would have cancelled it had it been any longer than seven days, but it was just the right length. I really struggled at times, so we didn't do as much in the evenings as we had managed previously, and limited our activity ashore. However, it was a good break and a change of scenery that did us both good.

The one element which continues to be a potential banana-skin for me is embarkation day. Sometimes it's fine as we miss the crowds, but as with this cruise, if we catch the embarkation rush it's a long difficult process which really hits me health-wise. There is the option of P&O's assisted boarding system for people not mobile enough to board by themselves, but I can walk and board okay, it's just getting aboard for some rest as soon as possible that I need. I did try the assisted boarding before, but as well as feeling a fraud that time I used the wheelchair-based system, a few days later a passenger was quite rude to (the now walking) me. However, other than arriving early each time and hoping we miss the rush, it's difficult to see what we can do differently.

Chapter 9 – The Glass Ceiling

Friday 1 June 2007
I'm missing Macca's 40th birthday party tonight and I'm gutted. But I know it will be busy and noisy, and as much as I love him, I would just be a liability and an embarrassment. There will be lots of people I know there, but in a busy environment like a party, especially a house party, I'm not sure that's a good thing. In fact I'm terrified at the thought of seeing some of them, as it would be the first time since I became ill and I would be far from my best - and even my best isn't great. In all probability the volume of music and people would just prove way too intense for me, cognitively I would become a five-year-old, and then my head would start banging. And that's best-case scenario. Realistically, I could also start shaking at some point or end up doing some kind of dying swan act, and leaving early. And I'm not even the entertainment.

I do want to go to such events, and especially to Macca's 40th as he's been a really good mate, and I feel like I'm letting him down. However, even if I was to be miraculously healthy at such a shindig, the fatigued me seems to lack that little filter that normal people have, that determines what's appropriate and what's not. You know, that little thing in your brain which stops you from saying every single thing that enters it. Sometimes it just filters out the boring, mundane stuff. And sometimes it prevents you from doing something stupid in front of the host's elderly relatives. But at the very least it rephrases thoughts like "Blimey, you've piled on some weight" into a more suitable, less offensive equivalent. My filter is, at best, intermittent and the more tired I get, the less it seems to work.

So, you see Mac, I'm actually doing you a favour by not going to your party as the extent of bemusement, offence, or just general boredom amongst your guests will be significantly reduced by my absence.

Monday 18 June 2007
An advantage of not going to Mac's party was that it could easily have knocked me out for weeks health-wise, and meant me missing a long-standing arrangement to visit my cousin Tracey and her fiancé Tim, in Colchester this last weekend. You see, at my Aunt June's (Tracey's mum) funeral two years ago, we talked about how Tracey and Tim's house, just outside Colchester, was so remote and rural that they thought it would be perfect for Mandy and I to have some rest and relaxation. In fact, from

pretty much the point I became ill until she died in 2005, June had said the exact same thing. So actually this whole weekend in Colchester became something that I felt I wanted to do in memory of June, even more so as, ever since Mandy and I had married in 1997, June had regularly invited us up to Colchester without us once taking her up on the offer. And after two years in the planning, and waiting for a good run health-wise, our weekend with Tracey and Tim had finally arrived. My biggest problem, as I knew it would be, was the 150-mile journey there and back.

Fortunately, aside from the thumping great obstacle of getting across London, the train journey to Colchester was very straightforward, with regular direct trains into Paddington Station and out of Liverpool Street Station. Thus, by travelling at a quieter time of the day, most of our journey was okay. However, the opposite was likely to be true of the London Underground and so we had already decided to avoid that at all costs and take a taxi across London instead. That proved to be the hard bit, as although quiet, it was a far from comfortable ride - very busy and stop-start - and the driver even fleeced me for £10 more than the fare we agreed on when he picked us up. But eventually we got to first Liverpool Street, and then Colchester, and I was feeling relatively alright.

After a kip and a quiet lunch at Tracey and Tim's, we enjoyed plenty of the rest and relaxation that both Tracey and her mum had suggested for so long. The house's location is idyllic, right out in the sticks, down a no-through-road country lane, and surrounded by open fields. Even the style of the house was the part wooden, almost New England style we had always hoped for ourselves one day.

After a nice lazy afternoon relaxing in the sun and enjoying that beautiful setting, the four of us headed to a local pub to meet Tracey's dad, my Uncle Ray, for dinner. It wasn't too busy or noisy in there so we found that we quickly relaxed, and had an enjoyable meal and a good laugh. Obviously it felt a little strange being with the three of them together like that without the lovely June, but Ray and Tim, like a well-practiced double act, kept us laughing throughout.

The following morning I was struggling a bit, and in anticipation of that Tracey packed Tim off to play cricket. The weather was still fantastic, so we had a late breakfast and chilled all morning in the garden. I'm pretty sure my head was at that dangerous stage between being too tired to talk any sense but not fatigued enough to actually shut up. Either way, we chewed the fat for a while on everything from the much-missed June, to wider family events, and life in general.

As the weekend progressed I started to feel worse as that long journey caught up with me. Knowing that the delayed fatigue of CFS would mean worse was still to come, and not wanting to be a burden to Tracey and Tim, we had arranged for our cruising friends, Richard and Joyce, to pick us up in the evening. Richard and Joyce only live about ten miles away and had offered to either put us up for the night, if I was up to that, or even drive us home if that's what we needed. Not wanting to be a pain, we opted for the former in the end and we enjoyed a quiet but pleasant evening with them, before they dropped us at the station the next morning. All in all it was a great weekend, visiting not just Tracey and Tim, but Richard and Joyce too. Which I'm glad we managed actually, as I'm not sure I can do that journey again anytime soon. I'm not feeling well at all now, and will need some time to recover, but the longer I have CFS the more I realise that sometimes I just have to put myself through it. Otherwise life will just pass us by.

Friday 20 July 2007
Right, all recovered from the Colchester trip I think, after a month of Base Level activity. I'm now ready to use my daily Pacing again to try and slowly build up towards a decent level of activity. However, this time, rather than simply alternating my activity and rest periods, I am going to try "switching" activities too.

You see, to date, after my daily walk for example, I would rest for 60 to 90 minutes before spending, say, 20 minutes on my emails. I would then rest for another 60 minutes. That is the method of Pacing which I have found works for me the best, as whatever the activity, an immediate rest after it allows me to recharge. However, there is also a theory that, rather than resting after each activity, you should immediately switch to a different type of exercise. The logic being that by immediately switching from, say, a physical task to a mental task, you are resting that part of you that has just been exercised, whilst encouraging your body to get use to a longer activity period overall.

I think it's something that's worth a try, as I keep getting stuck at the same point using my normal Pacing method, but I have concerns. For instance, a bodybuilder may spend time exercising his arms and then switch to his legs. It's not as simple as that with CFS, as in my experience one type of activity seems to also fatigue those elements you need to carry out the other type. It's why, if I stick the television on when I come back from my walk, I struggle to concentrate on the programme being shown even if, in all other respects, I am resting. But it's worth a try.

Monday 8 October 2007

Well, after another summer of very careful Pacing, I once again fell flat on my face and had another relapse. Not as bad as the last one, as I recognised what was happening and immediately went back to Base Level activity. I'm glad to say I'm feeling stronger now, but a definite relapse and a rough old time of it as a result. It also means that the switching element of Pacing, which I experimented with this time, isn't the answer. In fact, I couldn't even get back to where I was last year by using switching, so halfway through I reverted back to my normal Pacing method of alternate activity and rests.

Once I made the change back to my usual practice, and got back to my normal Sustainable Level, things actually went very well for a while. But again, a few weeks into exceeding this level, the problems started. This time I tried to use everything I've learnt to date to avoid the relapse, but other that recognising it earlier, I wasn't able to avoid it. I think I now know enough about how my body and mind reacts to CFS to manage it quite well, but short of giving up, I don't know what else I can do to progress further. If I try, it results in another relapse. I just can't seem to avoid them. And I have to avoid them as they are not doing me any good at all, and it's not fair on Mandy. It feels like I'm stuck.

Monday 5 November 2007

Today Mandy and I met with Martin Lee, my CFS doctor. In normal circumstances, I'm sure Martin would have been forced to cease his involvement with my case by now, as he has a whole string of newer patients who are in even more need of his help. However, I think he can see how desperate I am to get better, and how much I appreciate any support and guidance he can still offer, so we do still meet occasionally. This time it's been well over a year since I have seen Martin, so we had a lot to talk about and review.

I quickly brought Martin up to date with my continued use of Pacing, and the relapses I had when I pushed too far. As a relapse has occurred at pretty much the same point in the process every time, Martin explained that I may have hit what, in CFS circles, they refer to as the glass ceiling. That came as a shock to me as the only glass ceiling I had ever heard about was the one that disgruntled career ladies moan about, when some spotty man-child gets promoted instead of them. Martin laughed and explained that, in CFS it's used in similar terms – i.e. that the glass ceiling represents the invisible but very real barrier through which further progress looks achievable, but all attempts to operate beyond it prove unsuccessful. It doesn't mean I should give up trying to progress, but I need to tread very carefully when I approach this level.

As a result of seemingly hitting this glass ceiling repeatedly, we also reviewed whether Pacing was still the right approach for me. We both felt it was. Martin explained that, given how ill I was when I first saw him, and particularly due to how long I initially went undiagnosed at the start, he felt that I had done incredibly well to get as far as I have. The level of Pacing I refer to as my Sustainable Level is a point that he was unsure I would get too, and represents a quality of activity that many in my situation fail to reach. In that respect Pacing has worked very well for me. Also, other than perhaps Cognitive Behaviour Therapy and Graded Exercise Therapy – neither of which worked for me previously, but that I use small elements of – there is currently no other NHS recommended treatment available for CFS.

From my point of view, Pacing has given me a better quality of life, even if it hasn't given me back the quality of life that I had before CFS. Therefore, in the absence of anything else that comes anywhere close to giving me the same thing, I will stick with it. I'll never give up trying to push beyond this glass ceiling, if that's what I have hit, but it's important to be aware of its existence. If I can't get beyond it, then on the plus side, the Sustainable Level I have successfully managed for long periods represents a life that, if I have to, I can live with. The downside is that it's difficult to see any possible form of employment that can incorporate the amount and regularity of rest spells a typical day at that activity level requires.

Sunday 16 December 2007
Yesterday, we went to see Mamma Mia, the musical, in Bristol. That was a pretty big step for me as it meant attending a busy event in an unfamiliar location, and a reasonable distance away. It was intended as an early Christmas present for Mandy, but I also wanted to try using the train again to see how I got on. You see, as hard as the Colchester trip

was in June, the first train element of that trip felt okay. If such a train journey is a) short, and b) direct, I think it's something I might be able to handle during a good spell. Bristol, being just three stops and 30 minutes down the line, ticked one box and my current, mostly problem free, activity level ticked another. I could almost hear the drums Fernando.

As always, the day was planned out with military precision. Our train tickets were booked in the quiet part of a train leaving at the least busy time. Also, my brother Phil and his wife Karen, who had (been) volunteered to come along, joined us so they could provide Mand with much-needed support should I go "rogue" at any stage. Once in Bristol, we jumped in a taxi and then went for lunch at a small restaurant close to the theatre. So far so good, and the small CFS-related problems I had experienced thus far, I had kept successfully hidden I think. We got to the show itself early, again to avoid the crowds, and took our seats, which had been carefully selected in consultation with the theatre itself. I'm sure the D-Day landings hadn't required planning of this precision, but it had worked, we got there okay, and although our seats were up with the gods, everyone was having a good day.

The show itself was good too. I did wonder beforehand how Abba's songs would be squeezed into a storyline written 30 years later, but on the whole it worked, and certainly no "Super Troopers" magically arriving on the little Greek island of the story's setting. One song did feel a little crow-barred in however, when in reply to the very leading line "We need to talk", the Mum character very predictably says "I don't wanna talk...(pauses for music to kick in)...*about the things we've gone through*". And, frankly, you can hardly blame her, as she appears to have slept with so many fellas that at least three of them think they are the biological father of her teenage daughter. Floozy.

It was a good fun show though, which we all thoroughly enjoyed, and we had a nice day. The bonus is that, based on how I'm feeling today, a 30-minute train ride appears to be do-able, as does lunch and a show, even if, as I suspect, I will feel worse tomorrow. It means taking some sensible precautions, and as usual getting loads of extra rest in the week before and after such a trip, but I'm really pleased it went so well.

Friday 15 February 2008
I've been treading very carefully since Christmas, as symptom-wise things started to worsen slightly, and so I treated that as a warning sign.

So far it's worked: the CFS symptoms have settled down again to the point where we've even gone out twice in the last fortnight.

Firstly we attended my niece, Jessica's, 18th Birthday party, which despite the headache that having all of our wider family in one room can be, was great, and I was chuffed to be there. It did feel a little like I spent half of my time outside the main venue of the party, due to struggling with the volume of people and the music. And the other half of the time trying to stop my mum castrating my sister's ex-husband, but I'm glad we went. It's hard to believe that my nieces and nephews are now practically all adults.

Secondly, Mandy and I went to a great little Italian restaurant to celebrate our anniversary. It opened up last summer in what used to be our local pub, and where Yeti and I used to play pool. Mandy's favourite food is Italian, so to have a good Italian restaurant just down the road, especially when your husband is generally averse to going much beyond that distance, is brilliant. We've been to La Carbonara a few times now, and whilst I still need to go along at quieter times (it's very popular), it really is good having it so close. Both the Spring Chicken and the Steak Rossini, the house speciality, are excellent.

Whilst we were there, Mandy and I got onto the subject of my health (romantic hey?) and how best to approach my CFS now that we know there's the possibility of a glass ceiling. It was a useful discussion as Mandy is the one person who sees the impact of my CFS on a daily basis. Her view, having seen me relapse multiple times now, is that the illness would be much more manageable if I just kept to that sustainable level of activity I have shown I can achieve relatively consistently. However, that level of activity won't enable me to regain employment, my independence, or any real life outside these four walls, and so she says she fully supports me if I need to keep trying to get more of my life back. It was just what I needed to hear.

Friday 18 July 2008
Martin Lee phoned me this week to say he and the CFS clinic is now operating from the Intermediate Care Centre of the local hospital. Their CFS care is still aimed primarily at newly-diagnosed cases, and giving those people the support and knowledge they need to recover from the illness, but it's good news overall. As yet it's unclear to what extent they will be able to assist long-term sufferers of CFS like me, but Martin

reiterated that he's still there if I need him. In fact I asked his advice on something right there and then, that I've been agonising over for a while.

My cousin Tracey is having a 40th birthday bash in Colchester in a few weeks' time, but as much as I would love to go - and really feel I should after she and Tim were so good to us last year - I just can't see how I can. Martin and I talked through the obstacles, such as my difficulties with crowds and noise, and how I was so ill after the last time I travelled there. It was useful to speak to someone who understands the predicament, and he came up with a couple of points for me to think over, but I'm still far from convinced.

Tuesday 29 July 2008
I'm pleased to say that Mandy and I made it to Tracey's 40th birthday bash at the weekend after all, and it was absolutely brilliant. It was a medieval-themed garden party, with everybody in period dress, and involving everything from jousting (on bicycles cunningly disguised as jousting horses) to the most amazing spit roast. Somehow I had managed to buy the exact same knight's outfit as my Uncle Eddie, but crucially I had by far the longer sword. It was a brilliant do.

We nearly didn't make it of course, because the nearer the event got, the bigger the CFS-related obstacles seemed to feel. But by analysing how things would work on the day, and including a couple of the ideas Martin Lee suggested, I convinced myself it could all work okay based on three key points:

- First and foremost, Tracey's event was being held outdoors in her sizeable garden and the farmer's field behind. As such, I could avoid any crowding, and whatever noise or music there was could be easily escaped.

- Secondly, my other cousin, Jill, had offered to drive us up and – crucially given the delayed fatigue of CFS tends to kick in 24-36 hours later – take us straight home again the following morning, before I started to feel too bad.

- I found, and booked, a Bed and Breakfast a few hundred yards up the road from Tracey and Tim's house, which I planned to escape to for regular rests when needed.

And, do you know, aside from turning up at the B&B to find the owners had split up and closed the establishment a few days before, things worked really well. Luckily there were enough tents and caravans present at Tracey and Tim's place for me to still escape for a rest when needed, and although personally I didn't sleep a wink, for us to have a bed for the night. Yes, I'm shattered and feeling really rough, but I did so well when I was there that I'm over the moon. I really do hope there isn't this glass ceiling preventing me from doing such things more frequently in future, as I'm not sure I could handle that. But for now, I'm just so happy to have been there, and that is thanks largely to my cousin Jill, and her husband Andy, as we wouldn't have made it without them.

Sunday 24 August 2008
It was Mum and Dad's 50th wedding anniversary this weekend so, with them not wanting too much fuss, we just organised a small meal at a local pub for friends and family yesterday. However, what Mum and Dad didn't realise until very recently, was that my cousin Mark and I had arranged for some surprise guests from Cape Town, namely Uncle Tom and his wife Ethel. Tom is my mum's elder brother who emigrated to South Africa in the 1950s, and aside from a short visit in the early 1980s, hadn't been "home" since. But thanks to Tom and Ethel's son Mark, who's presently working in Southampton, all three of the Cape Town branch of our family were present on Mum and Dad's special day.

It was lovely seeing the looks on everyone's faces as they met up after so many years, especially Mum and her brother Tom, who always seem to have had a special connection. Mum and Dad had been to visit Tom and Ethel in Cape Town, but with them all getting that much older, it had been some years since they had seen each other. And I think they all suspected this would be the last occasion they would do so, which only made the day even more special. Add into that mix some friends and family, who again due to advancing years Mum and Dad hadn't seen for a while, and it turned out to be a really great occasion.

As usual, Mandy and I were the first to leave, but this time for a very specific reason. I wanted to get home and rest so that I would feel well enough to have Tom, Ethel and Mark join us for one of Mandy's Sunday roasts today. And it worked. Mandy did us all proud with a meal that, not just Tom, Ethel and Mark seemed to enjoy immensely, but semi-regular Sunday roast attendees, Mum and Dad, too. Afterwards we all sat back contentedly with our full stomachs, and just enjoyed the company. Tom made Mandy's day by saying it was the best roast dinner he had ever had, which even allowing for it not perhaps being as regular a fixture on South African dinner tables, is quite a complement.

Alas, far too soon it was time for them to start making their way home, first to Mark's place in Southampton, and then in a few days' time, onto Cape Town. There were a few tears shed, especially by Mum, but it had been great to see them all. It had been a really special weekend and we were really sorry to see them go, even though the symptoms of my CFS were starting to kick in big time. Whilst I had been sensible enough to plan in some rests, which had no doubt helped, as they drove away my head in particular felt really bad. But, as I'm starting to realise, some things in life are worth doing no matter how difficult they may be. And believe me, two family meals in two days, and all the extra talking and concentration that involved, was really hard.

Wednesday 10 September 2008
I've been feeling rough the last few weeks, but the good news is I have avoided a full relapse. Whilst it was a busier summer than I've been used too, I decided after Tracey's party to just keep my activity level below this apparent glass ceiling for a while. And I felt better for it. So maybe it's best after all, to stay at the sustainable level of activity I know I can achieve, and just occasionally up my game for the day or so I need for special occasions. That's still hard to do but seems more achievable than trying to consistently be more active than my body is telling me it can be. Had I tried once again this year to consistently exceed my sustainable level, then I suspect a full relapse would have happened, and I may have missed out on some pretty important events.

Sometimes, when I'm feeling a little rough or sorry for myself, I get a sudden urge to "Google" all the latest CFS-related research and findings, even though the concentration that requires, ironically, can exacerbate my symptoms. I also know, from the numerous times I have done this previously, that I will find little if anything that I haven't already tried, as I already receive quarterly bulletins from the ME Association. In any case, medical studies and tests take so long to be approved, licensed or shown to be reliable, that it's many years before any doctor can justifiably recommend a new treatment. But at least by checking I feel like I am doing something towards getting better. And if there is indeed a glass ceiling preventing me from getting better, then new treatments may be my only hope.

Thursday 27 November 2008
Last month we went on a cruise on P&O's new ship, Ventura. For the first time, the cruise didn't go well. In fact, health-wise it did much more harm than good. If that cruise had been our first cruise, I'm not sure we would ever have cruised again. But for once my CFS wasn't the cause.

The problem was with our cabin and that, unbeknown to us, it was situated under a pantry. Consequently from about 4am to gone midnight we were regularly disturbed by the noise of things being banged around on noisy metallic surfaces. It was so loud that on one of the many occasions I phoned the Reception Desk to complain, the chap answering the phone immediately asked "what is that noise?" even before I could explain what I was phoning about. It meant that sleep was constantly interrupted, even when I popped back to the cabin during the day. It wasn't just me and my CFS-related noise sensitivity, poor Mandy was exhausted too.

Unfortunately the cruise was full. So although they sympathised, P&O were unable to offer us an alternative cabin until three days from the end. Although over the years we had had an occasional procedural issue with P&O Head Office, this was the first time we had experienced anything other than excellent service on board. They were useless, and the lack of sleep meant the CFS flared up so badly that I am still getting over it now. It's a shame: Ventura is a beautiful ship, and to a certain extent we were unlucky to be the ones in that cabin, but she's six months old now so she shouldn't still be having teething problems like that.

Monday 19 January 2009
I spoke to Martin Lee today and asked for his advice about my cousin Tracey's upcoming wedding. It's obviously a very important occasion and we really want to go, but there are some crucial differences this time compared to when we travelled to Colchester for Tracey's 40th.

Firstly, I'm still recovering from a rough end to last year as that Ventura cruise and the problems we encountered on it really hit me. Secondly, the number of people who will be there is a concern, as unlike her 40th, Tracey's wedding will be mostly indoors, with everyone in the same room or area. That will make it feel busier, and I don't think it would be as easy to discretely escape when things get too much for me. But as much as those issues are causing me concern and anxiety, I would still give it a go if it wasn't for the getting there and back.

You see, for many months my uncle, Eddie, had said he would happily take Mandy and I up to Colchester with him and his wife Margaret, and, as proved so crucial before, bring us back the very next day. That would mean that no matter how ill I feel, I would be back home before the worst of the delayed fatigue of the CFS hits me. The spanner in the works is that Eddie and Margaret have now decided they want to stay in Colchester for a few days after the wedding. So with no other locally-based members of the family going to the wedding, we're stuck. Mandy drives, but isn't a confident driver by any means, and would need a cognitively dysfunctional me to navigate. It's left us in a real pickle.

Martin advises caution. He would be happier if I was a) feeling stronger, b) had a firm idea on where and when I will rest during the day, and c) have direct, stress-free, travel arrangements in place. What concerns him is that currently, not only do I fail on all three counts, but even when I was able to tick all those boxes last time I went there, I was still ill afterwards. In short, it's my body and I know it best, but based on how I am doing at the moment, Martin feels it could result in a real set back.

Sunday 1 February 2009
Mandy spoke to Tracey today to explain that we are really sorry, but we won't be able to make her wedding. I initially tried to put everything in a letter to her as I felt so bad. I then decided to phone Tracey instead. Only, due to stressing over the situation for days I wasn't exactly at my best. Mandy therefore offered to phone Tracey for me, saying she could read from my letter to get across how gutted I am. And that's what she did. And Tracey, of course, said she understood. So why do I feel so crap for letting her down?

I also feel angry. Angry at my CFS, angry that I'm still not better, and angry that I can't just go to a wedding for a couple of hours, even if it is the other side of the country. I also feel angry with Eddie. I keep reminding myself that I am the problem here - it's me and the CFS that's the issue. I shouldn't be too hard on Eddie, it was good of him to offer in the first place. It's just so bloody frustrating. I'm not at my best health-wise at the moment, but I wanted to go despite how ill I may feel afterwards. I really hate this illness.

Tuesday 21 April 2009
As gutted as we were to miss Tracey's wedding in Colchester, we were over the moon to be able go to another important one in Devon last

weekend, on account of us getting some much-needed help. Skelts got married to the lovely Tabitha, or "Tabs", and this time it came together brilliantly. Well brilliantly for Tim and Tabs, me and Mand, and also Kenty and his wife Claire. But a small hiccup for Mac and Michaela, which was a bugger because everything had worked out so well otherwise.

You see Skelts had booked Mand and me the best, most handily-located room in the country hotel where they were getting married. This, bless his little cotton socks, was so that I had a nice quiet room to go and regularly rest in throughout the day. That fact, together with Mac and Michaela kindly driving Mandy and I the (one hour and thirty minute) journey there and back, meant I was feeling extremely grateful. Mand and I quickly checked-in on arrival and were directed to a nice plush, newly renovated room. Unbeknown to us, Mac and Michaela were then shown to a (yet to be renovated) room which the receptionist rather alarmingly described as "not our best room". In short, it was smelly, dirty and still giving off the ambiance of the wolf pack that appears to have been its previous occupants. Armed with a refund and a recommendation from the guilty-looking receptionist, they were soon on their way to a farm a few miles away that offers bed and breakfast. As grateful as I was to Skelts for organising our room, we now felt awful that the Mac's, without whom we wouldn't have been there, had been forced elsewhere.

Anyhow, the day was a good one (I always enjoy your weddings Skelts!), the happy couple looked, well, happy, and their three kids from their respective first marriages were so excited they looked like they might burst. It was the perfect setting too, with a beautiful garden for the photos and, not being family, the very un-photogenic me was pleased that we weren't asked to be in many. Which is probably just as well as a combination of the bright sun and the glare from my new shoes could have made things tricky. My shoes weren't quite patent leather, but once in direct sunlight they were so bright it was if some ancient religious cult was channelling the power of the midday sun through them. Suffice to say, for the rest of the day I was ribbed constantly over the shininess of my shoes to the point where, come the evening reception, even the DJ asked me to stand a bit further away, as I was apparently detracting from his pyrotechnics.

By then I was already well on my way to acquiring the (hopefully temporary) nickname of "Three Sleeps", on account of my regular trips back to my room for a rest. It worked well though, and even when I returned from the middle one of those rests to find the DJ was doing his utmost to make the music louder than my shoes, our small party had settled in a great little spot right outside the main hall. This quieter location was clearly secured with me in mind, and without any prompting at all, bless them, on mine or Mandy's part. I was so touched I nearly bought a round. It was a brilliant location there and worked so well all night that, for a change, I wasn't the first to leave. In fact, although it's a bit hazy, and I definitely had that third sleep at some point, I'm sure I was up long enough to guiltily wave off Mac and Michaela's taxi as they shot off to their farm house at the end.

Next morning I was pretty foggy and my head had started really banging halfway through the night, but I was okay. I also think I strung enough coherent words together, when running into Skelts and his family at breakfast, to make them think the same. Just as I was starting to really struggle, Mac and Michaela turned up with tales of how they were awoken to the sound of their breakfast being freshly slaughtered, but by all accounts it tasted great. I couldn't even face talking about breakfast, let alone eating any, and so I was glad that we were soon on our way. My plan on the way home, as it had been on the drive down, was to save energy and not to talk much. But being so pleased with how the previous day had gone, I'm pretty sure I was on turbo-annoy much of the way home. Little of it made any sense of course, and my inappropriate filter had long since given up the ghost but, hey, I don't get out much.

Saturday 9 May 2009
We took Mandy's mum out for lunch at our local Italian today, as it is her birthday. I'm still resting after Skelts' wedding, but having that Italian restaurant just a short walk up the road meant it wasn't too taxing, especially at lunchtime when it's quiet. Mand's mum loved it (especially her Lasagne), and the owners of the restaurant, Sue and Lino, made a real fuss of her. We've got to know them, and their two lovely boys, quite well and they are nice people who really value their regulars. In fact, their boys Oliver and Luca are quite the characters who do as much, if not more, to charm the customers as their parents do. We're so lucky to have them located so close to us, it's almost like having a social life again – albeit a quiet, lunchtime-based one.

Still, it's back to recovery mode tomorrow. I'm nearly there I think, but am still feeling a bit woolly and have a tough week coming up – you remember that new kitchen I said we needed a couple of years ago? Well, it's being fitted next week. We've planned it so that it should all be over in five days, and hopefully won't be too noisy, so fingers crossed it will all go okay.

Monday 18 May 2009
It seems I spoke too soon about the fitting of the new kitchen going okay. Taking the old one out went well, but the small amount of the new one they were able to fit today looked kind of pink! The look on Mandy's face when she came home from work confirmed my worst fears – it was the kitchen we had ordered, but the colouring of the wood was vastly different to that we had viewed in store. A quick trip to the showroom to compare one of the off-cuts with the version on display, and we were proved right. To her credit, the sales lady we spoke to immediately agreed that the difference in colour was huge, and beyond the variation it's reasonable to expect even with a natural wood kitchen. The bad news is, a new replacement kitchen will take six weeks, and they've already put our old one in a skip.

Thursday 28 May 2009
Well, after a pretty stressful ten days trying to get our kitchen situation rectified, the fitters finally returned to fit our kitchen today. Not the original kitchen style we had chosen, as that would still take another four weeks to arrive, and also no guarantees were forthcoming that a direct replacement wouldn't also be pink. So the kitchen that's being fitted from today is a different, more expensive one. But although the cheeky buggers first made me pay the difference in cost, this one was immediately available, albeit on a drip-feed basis over the next two weeks. My instinct was to demand they pay the difference given their misrepresentation of the original kitchen, but I thought let's just get a (non-pink) kitchen fitted, get our house back, and argue the toss when I'm feeling stronger.

It just goes to show that no matter how carefully you plan something like this, and go to great lengths to get assurances from people over how long it will take, it only takes one cock-up and you're screwed. Due to my CFS, we had avoided replacing the kitchen for some years, but having planned things so meticulously and turned down firms that couldn't assure us of a one-week fitting, we finally went ahead. As it is, ten days into this, we have no kitchen, I'm exhausted, and Mandy is itching to test the "soft closing" mechanism of our new cupboards on someone's head.

Wednesday 10 June 2009
I finally signed off the kitchen as completed today. The last part is actually being fitted in a couple of days' time, but whilst the fitters have left small scratches all over the work top (it isn't suitable for storing their collection of power tools on, who knew?!?), I just want to draw a line under the whole sorry experience. I'll never have any more dealings with that company, and it's my sincere hope that they never have the need to darken (or pinken) our doorstep either. The whole experience was exhausting.

We did at least get some recompense from them, courtesy of our journalist friend Brian scaring them witless. It doesn't come anywhere near compensating us for the stress and impact on my health, but even me trying to keep Brian updated proved incredibly hard work once the CFS kicked in, so I'm just glad it's all over. We basically got the more expensive kitchen for the price of the cheaper one we originally ordered – or at least that's the way I'm trying to look at it. Yes it took a month to fit, yes it's scratched, and yes I feel like I've gone ten rounds with Mike Tyson. But it's useable, looks okay and isn't pink, so we'll settle for that. And if Mandy mentions anything about doing the bathroom next, I'm afraid I cannot be held accountable for my actions.

Sunday 19 July 2009
We went over to see our friends Charley and Andrew today, and although a brief visit, we had a great time. I was still feeling that whole kitchen palaver, but we wanted to pop along for a bit as Charley and Andrew were holding their annual air show barbeque. The air show in question is at the local American Air Force base which, quite handily, Charley and Andrew's house is in close proximity too. It's in a beautiful setting out on the Wiltshire and Gloucestershire border, surrounded on all sides by open fields. We love it.

Charley and Andrew always lay on a truly lovely afternoon of amazing food and just all-round excellent hospitality. In fact, I was sleeping off that excellent hospitality for much of today. They invite a small number of other friends and family too, so it's a pleasant mix of nice people that are good fun without being overwhelming. It's such a great location out there too. Every time we visit them, we drive away even more determined to bring our own plans for rural living to fruition. Much as we love our house, I just wish we could pick it up and plop it in the middle of a field somewhere, well away from the noise and activity that I find so exhausting now.

Friday 21 August 2009
We are off on a cruise next month and I'm halfway through the four weeks of extra rest I have found I need to prepare for a two-week cruise. It's basically a longer version of the extra rest I find I need to have both before and after a one-off event like Skelts' wedding, and it seems to work for me. In actual fact, I am still wondering if I could actually attend more of the events that really matter if I stop trying to push myself. When I am not trying to go beyond this glass ceiling I do feel better day-to-day, and have more energy for the times when I need it most. Maybe I should just accept that this is as far as I am going to progress.

However, that would feel like giving up, or resigning myself to my current predicament of being too ill to work again. It would feel defeatist. I know my employer and their doctors effectively reached this conclusion when they retired me, but I'm not there yet. I'm not sure I ever will be. I mean, if I give up, what do I focus on or work towards? All of my life I have been encouraged to strive to succeed, and taught that anything is possible if you work long enough at it. To stop trying therefore feels wrong, even if it is the easier and possibly more sensible option.

Chapter 10 - The Menace in Venice

Sunday 13 September 2009
Today we are on P&O's Oriana for a 17-night cruise to the Adriatic and back, with an itinerary which includes two of our favourite ports, Venice and Dubrovnik, but also takes us to some promising new places like Split and Lisbon. Indeed, my excitement at going on this cruise is surpassed only by Mandy's, who has been counting down the days since she kicked the last kitchen fitter out of the front door in June. Relaxation, sea and sun, not to mention some extra on-board credit (i.e. handbag spend) due to the noise problems we had on Ventura last year. It should be a good one.

Unusually for me, I've done a little research thanks to an online cruise forum I found on the P&O website. It provides loads of interesting information and tips from other cruisers, and having registered with a hastily thought up user name (Dennis The Menace), I'm finding it quite handy. The forum is also quite funny at times. Being on the internet, it attracts a few fruit-cakes, but the majority of users are normal friendly types, who just share a love of cruising. It's a real find, but I'm not so sure Richard and Joyce (who have joined us again this cruise) will agree after 17 solid days of me repeatedly saying "Do you know, on the forum it said......"

Anyway, after my normal post-embarkation rest, we explored Oriana to try and find out for ourselves just why everyone seems to love her so much. I think for some it's that she's one of an ever-decreasing number of ships these days that are both smaller in size and traditional in style. Other passengers use phrases like "warm atmosphere" and "friendly ship", but surely those are things created, at least in part, by a crew not a ship. And most of this crew have also been on other ships to which such compliments are much less frequently bestowed. Whatever it is, we have 17 glorious days to find out.

Monday 14 September 2009
We started with an early night last night after first joining Richard and Joyce for dinner at a nicely-positioned table for four in the Peninsular Restaurant, followed by a swift, post-dinner drink. It's funny, we don't see Richard and Joyce very often between cruises, because of the distance between where we live, but as soon as we join up on a cruise ship together we all seem to carry on where we left off. They know my

limitations well by now, and when my brain goes blank and my eyes glaze over, they realise it's nothing personal, just the CFS. Although Mand and I still tend to do our own thing during the day, and ensure I get lots of rest for example, we spend most evenings with Richard and Joyce, and they are really good company without being too taxing energy-wise. They've become good friends and our cruises are better for them being there.

That early night must have done me some good, as I won this morning's Wii Tennis competition in the Lord's Tavern Pub. I have to confess, having done embarrassingly badly at both Wii Tennis and Wii Bowling when trying them for the first time on the last cruise, I ensured I got a little bit of pre-cruise practice in this time. I'm glad I did as I now know, contrary to the Wii adverts on the television suggesting you need to leap around like Mick Jagger after a curry, a flick of the wrist is really all that is needed. I did still lean on my (newly acquired) foldable walking stick for balance with my left hand, but even if I do say so myself, I pretty much kicked arse. To be fair, I was probably the most competitive there, and definitely the only one adding their own Maria Sharapova-like squeal to every single shot, but a win is a win. And my winner's faux leather toiletry bag, with a P&O insignia no less, will now remind me of that fact whenever and wherever I unpack my travel-sized toothbrush.

Returning to the cabin with my "trophy" under my arm, I came across a couple having a right old barney in one of the lifts. I initially thought they were a married couple going at it tooth and nail, so I just assumed they were having a domestic and that they should be left to it. However, as I drew level with them I could see that a middle-aged lady was struggling to reverse a more elderly man's wheelchair out of the lift. As a result, the elderly man was giving her all sorts of grief. It was causing quite the spectacle, and a number of passengers had stopped to see what the commotion was, which must have just made it even worse for the lady on the receiving end.

Seeing that the wheelchair's problem was the very slight "lip" between the level of the lift floor and the carpeted floor of the deck she was trying to access, I offered to help. She gratefully accepted and so, with a slight lift on the wheelchair's handles I reversed the clearly frail, but still cursing, gentleman out of the lift. The lady was grateful, but clearly at the end of her tether, so I offered to wheel the gentleman the remaining distance to their cabin. Whilst we walked the lady dropped her voice slightly so only I could hear, and explained that her father wasn't normally so rude, that he was just tired and grumpy after a long couple of days. Bloody hell I thought, this is me and Mandy in 30 years' time! But she looked relieved to have got her dad back to their cabin, and he seemed much happier, so hopefully their day got better from then on.

Tuesday 15 September 2009
After a cloudy but enjoyable first sea day yesterday, we decided to indulge ourselves last night. Yes, as if we didn't feel spoilt enough already spending the next two and a bit weeks on Oriana, it was the second night in and we were already dining at Oriana Rhodes in celebration of Joyce's birthday. Once again it was a fantastic experience. If anything, I think I might even prefer it to the Gary Rhodes venue on Arcadia, due to its location in the beautifully light and airy Curzon Room, and it being right next to our favourite bar, Tiffany's, at the top of the Atrium.

The food is certainly on a par with its sister restaurant on Arcadia, with our starters of Crispy Lemon and Parsley Chicken and Butter Poached Prawns kicking things off nicely. It was followed by a Steamed Lobster and Sole Papiette that saw me withdraw from the conversation completely for a long spell, as I gave it the undivided attention it deserved. Dinner in the Peninsular Restaurant on our first night was good, but this was fantastic, and a great way to celebrate Joyce's birthday. I wonder if we can celebrate it again tomorrow night.

Oh, and I saw that elderly chap in the wheelchair and his daughter sat on the Prom Deck earlier. He was fast asleep but his daughter gave me a smile and indicated I should take a seat next to her. Speaking quietly, so as not to wake him, she couldn't apologise enough for her father's behaviour yesterday. Obviously I said it wasn't a problem, and if I could help again, just to let me know. She then went on to say her name was Maureen and that her father was terminally ill, which is why he gets so tired and grouchy, especially with her. She wasn't at all sure about coming on this cruise in the first place, she said, but it seemed the best option as her dad desperately wants to visit the grave of his best friend, about 60 miles outside of Venice. I was interested to know more, but Maureen's dad started to stir and complain of being cold, so after first checking they didn't need any help moving inside, I bid them farewell and went to find Mandy.

Wednesday 16 September 2009

Today we were in Malaga and, given I had always pictured it as simply a place full of nice beaches, and seafront bars full of us Brits, we were pleasantly surprised to find it is much more than that. I should have realised really, as due to the little bits of information I gathered from my new cruise forum, the place clearly has a long history and is even the birthplace of Pablo Picasso. What that means is that there are plenty of museums and galleries, if that's your bag, but we prefer the outdoors where there was still plenty to see. After first getting our bearings by having a 30-minute ride on a horse-drawn carriage pulled by the most glorious looking mare, we had a leisurely walk around the Old Town.

Straight away we started coming across beautiful old buildings decorated by large displays of flowers and hanging baskets. In particular, we had a good look around the beautiful old cathedral known locally as La Manquita (or Lady with One Arm) on account of one of the intended towers having never been built due to funding issues. In fact funding was such a problem, and the still incomplete cathedral was built over such a long period, that it incorporates at least three different types of architecture, but they all look pretty stunning. The old town in general was very pleasant actually, so we decided to stay for lunch at one of the many little cafés, and had a local speciality called "Coquinas" – basically clams in lemon, garlic and olive oil – which tasted amazing.

After that, and with conserving energy for the four best ports in mind (three of which are grouped together in the middle of the cruise), it was back to the ship for some rest and relaxation.

Thursday 17 September 2009

This morning I ran into Maureen coming out of her cabin and she was looking pretty worried. Her dad had had a bad night and she said they might have to fly home. Her dad is still adamant he wants to stay on board, at least until Venice, in order that he can visit his friend's grave near Treviso, but she's not sure he's strong enough to do that. She's talked to the ship's medical team and they have suggested she gives it 24 hours before making any decision, which she will do. Such a shame, it's clearly a journey that means a lot to her dad, but it's proving really hard for both of them. I checked that they had had some breakfast delivered, but I'm not sure what else I can do. I really hope her dad has a better day today and that they get to complete their trip. The medical team are keeping close tabs on them, so that's the main thing.

Anyhow, back to yesterday and once back on the ship the afternoon temperatures were hitting a nice 23 degrees, which meant that, together with that cooling breeze, we had a relaxing few hours in the semi-shade of the Prom Deck. Then just as I was wondering if those Coquinas were going to be enough to see me through to dinner, a couple of restaurant waiters literally brought afternoon tea to us. Well, a smaller version of an afternoon tea anyway, as thanks to the little wooden tea trolley they were pushing, they had freshly-made sandwiches, cakes and pots of both tea and coffee. It was great. It was, as I say, a much smaller version of afternoon tea, but they set themselves up halfway along the deck, and passengers just popped over to them in twos or threes, were served a drink and a snack, and took them back to their sun chairs. Very civilised. I had not seen it happen before but it looks like it's a regular thing on Oriana, I suspect due to its extra-wide Prom Deck.

Later on, having enjoyed another fine dinner in the Peninsular Restaurant with Richard and Joyce, we went along to one of the Abba-themed shows (performed by the on-board production company, Headliners) which always seem to go down well with passengers. And this one was no exception, it was excellent. Then it was off to Tiffany's for a nightcap where, due to the same three or four waitresses seemingly there every night, they take very good care of us and share in a few laughs. One of them doubles up as the sommelier in the Gary Rhodes restaurant next door, and looks just like Lucy Liu off of Hollywood.

Friday 18 September 2009
It was a nice lazy sea day yesterday, enjoying temperatures of 26 degrees or so if you could stay out of the slightly chilly wind. That's something we managed quite successfully on the decks at the aft end, and the mixture of the moderate temperature and cooling breeze meant that I stayed there, on a lounger next to Mandy, for much longer than I normally do. Boredom, overheating, or the need to stretch my aching bones usually sees me depart long before Mandy's digging me in the ribs asking if I'm hungry. And of course what she really means is that she's hungry and it's time to seek nourishment.

After lunch I managed to win my second faux leather toiletry bag, with P&O insignia no less, when I won the Wii Bowling. No walking stick needed this time, just the patience of a saint, which I have to say, Tori from the Entertainment Team showed she had in spades. You see, a number of elderly passengers decided to have a go, and not only was it the first time any of them had used a Wii, but quite possibly an electrical item of any description. It took ages. One lady in particular took ten minutes to bowl two balls. Poor old Tori must have shown her a dozen times how it worked, but the Wii version of the lady shown on the TV screen just kept throwing the balls over her head and behind her. It was purgatory at times. But I stuck with it, if only to ensure Tori didn't throw herself overboard, and I came away victorious. Get in there, my son.

Saturday 19 September 2009
A quick update on Maureen and her dad – he's feeling better but they intend to leave the ship tomorrow, once we get to Venice. They initially have a car booked first thing tomorrow morning, to drive them to the military cemetery near Treviso, and then to take them onto the airport where they have a flight home booked. When I enquired about the military connection, Maureen explained that her dad's best friend was actually killed when they were fighting in Italy together during the latter stages of the war, and her father desperately wants to go back and visit his grave whilst he still can. I must confess, whilst I know about Monte Cassino, I didn't know there was any allied fighting anywhere near as far north, and feel pretty embarrassed that I haven't put it all together sooner. Belatedly, it's now crystal clear to me why this trip means so much to Maureen and her dad. Maureen assured me that the crew are helping them disembark in the morning, so we said our goodbyes and I asked that she give her father my best. I think I might get up early tomorrow though to make sure they get off okay.

Anyhow, enough of me being as thick as two short planks, we are in Dubrovnik today and Mandy is convinced that she will see the little ginger kitten we found, and took to the vets, the last time we were here. I did try pointing out that, as that was 2006, he would no longer be a kitten. Also that the vet had assured us she was taking him to a good home, so he's unlikely to be back in an old town full of just shops and restaurants. But she seems sure she'll see him (and presumably recognise him) and if it means she spends less time looking in shop windows, then I shouldn't knock it.

Sunday 20 September 2009
Well, it's 9.15am and I have just seen Maureen and her dad off the ship. In fact I'm pleased to say that a whole group of us gave them a really good send-off. You see, when I turned up at their cabin I found an officer and a number of the crew doing a fine job of reversing Maureen's dad

out of the cabin door. For the first time Maureen looked relaxed and stress-free, and her dad looked like a different man - happy and healthy, with a real glint in his eye, and proudly wearing his regimental blazer and beret. Clearly this was the day he had been waiting for.

Not wanting to get in the way, I joined the end of their little convoy, as did the half a dozen other passengers who had also turned up to see them off. Surreally, we all then separated briefly, as we each made our own way down to the bottom of the Atrium where a small party of officers in full dress uniform had gathered. One of them came over and invited us passengers to say our goodbyes – at which point I gave Maureen a peck on the cheek and shook her dad by the hand – and the officer then suggested we all wave them off from the Prom Deck. When we got there, Maureen was already stood on the dockside next to all of the officers we had just seen downstairs, only now they were all stood in a line, to attention, and saluting Maureen's dad as he was wheeled along the walkway and past them towards the waiting car. I don't mind admitting I found the whole thing quite moving. Even more so when I realised a number of other officers, dotted at various points along the Prom Deck, had also interrupted their day to salute an old soldier. And with that, Maureen and her dad were helped into the car and went on their way. God bless the pair of them.

Anyway, back to Dubrovnik, and yesterday's stroll around the old town felt completely different than the last time we did it. In 2006 it was raining and so the marble-like paving of the old town made it quite dicey under foot. This time it was 27 degrees by 10am and the sun really brought out the colour of the buildings, and their terracotta-coloured roofs reminded me a lot of Florence. We didn't see any kittens this time however, even though Mandy insisted we stop for a coffee in the old harbour where we found little Luka.

But where last time our exploring inside the city walls felt a little rushed, perhaps due to a mixture of dodging showers and rescuing sick kittens, yesterday was much more leisurely. This time we discovered a number of smaller streets where the properties took on a more inhabited look, although I suspect even these are holiday lets rather than permanent residences. Mandy was also able to scratch her retail itch, via some of the shops, and we managed to find the other city gate, the Ploce Gate. Although not as pretty or central (and therefore not as busy) as the main Pile Gate, the fort and old stone bridges there made me come over all medieval. Alas, I resisted the urge to slap my wench heartily across her rear and demand she serve me some mead, opting instead for the frankly less life-endangering enquiry "ready for some lunch and a glass of Chardonnay, my sweet?"

Back on the ship, and having fought the fight of a hundred shuttle buses (a fair few ships in port today), Mandy did indeed drink a large Chardonnay with her lunch, before I parked her on a sun-lounger out on the aft decks. And it was there that we laid for much of the afternoon, occasionally snoozing, and me wondering how Maureen and her dad were getting on. Fingers crossed everything went okay for them, and that their trip back home is a smooth one.

Monday 21 September 2009
So yesterday was the first of two full days in Venice, and having covered some of the main sights the last time we were here, the plan was to have no plan. We almost tried to do too much last time, so yes, hordes of tourists permitting, a relaxed meander was the only point on the agenda. And as if by magic, this time P&O had arranged the option of the unlimited use of a cruise launch (i.e. a large water taxi) direct from the ship to a drop-off point at St Mark's Square, which would very much facilitate our relaxed approach to this visit. It meant that we could go to and from the ship for a rest a) easily, and b) as often as we wanted over the next two days.

First off, we wandered into St Mark's Square, and were just passing the Basilica when we realised there was a Sunday morning mass about to start. We nipped in and found that the Basilica's inside is as amazing as its exterior, all lit up and full of mosaics and precious artefacts. Of course the mass that followed was mostly in Italian and Latin, but it was just about possible to follow, and it is something I would recommend to anyone irrespective of whether they are religious or not. I'm glad we went in.

The other advantage of Sunday morning was that Venice was pretty quiet and really peaceful to wander around. Or it was until one of the smaller canals we decided to walk along had a water ambulance shoot along it so fast, and so suddenly, that Mandy nearly had to call an "ambulanza" for me too. Having narrowly avoided giving me a heart attack with that siren of theirs, they pretty much drowned me as well with the amount of water they threw up as they went by. Although if the truth be known, it was quite invigorating, and combined with me thinking I recognised the paramedic from the Venice documentary we've been watching on the telly at home, I was shrieking like an over-excited schoolgirl. Mandy, on the other hand, found my reaction quite pathetic, and didn't even stop to thank me for (unintentionally) shielding her from that spray of water, before she hurried off down the canal.

The reason Mandy was hurrying off into the distance was, it turns out, because she had spotted a shopping opportunity up ahead. I forget which shop exactly, but it was certainly one of the high-end fashion brands with high prices to match, that pop up all over Venice, and other than a wide range of souvenir shops, seem the only type of shopping available here. Sadly for Mandy, it was still Sunday, and so with many of the shops closed, she had to be happy with a third type of shopping – window shopping, surely the kind favoured by men everywhere. Anyway, after all that wandering we decided to pop back to the ship for some lunch, and a much-needed rest, with a view to going back ashore in the afternoon or the evening. In the event, I felt so shattered we made neither, which whilst disappointing, was okay as we had another whole day in Venice to follow.

Tuesday 22 September 2009
We were up and about early for day two of our stop-off in Venice, and keen to make up for only making it ashore the once on Sunday. Having been so excited about seeing Venice again, and having had such a gentle wander around on Sunday morning, it was galling that I should suddenly feel so fatigued come the afternoon. What we did do yesterday however, just in case the same thing happened again, was to decide on the one thing we wanted to do most. Amazingly, given the shops would be open, Mandy said exactly what I was thinking – The Doge's Palace. We had admired it a few times from the outside but the queues to go inside had always proved too long. If we got there early however, we were told queues aren't an issue and that, for someone whose original plan was to have no plan, sounded like a plan.

So after taking the cruise launch into St Mark's again, we marched straight off to sort our admission to the Doge's Palace. Despite it being quite early it was already busy, and my heart sank in anticipation of a long queue. Luckily, we got talking to one of the guides and he said we should opt for the "Secret Itineraries" tour, which would permit us to come back at a designated time and avoid any queuing. It also meant a guided tour with greater access than the normal admission permitted. I couldn't say "grazie mille" quickly enough, I can tell you. And when our new friend, Luigi, returned with our tickets, they were for a tour just 30 minutes later, enabling us to sit in a quiet corner and have a rest first.

The tour of the Doge's Palace was terrific. As nice as the outside looks, the inside is even more beautiful and the sheer size of the ballroom in particular comes as a real surprise; it's like walking into a very opulent Tardis. There's so much to see too, everything from ancient catacombs to grand marble staircases. The highlight for me was crossing the Bridge of Sighs to and from the prison cells. It was here where they tried to show Casanova the error of his ways. Although I must admit, when the guide used that phrase all I could think of was that famous George Best story about Matt Busby walking into George's penthouse suite, seeing him laid on a bed strewn in casino winnings, and containing Miss World, and saying "Oh George, where did it all go wrong!" But as much as Casanova and I have got in common (I wish!), the only sighs I made as we crossed that bridge the second time was because I was feeling increasingly in need of a rest and some fresh air. We therefore cut our tour a little short and headed for the exit.

Once outside the palace, we skirted the edge of the piazza and headed for the Grand Canal where we grabbed a coffee and watched the Venetian world go by for a bit. As luck would have it, we were sat overlooking one of the Gondolas that are used, mostly by locals for one Euro a time, to ferry people across the Grand Canal. I think they are called Traghettos, and basically cross the canal every five minutes or so, only this one came complete with its own little Dachshund who, every crossing, would stand right at the bow and bark at any other shipping that came near. It was really cute. After a long rest I was still pooped and so, reluctantly, we headed back to the ship for a lazy afternoon. However, all visits to Venice end on a high note, courtesy of the best sailaway going, and yesterday's early-evening version was no exception. What a fantastic place, a real favourite.

Wednesday 23 September 2009
Yesterday we were in Split, which despite being Croatia's second biggest city, I have only even heard of because of its once-brilliant football team, Hadjuk Split. And, surprisingly, that very connection was to make yesterday a day I won't forget in a hurry.

You see, as we tendered in from the ship, I could see this huge red lorry on the esplanade, looking very out of place in front of the Roman buildings behind. As we got closer, I could see that this out of place red lorry seemed to have the insignia of the Champions League emblazoned across it, which was confusing as, for some years Hadjuk Split had had only minimal involvement with Europe's richest football competition. Then as we hit land (and I think the pilot of the tender must also have been a football nut as we did, literally, hit land) I spotted the Champions League Trophy that my team, Liverpool, had won just a few years ago. The trophy must be on some kind of tour to the footballing cities of Europe and I couldn't believe my luck. I couldn't have planned it better if I had tried.

Anyway, ignoring Mandy's suspicious looks, which seemed to suggest I had known about it all along, I approached the lorry to see what the "scoot" was. In short, the red lorry was the equivalent of an armoured truck from which a large, mainly glass, display case had been unloaded, and which contained the trophy on a pedestal. But this display case was so big (about the size of our cabin) it enabled people to enter, one at a time, and watched by four strapping security guards to ensure no-one touched it, have their photo taken standing next to it.

Of course, when it came to my turn, me being me, and with Mandy poised ready with camera in hand the other side of the glass, I leant towards the trophy and pretended to kiss it, albeit still a good few inches away. Well, two things happened at this point. Firstly, I got an almighty cheer from the small crowd outside followed, a millisecond later, by four massive security guards rushing at me like I was about to stick the trophy under my arm and leg it. Ignoring the fact that, due to my post-Venice fatigue I was hobbling around on my foldable walking stick, and that I had not actually made any contact with said trophy, they whisked me out of there so quickly my feet hardly touched the ground. But it was worth it, as Mandy took the photo of every football fan's dreams - and which will soon have pride of place in whichever of the deepest, darkest corners of our house she reluctantly permits me to display it in. If I can find a way of airbrushing out the walking stick then even better.

Split itself was pretty surprising too. The esplanade, or "Riva" as it's known, runs the length of a gorgeous harbour bursting with so many yachts it feels more like the Cote D'Azur than the relatively recently war-torn former Yugoslavia. The central tree-lined walkway for instance looks more Cannes than Croatia. And it comes complete with large outdoor armchairs carved out of sizeable chunks of marble, and matching mallets with which to crack the huge communal supply of almonds on offer. With or without a dirty great Champions League juggernaut (and its four marginally smaller security guards), the Riva looks lovely, and I can see why it provides the main meeting point for the locals.

But the best bit of the Riva, by some distance, is its backdrop of your common-or-garden Roman palace that, despite it surely approaching its 2000th birthday, is aging even better than Cliff Richard – which is amazing when you consider the palace, its walls, even its original stairways and corridors, form the main infrastructure of a fully working, living town to this day. Cafés, bars, shops, even residential apartments, have sprouted from just about every Roman nook and cranny, to the point where the Palace's large central courtyard has become a café's multi-tabled terrace with perfectly intact Roman columns and arches on all four sides. Surely the most resplendent, alfresco beverage we will ever have.

So yes, whether it's not kissing the Champions League Trophy, my subsequent aerodynamic eviction from the "trophy room" or just the beautiful living museum that is Split, it was a memorable day. God, I need a rest though, that's Dubrovnik, Venice and Split on the trot now, and I'm shattered.

Thursday 24 September 2009
Why is it that gay fellas always absolutely love Mandy, but think I'm some oik who sounds like a farmer and has the dress sense to match? Case in point: during my pre-dinner saunas this cruise, I've been chatting with a gay couple called John and Ed (or as John puts it "I'm not gay, but my boyfriend is"), having a few laughs, and getting on really well. Then this afternoon, Mandy and I ran into them on the Prom Deck, and I might as well have not been there.

"Oh, you must be Mandy" said Ed. "Oh, you are absolutely fabulous aren't you".

Not to be outdone, John then chipped in with "I love what you're wearing Mandy, is that Christian Dior?" and "Wow, your hair is simply gorgeous".

I know she's my missus, but it was nauseating. They must have fawned over her for a good few minutes before I was able to interject with a lame, but understandable: "Oi, and what the bloody hell am I then, chopped liver?"

They still barely acknowledged me, so I sarcastically continued the conversation by myself, making up their replies and mimicking the slightly camp tone to Ed's voice - "Nice to see you too Den", "Ooh, your arse looks great in those shorts" and "That Mandy is a lucky girl."

The cheeky devils still barely batted an eyelid, but eventually they took the hint and cleared off. Bleeding charming that is, I'm the one who's been chatting to them all cruise, but one sight of my, admittedly gorgeous, missus and I'm yesterday's news. I tell you, if they are in the sauna later, I'm just going to sulk in the corner.

Anyhow, we were in Corfu yesterday but I didn't make it ashore. I'm hurting in places I didn't know could even hurt, and these last few days I've taken so much paracetamol it's getting silly. That's okay, we've now got some more sea days to recuperate, and I've gone ashore in three of the "big four" ports so far. We don't hit the fourth, Lisbon, until Sunday, so fingers crossed.

Saturday 26 September 2009
Right then, we've now been aboard her for two weeks so I've been thinking about what it can be that makes Oriana such a popular ship. I think for me, it's a mixture of her size and layout that makes her different. Indoors, Oriana isn't tiny but she's small enough to have a number of quiet little areas to sit and relax, and bars and lounges to socialise in, that are not part of the main thoroughfare as on many other ships. Outdoors, she has that extra-wide Promenade Deck, which has plenty of room for both those who like to sit and mellow, and those who like to walk a few circuits. But the best bit of Oriana, I think, is her tiered aft end which looks-wise gives her a real elegance, and more practically speaking, provides the outdoor relaxation most enjoy but with the added benefit of a spectacular view over her wake.

She also has good facilities for a smaller ship, such as the purpose-built Chaplin's Cinema, a good theatre, and best of all, a Gary Rhodes dining venue. Actually, speaking of the Oriana Rhodes restaurant, we made our second visit of the cruise there last night in all our formal night glory. I know I'm starting to gush about Gary Rhodes now, so suffice to say it was just as good as the other night. Well actually I must mention one dish, the Roast Chicken and Stuffing Ravioli (with chestnut cabbage and crispy bacon) which was sooooo good. And oh yeah, the Rhubarb and Custard Cheesecake was awesome, not to mention Mandy's favourite, Red Snapper. But that's it, I won't mention the Rhodes restaurant again. Honest. Although I swear the nice sommelier lady looks more like Lucy Liu than Lucy Liu does.

After dinner we went to the Headliners show called At The Hop, which promised to be a "whirlwind journey back to the time when Rock n' Roll was born" and "an explosive, colourful, jumping and jiving trip down memory lane". And I have to say that, aside from the "trip down memory lane" bit (and to be fair, in our case, that would have required hypnosis and past life regression), it delivered on every point. It was really high-paced, great fun, and had so much twisting and shaking going on, it was a miracle we didn't all wake up this morning with cricked necks. After a quiet old few days, it was just what we needed.

Then, as we headed to Tiffany's for a nightcap, we ran into John and Ed looking resplendent in their matching black tuxedos. Well okay, all black tuxedos tend to match, but what I mean is that these had been tailored to look exactly the same, as had their shirts, ties etc. Courtesy of their shaved heads, semi-permanent designer stubble, and their sharp suits, they looked like a couple of smartly dressed bouncers, and after inserting "slightly camp" in the middle of that sentence, I told them so. John just laughed it off, ruffled my hair like you would an over-enthusiastic terrier, and said he'd take it as a compliment. Ed, on the other hand, and clearly the less enthusiastic suit-wearing half of the couple, said "If I had my way darling, my formal night wear would consist solely of a black leather waistcoat and matching arseless chaps". Silly sod, doesn't he realise the head waiter would ask him to stick a jacket on.

Sunday 27 September 2009
This morning we came out on deck to a strange humming sound that we soon realised was being produced by Lisbon's answer to the Golden Gate Bridge, the unusually named 25 April Bridge (in recognition of the 1974 revolution), under which Oriana was moored. Now, having spent the first four days of our honeymoon in San Francisco, neither Mandy nor I could remember any such hum there, and it was only on closer

inspection we noticed that we could actually see the underside of the cars crossing the bridge. Unlike its Californian cousin, the 25 April Bridge has no proper road surface other than the metallic "mesh" of its structure, which is totally safe and effective, but it hums as the cars go over it. The bridge has its similarities to the Golden Gate however, and, combined with the huge Rio-esque "Christ the King" statue across the river, Lisbon initially has a real Americas feel to it.

After a swift breakfast it was time to explore, but we initially made the mistake of taking the free shuttle bus into the city centre on a very sleepy Sunday morning. That's not to say the centre itself wasn't nice, in fact the square we were dropped in, Praca dos Restauradores, was very nice despite its name suggesting it's the location of the local Burger King. The word "Restauradores" actually refers to the Portuguese War of Restoration, when they finally evicted the Spanish, and the praca (or square) commemorates that. It's a grand old praca to be fair, and as well as a number of lovely old buildings and an obelisk, it also contains a palace. Ironically however, for such an old square dedicated to a war in the 1600s, the stand-out building for me is an old art-deco cinema called the Eden Teatro, built less than 80 years ago.

But it was really quiet in the centre, with very little going on and very few shops open. So we jumped on the hop-on-hop-off bus, and although that took us pretty much straight back to where the shuttle bus had picked us up from, we jumped off a bit further up the river where we found some of Lisbon's more famous sights grouped together. That meant, initially, a visit to the Belem Tower which is, for want of a better description, a tiny little castle which is really decorative and in amazing condition for something built in the early 1500s. Before the path of the Tagus changed, it was situated in the river itself, to see off potential invaders. But now it stands proudly on its bank, as does the Monument to the Discoveries that was built just down the river in 1960. This is a stunningly detailed monument, built in the shape of a ship's prow, and depicts a range of explorers from Vasco da Gama to Henry the Navigator.

By this time it was fast approaching lunchtime, and I needed a rest, so we thought we would go back to the ship. Only everyone else must have been thinking the same thing, as when we went to catch the hop-on-hop-off bus, there was a queue a mile long. So we, and a number of others, set out to walk the apparently short distance back along the river bank to the 25 April Bridge, and therefore Oriana. Only it wasn't anywhere as close as it looked. After 30 minutes, and a nice (if tiring) walk along the Tagus, that bridge didn't look any damn closer, and a number of people in addition to ourselves were saying as much. It was really deceptive. We could all see the bridge, and hear the cars crossing it, and we knew Oriana was parked underneath, but having walked so far already, we belatedly realised it was much further away than it looked. Cue a number of hastily hailed taxis for the lightweights, and a promise to the die-hards (continuing the journey on foot) that we wouldn't let Oriana leave without them.

Monday 28 September 2009
Today we were in Vigo, and as beautiful and green as it looked (it's a cooler, wetter climate than the rest of Spain) I'm afraid we didn't go ashore. That's three out of the eight ports this cruise where we have not gone ashore (as well as Corfu we also missed Palma), but health-wise, it's been hard this time, and that misguided attempt to walk back to the ship yesterday has just about finished me off. But we got to spend considerable time in all of the places we were most looking forward to this cruise, namely Dubrovnik, Venice, Split and Lisbon, so I can't complain.

Mandy, of course, still refuses to go ashore without me, but said she was quite content with us having a restful day today, especially as it was the Guess handbag sale in the Atrium this afternoon, and if I was going to be her "wing man" I was going to need my strength. Sadly, in the end the Guess handbags were a bit of an anti-climax, with most the bags being quite gaudy (damn near Gaudi a couple of them), but Mand found a handbag and purse she liked, so she's mucho chuffed. And both were secured without her putting any other passengers in the sick bay (this time), so all good, and I was soon back to, and prostate on, my sun bed contemplating how many handbags one woman could possibly need.

Tuesday 29 September 2009
It's our last day. And so today I will mostly be crying. No, scrub that, let's not forget we're on a cruise ship after all, so today I will mostly be eating. And then on the mostly scale of things I will mostly be doing, I will mostly be crying.

Yesterday however, was as lazy a day as I had hoped, and it seemed to just fly by, as the latter days of a cruise always seem to. Before I knew it, it was early evening and I was having my pre-dinner sauna with John and Ed, who took great joy from the fact that I didn't know what a "Friends of Dorothy" event was. Such events have regularly appeared in the on-board newspaper this cruise, and I just thought who the hell is this Dorothy woman, why is she so damn popular, and how come she gets to have so many parties?

Once they stopped wetting themselves laughing (never a nice sight in a sauna), John and Ed explained that "Dorothy" is a reference to the film The Wizard of Oz, or more specifically the actress (and gay icon) Judy Garland. In the film, Dorothy befriended characters who were "different", such as the gentle lion (at this point, and rather worryingly well rehearsed, John and Ed sang in tandem "I'm afraid there's no denying, I'm just a dandy lion") and this resulted in the term "A Friend of Dorothy" becoming gay slang for saying you are gay. Thus, an event for The Friends of Dorothy is basically an opportunity for gay guys and gals to meet up socially.

So, there you have it. A Friends of Dorothy event is basically gay networking, and whilst it sounds a damn sight more fun than bridge, no I'm not allowed to go along. Not even if I pretend I once had a dog called Toto. Or, apparently, even if I know all the lyrics to Somewhere over the Rainbow. Sod'em, then.

Wednesday 30 September 2009
Back home now, and I'm pleased to say that when we arrived our cats were doing pretty good impressions of being dandy lions themselves. And all our non-feline loved ones are fine also. Another great cruise, and although I'm tired, both Mandy and I feel so much better for it.

Chapter 11 – My Worst Nightmare

Friday 13 November 2009
I saw my GP recently and he took the opportunity to have a brief "how's it going" chat, so I shared my fear that I may have fallen off the NHS radar as far as any future CFS treatment was concerned. He therefore suggested he write to the CFS Clinic at the local Intermediate Care Centre. He said it wouldn't do any harm to remind them I'm still here and still ill, particularly as Martin Lee isn't working there now due to his own ill health. Martin has been really ill actually, and has had us all pretty worried about him. I hope for his own sake, after a career of looking after others he now puts himself first.

My GP has been really supportive. I don't see a lot of him, as prescription drugs have little effect on CFS, but he's always keen to help if he can. That usually means I see him once, sometimes twice a year, as and when individual symptoms are proving a particular problem. That said, he always stresses that I should highlight to him any significant change in my symptoms, as CFS could, over time, mask other health issues. That means he's referred me to a non-CFS specialist on occasion if a new symptom develops or becomes more of an issue, if only to ensure there is no other cause. It's a balanced and proportionate approach that, when my heart started regularly palpitating like a love-struck teenager for example (as is often the case with CFS, and was initially quite worrying), I have found reassuring.

Wednesday 29 December 2009
We were over at Ivan and Cassie's today for lunch which was a real Christmas treat. You see, not only did Ivan cook a terrific lunch, but they have a new home. After many years of living in that beautiful little cottage, just down the road from the private school where Cassie teaches, they now live in the school itself. Not very exciting you might think, until I explain that the school is in a magnificent old country mansion house, and Ivan and Cassie (and young Joe) basically have a whole wing to themselves. We were, of course, given a tour, and it's a truly stunning old house set in the most beautiful grounds.

In addition to Cassie's teaching duties, she and Ivan are now also part-time house-masters to the small number of pupils that opt to board at the school, thus the need to "live-in". But even though they are effectively living above the shop - and, when first asked, young Joe's opinion was "I hate school, why would I want to live there too?" - it's not difficult at all to see why they chose to make this move. I'm sure, over time, the situation will have its good aspects and not-so-good aspects, but it seems a terrific place to live, and thanks to the excellent school on site, has some brilliant facilities. Indeed, whilst Ivan was showing us around this amazing wooden panelled Great Hall that looked like it had been lifted straight from a Harry Potter movie, he explained that on Christmas Day they had 37 of their relatives sat in there feasting on his Christmas Dinner. As brilliant as that must have been, Ivan says the amount of time and effort needed is likely to mean it won't happen again anytime soon.

But as far as our smaller, five-person, lunch was concerned, it was great and hopefully something that we will get together to do time and time again. It's a bit of a journey down there for us, and so Ivan and Cassie are just as happy to come here, but it's a lovely setting, so as long as I'm not proving too much like hard work, I can't wait to go again.

Friday 22 January 2010
I had a letter from the Intermediate Care Centre today offering me a place on a CFS Management Programme, which runs on six consecutive Tuesdays starting in February. I'm pretty pleased about that, as aside from the occasional chat with the ever-dependable Martin Lee, I've felt pretty forgotten about. It should also put me right in the middle of what my local NHS is now providing to CFS sufferers in the region. But I have a couple of concerns.

Firstly, the weekly sessions are a full two hours long which, when taking into account travel there and back, will mean three long hours without a rest. Surely for a CFS programme these sessions should be shorter. Secondly, having had a chat with the lady who is going to be running the programme, it sounds like it's simply going to cover the same territory I covered seven years ago when I was first diagnosed. So I could be pushing my limits purely to hear stuff I already know.

However, as I say, this course puts me back on the NHS radar, which is what I wanted. And although after seven years it's quite sad to see that there's been no progress in the recommended approach to CFS, the good thing is that everyone in the region with the illness now gets offered this support. That's got to be good news for CFS sufferers as a whole and due, I suspect, in no short measure to Martin Lee's sterling efforts.

Tuesday 23 March 2010
The CFS Management Programme proved as hard as I feared it would be. Due to their length, and their impact on me, I was only able to attend four out of the six sessions, and didn't learn too much in the way of new information. I'm not kidding myself though - I might have been physically present for four of those sessions, but for large spells my brain often went into neutral gear. And when my mind goes blank like that, very little of what is being said goes in. I have to ask myself therefore, if such courses are worth the extra effort required. Perhaps it is time to accept that self-management really is the best way forward for me now.

Wednesday 24 March 2010
Mandy came home mid-morning today, and although she was trying to hide it, I could tell the moment she walked in the door she was upset. I immediately felt an ache in the pit of my stomach, even before she had a chance to speak. She composed herself and quickly explained that, unbeknown to me, she had found a lump in her breast last week, and had just come straight from a hastily-arranged appointment with a breast specialist. Although the specialist's immediate feeling was that he couldn't feel anything sinister, the mammogram that followed straight afterwards strongly suggested otherwise. They had put a needle into the lump, there and then, for a biopsy, and whilst they wouldn't know the results until tomorrow, from what they saw they felt it was very likely she had breast cancer.

I was stunned. Mandy just collapsed in my arms and cried so hard that the words of reassurance we both tried to offer each other were barely audible: "we'll get through this", "we can beat this", "recovery rates are incredibly good these days". Basically all the usual clichés I guess, but every single word tinged with fear. I tried to be strong for Mandy and not show her how terrified I felt. She's 41 for Christ's sake. She just doesn't deserve this.

We sat down on the sofa and Mandy told me everything: from when she first felt the lump last week whilst stretching, to then seeing a GP, to then getting an immediate referral to the local private hospital, courtesy of her employer's BUPA cover. The specialist, Dr Galea, had been quite surprised this morning after the mammogram suggested a tumour, but Mandy says he was already very positive about a good outcome to all of this. She needs to go back tomorrow morning for the results of the biopsy, but she said they seemed in little doubt that it is cancer.

I just can't believe it. Haven't we already had our share of misfortune? Poor Mandy already takes care of me and her elderly mum, pretty much by herself. This is the last thing she deserves. It's so unfair. I just can't believe this is happening.

Thursday 25 March 2010
Mandy and I went back to see Dr Galea this morning for the results of the biopsy, and he did indeed confirm she has breast cancer. I held Mandy's hand and tried to focus on what else he was saying, but other than knowing he was making some positive sounds, it just wasn't going in. Also, although the little focus I had retained at that point was 100% on Mandy, I suddenly started to feel like I was going to vomit. Mandy on the other hand seemed to be taking it all in her stride, and asking the occasional question. In fact, she did brilliantly. I'm not sure if she was just all cried out from yesterday, or just incredibly brave, but barely a tear passed her eye, and except for holding my hand so tight I thought it might fall off, she was composure personified. I was so in awe I didn't vomit in the end, but instead held Mandy as close and as reassuringly as I could.

Luckily, my brain got back into gear in time for me to hear Dr Galea explain that he wanted to remove the lump from Mandy's breast within the next two weeks, together with some lymph nodes from under her arm. He will then send everything off to be analysed, and depending on the results, Mandy would definitely undergo radiotherapy, and possibly chemotherapy too. He is also fairly confident that, given that the lump is relatively small, Mandy will not have to have her whole breast removed. It all sounds surprisingly straightforward and whilst ultimately it very much depends on what they find, statistically Mandy has a very good chance of a full recovery.

As we walked back to the car, Mandy and I talked about the positive points that Dr Galea had mentioned, and undoubtedly there were a number. I think, individually in our own heads, we were also batting around whether Mandy would be one of those people who don't get better from breast cancer. But, thanks to Dr Galea's own positivity, the overwhelming feeling was a good one. And as if to confirm that, whilst we sat there in our car reassuring each other, a little robin came and perched right on the windscreen wiper, literally inches from Mandy's face. It looked straight at Mandy for what felt like ages, but was probably only ten seconds or so, before flying away. "I don't know why, but I think that was my dad saying it's all going to be okay" Mand said.

Friday 26 March 2010
I've been reflecting on what Dr Galea said yesterday, and there is definitely much to be positive about. However, whilst I'm not letting on to Mandy, I've never felt as scared as I feel today. I mean, it's cancer! The single most hated word in the English language. And my beautiful wife has it. Just thinking about what she's going through - what she has yet to go through - is horrible enough, but to contemplate that there is even the slightest chance that I might lose her is terrifying. She is my life. And what if I am in some way to blame for all of this?

Nobody knows what causes cancer I know, but there is just no logical reason why Mandy should get this, other than perhaps stress. She doesn't smoke, she barely drinks and is a tiny slip of a girl with a very healthy diet. Neither does she have any family history of breast cancer. That just leaves stress surely? And the only stress in her life is me and this damn CFS. Or at least my obsession with getting better from it. One thing I do know is that I couldn't live without her.

Saturday 10 April 2010
Mandy had her operation to remove the lump from her breast last week, and Dr Galea was very happy with the procedure. The lump was a little closer to Mandy's heart than is ideal, but he was able to remove it okay, plus a little of the surrounding tissue so they can check that the cancer hasn't spread there. He took a few lymph nodes from under her arm for analysis also, as this is a common route through which breast cancer can spread. But he stressed that he was very pleased with how the operation went, and also added that whilst he was "in there", he gave Mandy's breast a slight lift. "Oh great, every cloud!" said Mand.

Actually Mandy's been in quite good spirits considering what a horrible and stressful time this is. I've tried to keep her smiling, and occasionally laughing – which surely you have to when your breast surgeon shares a name with a melon! She says she already feels happier knowing that the cancer has been removed. There are a whole string of tests to be done, and results to be analysed, but for now it's comforting to know her road to recovery has started. And it will be exactly that: a recovery. No matter how long it takes, and no matter what's involved, the recovery starts here. Whatever is needed I'll be there with her every step of the way.

Wednesday 14 April 2010

We went back to see Dr Galea today for the test results on Mandy's tumour. As it was, two out of the three results were good. Both the tissue that was removed from around the lump and the lymph nodes from under Mandy's arm were completely clear of cancer. Dr Galea explained that it's safe to assume therefore, that the cancer has not spread beyond the tumour he removed, which is excellent news, and obviously very important going forward. Psychologically this is a real shot in the arm, as in our minds it means that Mandy is now cancer-free, and the treatment she has will be more focused on stopping the cancer returning rather than killing off what's already there.

The not-so-good news is that the tumour was found to be a Grade 3 cancer, which is the most aggressive type, and therefore, worrying. But given that a) Mandy found the lump very early on, and b) all the evidence suggests the cancer has not spread, the fact it's Grade 3 isn't anywhere near as bad news as it could have been. Also, those two plus points mean that, statistically, the eventual outcome after treatment is looking very favourable.

Saturday 17 April 2010

It was my niece Jessica's wedding today. I was unsure whether to go as it's been such an emotional couple of weeks, and we're both exhausted. Also, both our minds are constantly thinking about what's ahead, so I was wary of attending such a happy occasion and not looking, well, happy. But Mandy was adamant that we needed to be there and she looked absolutely stunning, as did Jess of course. Of those present, only my mum and dad knew about Mandy's breast cancer, so actually the wedding provided a nice distraction.

It was a lovely day too. I always made sure we saw a lot of my nieces and nephews as they grew up, so to see the first of them marry was quite special. My smile did feel a little forced to start off with, but the occasion quickly rubbed off on us and we began to enjoy ourselves. In the end, I would have liked to have stayed longer, but as the toll of the last few weeks started to tell, we made our excuses and headed for home. As nice a distraction today was, it was good to get back home with our cats.

In terms of telling people about Mandy's health, we've told very few people so far and don't see the sense in doing so until we have all the results back. At least then we can speak from a position of knowledge and with an awareness of exactly what treatment Mandy will need to have. We've not even told Mandy's mum yet, and to be honest, I think Mandy's as worried about that as anything else. Mand's mum is elderly, lives on her own, and a worrier, so our instinct is to protect her from this as much as we can.

We are still waiting for the last two test results, and it's strange: having just spent ten days praying for all I'm worth that the cancer hasn't spread, I am now finding myself constantly hoping that the tumour is "hormone positive" and "HER-2 negative" – both phrases I was blissfully unaware of until recently, but those exact results would increase the statistical probability of Mandy's total, and sustained, long-term recovery, and help me keep her positive in the months ahead.

Thursday 6 May 2010
We had an appointment with a Dr Cole today who is going to be Mandy's oncologist. That basically means he'll oversee Mandy's treatment, whether it be just radiotherapy or chemo too. He also had one of the remaining test results to share with us, and we now know that the tumour in Mandy's breast was hormone positive. That means that the tumour was effectively feeding off of the female hormone oestrogen, and so if that hormone can be restricted through the taking of medication then, logically, such a tumour has less chance of occurring again. It means that, once all other treatment is complete, Mandy will be on a drug called Tamoxifen for five years, but out of the two possible results, it's the one which gives her the best statistical chance of avoiding reoccurrence, and so good news I think.

The downside of today was that, whilst the "HER-2" test isn't back yet, it already looks to be in Mandy's best interests to have chemotherapy in addition to the radiotherapy. That's a real blow. We had both been hoping to avoid it if possible, even though, in our heads, we know cancer and chemo always seem to go hand in hand. Even ignoring our own horrible mental pictures of Mandy experiencing months of sickness and hair loss, the fact her mum will have to see her go through it, is something that Mandy dreads.

Dr Cole was great. He was very patient and used computer software to clearly show us, statistically, how the chemotherapy provides Mandy with a better chance of both avoiding the cancer reoccurring and her long-term survival. It's not straightforward by any means, as Mandy still has a good prognosis even without chemo. It's her decision, but with a clear statistical swing in favour of the chemo, it's hard to ignore the logic. Dr Cole doesn't need a decision yet, he said for us to go away and talk about it, and then go back for another chat.

Monday 10 May 2010
It's our wedding anniversary today, but we saw our GP first thing this morning to ask his advice about the chemo. He just seemed the obvious choice given that he knows us both, and he's been so supportive in respect of my own illness. And I'm so glad we went to see him, as it turns out our GP's wife has had breast cancer, and so he had first-hand experience to share. His wife's cancer was at a similar age to Mandy's, and whilst he stressed that everyone is different, his wife had both chemo and radio, so he could comment about both in some detail. He explained that whilst neither treatment is a stroll in the park, chemo, although unpleasant, can look worse than it is. He couldn't advise us which route to take obviously, and we didn't expect that, but having been already leaning in the direction of having the chemo, Mandy has pretty much made up her mind.

When we were back at home this afternoon, Father Colin, our parish priest, dropped by for a coffee. We've only known him a couple of months, but he's a nice fella and seems to be genuinely concerned that we are having a rough time of things. He's always laughing and telling refreshingly inappropriate jokes for a priest, so he's good company. I first met Father Colin in March when, as I was walking past his church, I just decided to pop in and ask the big guy upstairs for some help, as at the time, Mandy's cancer had just been diagnosed and it felt like everything was going against us. As I entered, the mid-week mass was just coming to an end, so I sat quietly at the back and said a quick prayer. Colin said later that when he saw me come in, it looked like I had the troubles of the world on my shoulders. As the mass ended, and I went to make a swift exit, Father Colin came running up the aisle to say hi, and make me promise that I would return. I only normally go to church for christenings, weddings and funerals, but I did go back and Colin has since become a good friend.

Father Colin is only about 30 years old, but when you spend time with him he seems even younger. His naughty schoolboy approach to life and religion means he retains a real fun element to his personality that inevitably rubs off on those around him. Therefore, whilst we hadn't expected him today, he was the ideal company at a time when our heads were in knots, and just so full with information it felt like they might explode. He only stayed an hour or so, but we talked about our situation, had a few laughs, and basically felt so much better for his visit.

Thursday 13 May 2010
We returned to see Dr Cole, the oncologist, today and advised him that yes, Mandy would have the chemotherapy. I did, perhaps unfairly, first ask him what he would do if it were his wife or daughter in Mandy's exact situation, but subject to him saying anything negative, we had already decided chemo was the route to take. His answer was both professional and understanding of our asking of it, but essentially it echoed what he had already said to us. So chemotherapy it is, followed by radiotherapy, and then five years on Tamoxifen.

Given Mandy's concerns over the side-effects of chemotherapy, and how her mum would react to seeing the hair loss in particular, Dr Cole and his chemo nurse, Pat, talked to us about something called the Cold Cap. This is effectively a helmet which, due to its ice-cold interior, cools a patient's scalp during each chemotherapy session with a view to minimising hair loss. The logic being that, if the scalp is cold, then the blood flow and chemotherapy medication that reaches the hair follicles is significantly reduced. Pat warned us that it's not that pleasant, due to the very low temperature they use to create the cooling effect, but they have had some reasonable success with it, so it's worth thinking about.

After consulting their diaries, Dr Cole and Pat decided Mandy will have her first chemo treatment on 3 June. She will need six sessions in total which will take place at three-weekly intervals, followed by radiotherapy in the autumn. So as there is a long hard road ahead of her, Dr Cole has recommended that I take Mandy away for a short break before her treatment starts. Nothing too strenuous, just a relaxing break to put us both in a positive frame of mind for the months ahead.

Oh, and the HER-2 test on Mandy's tumour came back as negative. To be honest, we've had so much on our minds that we had forgotten about the final test result. HER-2 is basically a protein found in some breast cancer cells which stimulates them to grow and spread faster. As such, to have a test result of HER-2 negative is good news. In fact since we found out that Mandy's tumour was the most aggressive Grade Three type of cancer, all the other test results have come down in our favour – its size, the fact it's not spread, and that it's hormone-positive and HER-2 negative, all contribute to Mandy having a really good chance of avoiding reoccurrence in the foreseeable future. As scary as this whole situation is therefore, there is plenty to be positive about.

Friday 14 May 2010
This afternoon, Mandy put her mum in the picture about her breast cancer. Mand had, of course, been slowly telling her mum little bits of information since she was diagnosed, but she had avoided using the word "cancer", at least until we knew the full situation. She had played it all down as best she could, so as not to frighten her mum. But now that we know the full picture, Mandy decided she wanted, by herself, to tell her mum all about it. She was dreading it obviously, and did not sleep much last night as a result, but as things turned out, her mum took it better than we anticipated. In fact, she had pretty much already guessed.

You see, over the last month or so, the singer Bernie Nolan had announced her own breast cancer diagnosis, and so by following the story in her magazines each week, Mand's mum had gradually connected the dots to Mandy's own situation. She wasn't sure obviously, and was still upset to hear it, but with Bernie writing so positively about her breast cancer, it meant that Mand's mum wasn't as fearful as she might otherwise have been. Not an easy situation, and there's no right or wrong way to handle it, but even though we know she will worry, as mums do, the main thing is she is now fully in the picture.

Saturday 15 May 2010
Well, it took a while, but today I was able to get us the last available cabin on Arcadia's week-long cruise to Norway and the Fjords, which leaves next Sunday. I say available, but the cruise had been sold out for some time, and it was only by checking the P&O website several times each day that I managed to get us on it. I assume someone must have cancelled very late on, which is a great shame for them but a big bonus for us. And so Norway it is, which is kind of ironic as we think about going there every year, especially as we have friends who live in Bergen. But every single time, including this year (until we had to cancel), we had instead booked the guaranteed sun and warmth of the Mediterranean. That's understandable I think, but we're both really looking forward to cruising to Norway and seeing our friends. We've heard a lot about how beautiful the Fjords are too, so it should be a nice break and just what the oncologist ordered.

Sunday 23 May 2010

Hurray, we're back on Arcadia, and although it was a bit of a rushed eight days getting ready, Mandy always has a list for every eventuality. Scarily, I was handed my own sheet with the double-underlined title of "To Do List", with a little tick-box next to each task. So, fearful it would actually be me who was going to get ticked off, I just took a scattergun approach of charging and mowing everything in sight, in between rests, and hoped that I covered the most important tasks. On a serious note, it's good to see Mandy focused on something other than her treatment, and hopefully the next seven days will be the perfect distraction.

Arcadia is as lovely as ever and our cabin, an extra-large inside cabin on G Deck, is huge compared to what we've become accustomed to. We've not been on her since her maiden season four years or so back, but Arcadia is still as beautiful as before and has even acquired a new boutique cinema, which has the widest, most comfortable-looking chairs I've seen in many a year. I think we'll be taking full advantage of that over the next seven days.

The only small problem is not being allocated our requested table for two for dinner each night as, based on the 'last to book/last to be allocated a table' system, we've been placed on a big old table that's in a very busy position. Although that's the fairest way to deal with the numerous dining requests they get, I think, this cruise more than ever, we really need a quiet table for just the two of us. No biggy, the cruise had been sold out for ages after all, and the alternative dining arrangements that instantly came to mind, tied in nicely with my plan to spoil Mandy rotten on this cruise.

The last time we were on Arcadia, as well as enjoying eating in the main dining restaurant, for a small additional supplement we also dined at the Orchid and Arcadian Rhodes venues which were both fantastic. As such, as soon as I realised we hadn't been allocated a table of our own in normal dining, I went straight to these other two venues and explained we would like to dine at each on alternate nights for the duration of the cruise. They were obviously very pleased to hear that, so I pushed my luck, asked if I could pick our table for two myself, and then selected the best (and quietest) tables in both venues. When I went back to the cabin to tell the unpacking Mandy where we would be dining each night she grinned from ear to ear, she was over the moon.

Monday 24 May 2010
A good first evening on board last night, and the highlight was our visit to Arcadian Rhodes - it was more an experience than a meal, absolutely fantastic. From the point we arrived and were seated at our table, Mandy especially was made to feel like royalty by the maitre d' (I had earlier explained our multiple bookings by telling him it was a "special" cruise), and nothing was to prove too much trouble. Mandy was really pleased with the quiet window table for two I had chosen, and now that the restaurant was slowly filling up, I was even more convinced I had bagged the best one. It was perfect for us.

Mand, of course, looked absolutely stunning, and it was just as well we weren't sharing a table with anyone, as I advised her of this ad nauseam. In readiness for her chemo treatment, and particularly as she has decided to try the Cold Cap, Mandy had been advised to have her gorgeous long blonde hair cut shorter. And, although I could tell that this shorter style was making her feel a little self-conscious (Mandy's hair has been Rapunzel-like since she was a child), she looked great, as I knew she would. She was also displaying a smile wider than Arcadia herself, and between Gary Rhodes and me I think we managed to keep it there all night.

After dinner, we wandered contentedly along to the show, but what we thought was going to be a Headliners show was mostly the cruise director and her team on stage introducing themselves. We had not come across this in previous cruises, and actually it might be well worthwhile on the longer ones. But to use up one of just seven cruise shows/nights having a dozen entertainment officers say "Hi, I'm Mike from Cleethorpes and I run the Bingo" seems a bit unnecessary. To be fair, the Headliners did still do three short numbers, but their half of the 30-minute "show" wasn't really enough and just left us wanting more.

Tuesday 25 May 2010
After a nice relaxing sea day yesterday, today we stepped foot in Norway for the first time, in the shape of a beautiful little town called Stavanger. In fact Stavanger is a big industrial city, but you wouldn't think it based on its pretty little harbour, surrounded by its old town of little white wooden houses. And it's this older part of town, dating back to the 18th century, that the tourists, and particularly its cruise visitors, come to see. So as it was a nice sunny day, and Arcadia having dropped us bang in the middle of it, it was the old town we decided to explore.

After a brief visit to the charming little cathedral, we found ourselves wandering up one of the many little cobbled streets that lead up and away from the harbour. The wooden houses are quite small and so close together that as you walk around the tiny streets it feels like a life-sized model village, and just as peaceful too. Indeed, due to the snug layout of the houses, stretching right down to the harbour side, Arcadia towered above them at such close proximity it made for a startling contrast. Photo of the day had to be of the front of these stunning old buildings with the good ship Arcadia looming above and behind them, looking every bit like Captain Oprey had parked her right in their back garden. A lovely first port and I even picked up a bit of Norwegian:

"Good Dag" – Good Day
"Halo" – Hi
"Tak" – Thanks
"Ja, for sure" – Yes, that's right.

Our meal in the Orchid Restaurant last night was so good we can't wait to go back there again. If anything, its setting, right at the top of the ship and surrounded by floor-to-ceiling glass, is even better than that of Arcadian Rhodes. Its food wasn't far behind either, so combined with another great table, excellent service and a bottle of champagne arranged for us by our friend Olly, it made for another memorable evening.

Wednesday 26 May 2010
Today we were in Olden which Mandy says is the most beautiful place she has ever been too. It's a small village situated on a large glacier lake (or fjord) and has everything we imagined a fjord to have – amazingly clear turquoise water, surrounded on all sides by rising green vegetation which gradually gives way to first hard brown rock, and then soft white snow, above it. It's like seeing four seasons layered into one stunning vista. The fjord itself is the best of the lot for me, with its water so brilliant, and so clear, it really is picture perfect.

Unfortunately, the must-do excursion of the day, to visit the local glacier, was sold out well before we had even booked the cruise, but that's okay, it was beautifully warm and sunny at sea level so we settled for a gentle bike ride. Despite being surrounded by mountains, the road around our part of the lake was nice and flat, and courtesy of a bike-hire place right next to our mooring we were able to see maximum scenery for minimal effort, and just relax in our own company for a while.

After a lazy afternoon on board, in the evening we went to the Belvedere Restaurant for the Indian Buffet Dinner. The Indian evening is always a favourite of ours, and particularly given that we were dining every other night at Arcadian Rhodes or The Orchid, provided a nice alternative bang in the middle of the cruise. And it was good. Really good. The lads working in there were all in Indian-style dress, and the restaurant and tables were decorated accordingly, so it all looked amazing too. As usual it was all so nice that I ate far more spicy food than is probably recommended for the digestive system of a straight meat-and-two-veg lad from Wiltshire, but hey, I'm on holiday. Now if you'll just excuse me, my tummy is telling me I should go "powder my nose".

Thursday 27 May 2010
We were joined at lunch today by a gentleman who had been on yesterday's sold-out glacier excursion. He said it was "awesome" and urged us to do it next time we are there. I'm told it's possible to do the trip independently, but this cruise, more than any other, I want Mandy stress-free, and so didn't want her worrying about me having possible health issues halfway up a mountain without someone from the ship being around. But it's not a problem, we will definitely cruise there again one day.

This chap at lunch said he was surprised just how cold it was up at the glacier, and also that there was this fine wet mist in the air, both elements for which he found his t-shirt and jumper combination were ill-suited. He therefore bought a fleece top from the Nordic mountain equivalent of a street seller, which although very expensive, the guy selling them assured him it was a "traditional Norwegian fleece" and "waterproof". Anyway, long story short, this fleece absorbed so much of the wet mist that it doubled his body-weight. Not only that, but when returning to the coach, and stopping to wring out his traditional Norwegian fleece, he spotted a "Made in China" tag inside. He wasn't happy bless him, so I tried to be sympathetic. Unlike Mandy, who, having initially restrained herself admirably at this man's surprise that it could possibly be cold at a glacier, was now stifling a belly laugh over his fleece-buying experience. "You poor thing" said I, "you were, literally, fleeced". At which point Mandy's attempts at restraint completely collapsed, as she noisily projectiled a mouth full of Earl Grey back into its cup.

Anyhow, we were in Alesund today which was very nice, but I have to say it wasn't a patch on either Olden or Stavanger. Maybe we've just been spoilt by two ports that looked amazing in very different ways, but Alesund just felt a little dull in comparison. It did have its own mountain in the middle of town – known by the wacky locals as "the town mountain" – which is quite fun, and if you are willing and able to walk the 418 steps to the summit (or take a taxi) it provides amazing views. And actually, on reflection, the town mountain is pretty good, so I apologise Alesund, you aren't that bad after all, please let's just put it down to my recent over-exposure to stunning scenery. Still not a patch on Olden and Stavanger though.

Friday 28 May 2010
I forgot to mention yesterday, that after first savouring the sailaway views with a pre-dinner cocktail in the Orchid Bar (it's daylight until about 11pm in Norway at this time of the year), we went to the Orchid Restaurant for dinner. The whole meal was once again gorgeous and the staff in there are great too, really friendly. Amazingly, the same girls (Fe and Mary Rose) who served us last night, and worked until gone midnight, were up at dawn and serving us breakfast in Café Vivo this morning. But it was just a quick breakfast for us as we were off to meet our friend, and Bergen resident, Jules, as she had wangled a day off work at short notice.

What a surprise Bergen turned out to be, as despite it reportedly being the rain capital of Europe, we had the best weather we've had all cruise. Also, for a place that is Norway's second city, it was really beautiful and not city-like at all. Admittedly we didn't see huge amounts of Bergen itself as we were at Jules' house for much of the day, but I can thoroughly recommend the funicular railway to the top of Mount Floyen. It was quite cheap by Scandinavian standards, and such a clear sunny day up there that the views were fabulous.

In actual fact, once out of the centre of Bergen everywhere seemed to have a decent view. The houses especially were amazing. Lots of wooden chalet-type places, and every one seemed to have a view of the sea, a mountain, a fjord, or all three. Our friends live in Os (pronounced ooze) just outside the main city which, if anything, was greener still and more mountainous. Even the schools, from which we picked up Jules' boys, Dominic and Marcus, were located in forested areas on the side of a mountain. Unfortunately, Jules' Norwegian hubby, Thomas, was working, but we spent a really nice few hours with her and the boys at their lovely home, enjoying a traditional Nordic lunch of cold meats and pickles. We had such a good time, we very nearly missed the final shuttle bus back from the city centre, but it was a good day and great to see Jules and the boys.

Saturday 29 May 2010
Yesterday we had rearranged our plans to go to the Orchid for a second successive night (and third time in total) as it was their Tandoori night. The girls in the Orchid had been stressing to us all week how good it was, and they were spot on. Mandy and I both had a huge starter of Kandahar Lamb Chops and Mint Chutney which was just heaven, and we both thought the main course would have to do very well to come anywhere near. But Mandy's Tandoori Butter Chicken, and my Tandoori Sea Food Platter, went pretty close. The only problem was, with those two sizeable courses and the various little complimentary items they brought us, we were stuffed well before we even caught sight of the dessert menus. That's okay though, you don't opt for Asian cuisine for their puds, and we were very satisfied, so just settled for something small and fruity before a much-needed early night.

Today the emphasis was on rest and relaxation as we enjoyed our final day of the cruise at sea. Having never sailed this far north before we have been pleasantly surprised with just how calm the sea has been, and we've also been blessed with sunshine every single day. We even got to sit out on deck for a bit today, which was a bonus, although I did still take Mandy along to afternoon tea at one point as an extra little treat.

Anyway, it's our last night tonight and we get an extra hour in bed, so we're off for pre-dinner cocktails in a minute. Dining-wise, as great as the Orchid is, we reckon we have saved the best for last as we go to Arcadian Rhodes for the third and final time later. Mandy's been talking about it all day, so fingers crossed she enjoys it as much as I think she will.

Sunday 30 May 2010
What a great final night. The lads in Arcadian Rhodes welcomed us like long-lost friends (we hadn't been in there for three nights) and, this being our final night, they really made a special effort for us. The food was fabulous once more, with me going for Beef and Calves Sweetbreads, and Mandy had Roast Duck Breast and Caramelised Onion

Tart, in a kind of red wine and beetroot sauce, that had her moaning and groaning like a wanton Meg Ryan. They really did us proud in there, and I have to say that both the Gary Rhodes restaurants on P&O ships are amazing.

During dinner I asked Mandy to marry me again. Or at least I asked her if she would like to renew our wedding vows. I said that I love her and that I want all of our nearest and dearest to join us in celebrating that fact. She didn't so much answer me as cry. Well not cry exactly, her eyes just slowly filled up and then she dripped into her Caramelised Apple with Sweet Shortbread. Which I took as a "yes". There's no hurry, and nothing to arrange just yet; my idea is to have the ceremony when Mandy has fully recovered. But because she is such a planner, I know it'll give her a nice distraction during the months of treatment, as she'll be unable to resist planning it all out.

After leaving Arcadian Rhodes on cloud nine, and making sure to thank each of the lads in there individually for taking care of us (as we did with the ladies in the Orchid the previous night), we popped along to the show. In short, it was an Abba-themed show and so high tempo from start to finish that it was like Mamma Mia on acid. The singers were excellent again (especially the Chicken Tikka and Fernando numbers), but it was the dancers that stole the show with loads of high-pace stuff, and a number of solo and duo dances showing just what they could do. A great show and, as we agreed when we toddled off to bed shortly afterwards, a good way to finish the cruise.

Alas we're back home now with our two very happy and healthy cats, and I'm pleased to say it was a fantastic cruise. Norway was a revelation, and the look on Mandy's face as we awoke in Olden will stay with me forever – she still says it's the most beautiful place she has ever been to, and I have to say I agree. What's more, Operation Spoil Mandy Rotten was, I believe, successfully accomplished. This cruise really meant so much to us. It was just perfect, and has put us both in a really positive frame of mind for tackling what will undoubtedly be a tough rest of the year.

Chapter 12 - Chemo-Brain and Going Radio Ga-Ga

Friday 4 June 2010
I went along with Mandy for her first session of chemotherapy yesterday and we were lucky enough to have a room to ourselves, which was a real bonus. The chemo nurses, Pat and Rebecca, are really nice, and regularly popped in and out, not just to administer the chemo and check Mandy was okay, but quite often just to have a chat, which was good. In fact, with Dr Cole checking in on her too, and in between visits Mandy fast at work planning our renewal of vows, the time went faster than we had anticipated.

It wasn't a pleasant experience by any means, but the chemo treatment itself wasn't too bad, and Mandy feels better now just knowing what's involved. In practice, the hardest thing yesterday was the Cold Cap which, at minus six degrees, Mand says feels just like having a block of ice pressed against her scalp for three hours. Not pleasant at all, but she's adamant she wants to persevere with it, and on the plus side, she hasn't felt too sicky from the chemo so far, just a little "woosey".

It was hard seeing Mandy laid there with, effectively, poison being pumped into her veins. But for once the CFS is working in our favour, as my lack of employment means I can accompany Mandy to (hopefully) most of her treatments, and be with her at home afterwards. It means I can try to keep her occupied, positive and laughing occasionally. Or at least make her momentarily forget about the iceberg on her head during the chemo sessions themselves.

Saturday 19 June 2010
Our friend Olly phoned today, and I have to say his calls are invaluable. Not only is he a genuinely nice guy, but Olly himself is unfortunate enough to be receiving treatment for cancer himself currently, and sharing his first-hand experience has really been putting Mandy's mind at rest. We've not known Olly that long, and as he works as a restaurant manager on P&O Cruises for most of the year we see little of him. But we've got to know him quite well since we met him on a cruise a few years back, often phoning us from a faraway port to make us jealous. Unfortunately Olly has throat cancer, and so since he heard of Mandy's diagnosis, he has been on the phone regularly to give advice and allay her worries, even though he is currently undergoing daily sessions of radiotherapy.

Olly's phone call today was well timed, as Mandy's next lot of chemo is planned for Tuesday, and she's been worrying about it. She knows the first one was supposed to be the easiest one, but she's feeling really run down now, even more so than she did straight after the first chemo took place. However, Olly calmly talked her through his own recent experience, and although his own chemo was a different type and strength, she found it really reassuring. That's the measure of the guy. At a time when he has been going through a horrible time himself, he's taking the time to help Mandy in any way he can.

Wednesday 30 June 2010
Mandy's second session of chemo was delayed until yesterday after her white blood cell count was found to be too low last week, which explains why she had been feeling so bad. But they gave her some extra medication and sent her home for a week, which did the trick as she was able to have the treatment today instead. I went along with her again and kept her occupied, but I could tell this second session was harder. Also, the veins in her arms are proving more and more elusive for the nurses. I'm not sure if it's down to the number of blood tests she's now had, the chemicals in the chemo, or just her slim build, but it's proving difficult and painful.

On a good note, Mand found she was again able to put up with the freezing temperature of the Cold Cap, and both Pat and Rebecca, the nurses, said how good Mandy's hair is looking. She's been advised to be gentle with her hair and let it dry naturally, so she's curly for the first time in about 20 years. The combination of her curly blonde locks and her new "chemo tan" (which apparently is quite common, and is due to the chemo medication's red colouring) means Mand now looks almost surfer-like. Everyone that sees her is stunned by how good she is looking, often remarking that maybe they should try this chemo malarkey for themselves. That, as well as receiving so many flowers and cards that I've nowhere left to put them, is keeping her in good spirits. It's still early doors I know, but she's doing brilliantly.

Of course there has also been the football World Cup in South Africa to keep us entertained. Okay, keep me entertained. Actually Mand has dismissed all (i.e. both) my suggestions to turn the television over to a different channel, by saying "blimey, if you're offering to turn the football off, then I really must be ill", or, on the other occasion, just continuing to snore. But at least I offered. Joking aside, she's got quite into it, and aside from England pre-empting dismal failure by first showing just enough promise to give us hope, and the constant irritation of the crowd's vuvuzela horns, I think she's quite enjoyed it!

Wednesday 7 July 2010
Father Colin popped in today to say hi and check we are okay. Mand and I were both feeling pretty tired actually, and initially even Colin's cheeky grin was one I would happily have gone without for a few more days. However, I made us all a cup of tea, and Colin soon had us chuckling with his own unique blend of tasteless jokes and gallows humour. He didn't stay long, bless him, but he raised both our spirits, so I'm glad he came, even if we did promptly fall asleep in front of This Morning as soon as he went. A nice lad.

Although he's been to our house a few times now, this time I noticed a neighbour's curtains twitching as he left. So if anyone pops round with a Tuna Bake in the next few days I'll know the nosy old mare over the road is telling everyone Mandy received the last rites! Actually, on a serious note, we've only told our closest neighbours that Mandy is ill, and they will keep it to themselves, so the one across the road hopefully hasn't a clue what's going on.

Tuesday 20 July 2010
Although they now have to get a particular doctor to come and entice Mandy's veins out of hiding with something called a "butterfly", I'm pleased to say we had no delays this time, and Mandy's third chemo took place today as planned. Her white blood cell count is still causing concern, but the booster injections she's been having saw her through this time, and hopefully that will remain the case.

It's clear that Mandy does feel pretty ill for a good week following each chemo, and looks really fragile for most of that. Our cats, Frisco and Maui, know it too, and rarely leave her side as she snoozes in and out of consciousness each day on the sofa. However, with a little aid from friends and family, I find I am okay to take care of her for that week, and just as I run out of gas, Mandy feels better and ends up looking after me for a week. Then hopefully we both feel okay during the third week, and we perhaps pop out for a coffee or some lunch, as a treat, before we then start the whole process again. It's really hard if I'm honest, and it breaks my heart to see Mandy going through this, but I'm at least at home with her to help where I can.

Saturday 31 July 2010

Mandy and I went along to the annual Mela today, and it felt just like every other year we have been there. No real surprise in that I know, but that is what was good about it. Mandy has been talking more and more of just getting back to normal once her treatment is over, I guess as a way of putting her breast cancer behind her. And the Mela, given that we go every year, gave us exactly that - normality. We got there early as usual, grabbed some just-cooked Indian food from the three different stalls that took our fancy, and promptly ate it all sat on "our" quiet little bench in the corner. There was no mention of cancer or chemo, just us stuffing ourselves silly and soaking up some early Mela atmosphere. This being an Asian festival, even Mandy's head scarf blended right in. Just two ordinary Joes with nothing major going on, enjoying a curry. Nice.

Another distraction for me, and especially when Mandy has been recovering from her chemo sessions by sleeping the big sleep, has been the P&O cruise forum. It doesn't take too much effort, I can dip in and out as I like, and I've even started to contribute now and again when I think I have something to add or just want to join in the banter. It's been a real help, and as I say, a distraction during a difficult period. A few of the regulars who somehow worked out we were having a hard time of it, have taken me under their wing a bit, and rather than Dennis The Menace, I now get referred to simply as "DTM", which I think they mean affectionately. However, as someone pointed out, that's actually the brand name of a lubricant they use on the probing device used in rather unpleasant medical procedures, so they could just be inferring I'm a pain in the arse!

Tuesday 17 August 2010

Okay, chemo number four completed last week, and whilst they are now having to alternate which bruised and battered arm they plug Mandy's chemo meds into, it's another one chalked off. A very rough week followed this time, but the worst after-effects of the chemo do, at least, seem to be mostly restricted to that first week still. From then onwards Mandy says the fog lifts, she feels stronger and her appetite returns. She's lost a fair bit of weight, but then she says she just seems to lose her taste buds for a week after each treatment. Good news though, not only did she eat a whole dinner today, but late evening she had not one, but two chip butties. It really is a case of eating what she fancies, when she fancies it.

As soon as she feels up to it I'm going to take Mandy for some lunch at the Italian restaurant down the road. Wendy, an old friend of mine who has been through cancer herself, told me right at the beginning to try and make sure Mandy enjoys the days she feels okay, and ensure she rests the days she doesn't. Having Sue and Lino's restaurant so handy therefore has been fantastic, and they really do make each of our visits special. Being the school holidays, their two boys Oliver and Luca will be there too, and no doubt entertain us with stories of dragons, dinosaurs and Doctor Who, which beats cancer and chemo hands down. A great, and handy, place to escape too.

Thursday 26 August 2010
We had a lovely surprise day out today. Brian and Gill, our friends from Newbury, managed to get us a couple of tickets to a show called Copacabana, that was being shown in their local theatre, The Watermill. It's basically the well-known Barry Manilow musical done on a smaller scale, and is a show I had actually enquired about, only to find that all the tickets on the dates that avoided chemo, or recovery from chemo, were sold out. Then, as luck would have it, last week Brian bumped into a couple of the dancers from the show in the supermarket, congratulated them on their performance the previous evening (when he and Gill had seen the show) and mentioned us. Long story short, they had two of their cast tickets left for today and said they would leave them at the ticket office for us. How nice is that?

And we had a brilliant day. We initially went to Brian and Gill's house for lunch, during which we also got to see their charming teenage granddaughters, Emili and Faye, and their mum, Becky. After a smashing lunch, and Emili picking up her guitar and demonstrating some really talented vocals as she sang a song for us, Brian dropped us down to the theatre. The Watermill is, as its name suggests, a former watermill which has been lovingly converted into a theatre so beautiful that you would be happy to go there and just walk the grounds or have lunch, irrespective of seeing a show. It's on the small side, so its productions are also, but that just adds to its charm and intimacy. The show was great too, with lots of familiar Manilow numbers, and all in all, a really brilliant day.

Tuesday 31 August 2010
Chemo session five today and Mandy really dreads these now. When you think some people will have 12 or more sessions of chemo, I am so

thankful that Mandy is having just the six. That in itself is a massive positive and means that the end of the chemo really is in sight now. And it can't come soon enough for the veins in her arms, as even the "butterfly" doctor is starting to struggle now. Her veins seem to be collapsing to the point where they now just look like dark shadows on her arms.

However, our renewal of vows event is still providing the perfect distraction, and during today's chemo a smiling Mandy shared with me what she had in mind. In short, Mand wants it to take place around our 15th wedding anniversary in May 2012, at the lovely church where we got married, and conducted by Father Colin. She's got loads of little ideas on how to make the day even more special, and how we can also use it to say thanks to everyone that's helped us through a tough year. Indeed, she is already drawing up the invite list, so it's proving to be the nice distraction I hoped it would be.

We also spent some of the time reminiscing about our wedding day back in 1997 and just how broke we were at the time. It had looked like we would only be able to have a tiny wedding, as having only just saved up for and paid off the £15,000 negative equity on our flat, we were in a nice new house, but totally skint and mortgaged to the hilt. However, it had enabled us to move closer to Mand's mum, which was the priority. The sensible thing might have been to then wait a bit to get married, but having strived so hard to get it, I had always intended to propose to Mandy on the threshold of our new house. Things didn't quite pan out as I had anticipated though.

Firstly, on the day we pulled up to our new house in our rental van full of our furniture and belongings, it was clear that the carpet fitters, arranged by the builders as part of the purchase, were still fitting the carpets. Actually, scrub that: once I had poked my head inside, it was clear that the carpet fitters had only just started and were likely to be there for most of the day. Worse still, apparently you are not supposed to move furniture around on newly-laid carpets for at least 24 hours! So, long story short, other than a bed for us to sleep on, our furniture and belongings spent the night outside in the rental van, the cab of which ended up being where I made my ever-so-romantic (?) proposal of marriage. On the plus side however, I was able to take a thread from one of the carpet off-cuts and wind it around Mandy's finger as a temporary engagement ring, which not only proved fit for purpose, but also matched the fixture and fittings of our new abode.

So we were engaged, but broke, especially when I felt obliged to replace that (perfectly good) synthetic-fibre engagement ring with something more traditional. Then after considering how friends and relatives might react to a Bring Your Own Wedding Breakfast invite, Mandy's mum instead convinced her to enter the local Bride of the Year competition. And knock me down with a synthetic-fibre off-cut, after progressing through to the final 25 entrants, then final 10, then final 3, she only went and won it. And believe me, even the 13 years of stick I have received since, due to the local newspaper (mis)quoting me as saying "our eyes met over a photocopier", have very nearly been worth it – Mandy's and her bridesmaids' dresses, mine and the lads' suits, transport, flowers, even the day and evening receptions, were all provided for us. Neither Mandy nor I had ever won a thing, and haven't since, but that was like winning the lottery for us, and made not just the day, but the months running up to our wedding unbelievable. The girl done good.

Tuesday 21 September 2010
That's it, thank God. Or that's it for the chemo anyway. After a bit of a worry over Mandy's blood count again - in the words of her nurse, Pat, she "scraped through" the blood test - she was allowed to have her final chemo treatment today as planned. So we're all done and dusted now as far as the chemo is concerned, which is a tremendous relief as the warnings we had about its cumulative effects were dead right. Mand now has six weeks to get some well-earned rest before her radiotherapy starts in November. Strictly speaking she still needs to pass an interim blood test and have another scan to ensure everything is okay, but the feeling seems to be that this is just routine. So, a milestone of sorts, and whilst radiotherapy is no walk in the park either, Mand says she feels like there is some light at the end of the tunnel now.

As far as the Cold Cap goes, Mandy was able to persevere with it for all six of her chemo treatments, but as time went on she needed me to distract her more and more from the discomfort it caused. As her hair thinned (and it does still thin), the more the freezing inside surface of the cap came into contact with her bare scalp, which wasn't nice. But she still has a decent amount of hair there, so that enables her to use her head scarves creatively to make it look like it is thick all over. In fact, when we visit her mum, that's exactly the picture she presents so in that respect it's worked. It's a little smoke and mirrors, and with the benefit of hindsight, I'm not sure Mandy would have gone for the Cold Cap, but it served a purpose.

Sunday 26 September 2010
An old mate, Howard, and his partner Cath, popped two large containers of homemade soup in to us today, and their timing was perfect. Mandy and I were both really struggling, and I hadn't even thought about what we would eat. Then completely out of the blue, the doorbell went and there was Cath saying "We're not stopping, but we thought you could make good use of these". And courtesy of Howie being a chef by trade, and including loads of home grown fresh veg, those two soups tasted amazing. Cath has been through chemotherapy herself, so knowing how badly it affects your taste buds, she had prompted Howie to make the soups spicy. The tomato one especially nearly knocked my socks off. But Mand loved it, and coming so soon after her last chemo, was the ideal meal. We had the other soup today. Howie you beauty!

Sunday 3 October 2010
I took Mandy to the local cinema tonight to see a live transmission of the Les Miserables 25th anniversary concert from the O2 Arena in London. Mandy still looks really tired and pale, and I was struggling myself, but Les Mis has come to mean so much to us that Mandy was adamant we were going. In normal circumstances I would have tried to get Mandy tickets to attend the O2 show itself, or one of the other two live shows being performed simultaneously in London's West End, but this live screening was a good substitute. She cried, as she always does at Les Mis, and we were both pretty tired by the time we got back home, but she loved it. I really enjoyed it too, and even though it wasn't quite the same as being there live, I'm really pleased we were able to see it. So a successful night out and another little treat to keep Mandy smiling.

Wednesday 13 October 2010
Mandy and I popped along to church this morning. Father Colin does a short, 30-minute, mass on a Wednesday morning, followed by coffee and biscuits, which we've been to a number of times now. It's not too busy, which is great for me, and the dozen or so Wednesday regulars have been really welcoming. So much so that Mandy has been added to the prayer list whilst she's ill, and they are all taking a genuine interest in how she's getting on. I have to confess my concentration is so poor still

that, mentally, I often zone in and out when I'm there, and know few of the liturgies or prayers beyond the Lord's Prayer, but no-one seems to mind, and we both feel better for going. They are a lovely bunch there and seem genuinely concerned for our welfare.

We also got to talk to Colin about our renewals and he said he would be honoured to conduct the ceremony for us. In fact, he picked up the phone right there and then, and booked it all in with the parish office. It's still 18 months away but we're really looking forward to it, and are over the moon Colin will be part of it after being so supportive this year.

Tuesday 26 October 2010
Mandy had her first radiotherapy treatment today, narrowly avoiding her 42nd birthday. And just as our friend Olly had explained to her, it was very quick and easy. It took a little longer today as it was her first time, but normally she should be in and out in five minutes, which is great. It's just a shame that she has to travel to Oxford every weekday for a month to receive this five-minute treatment. I guess it evens out though: the hospital where Mand had her chemo was only ten minutes away from us, and whilst the number of radio treatments is significantly more, of the two I'm so glad the chemo was the local one.

As luck would have it, Marion, an old friend of ours, insisted on driving us today, as she knows the journey and the hospital very well. That proved a massive help, as not only did we have reliable transport there for the first (longer) appointment, but it removed any navigational-related stress too. In actual fact, due to my health (and therefore driving limitations), not only have we managed to compile a short list of similarly-minded lovely people willing to help out if necessary, but BUPA have said they will pay for a taxi each day. I was initially very sceptical about the latter, given that this could prove very costly for them, but Mandy says they initially offered her a daily Ambulance! Anyway she's got it all in writing, and we've booked a taxi for the rest of the week, so I guess we'll find out.

Monday 9 November 2010
Ten lots of radio completed now, which means Mandy's halfway through and very much on the homeward stretch treatment-wise. She's really feeling tired again, but that didn't stop her letting me take her to lunch down the road at Sue and Lino's to celebrate. Interestingly, she mentioned how tired she is feeling to the radiotherapy nurse on

Thursday, and after stepping away to count how many sessions she had now had, he came back and said "yep, you've had eight sessions, that's bang on where it gets you". So hey, at least it's normal.

The treatment itself isn't too bad, Mandy says, it's just the tiredness it causes – not helped of course by an hour each way journey on the crappy Oxford road, which feels like it is getting longer and longer. But Alan, our brilliant taxi driver, is like a daily ray of sunshine, and especially on the occasions when I've been too unwell to go to Oxford with Mandy, he's kept her smiling and positive, which helps a lot. Also, having had two weeks of quite erratic appointment times for her radio, the remainder of her appointments are all at 11am, so things should now settle down into a routine. That means Alan will pick us up at 9.30am every morning and we'll be back home and resting just after midday, which is good as Mandy is now visibly wilting more each day.

Monday 15 November 2010
Another radio treatment completed today which means Mandy has just five left to go now. And thanks possibly to the two day break from treatment over the weekend, Mandy seemed to get a second wind today. On the trip there especially, we had a really good laugh and joke with Alan our driver, and between us we even managed to come up with all the answers to our daily pop quiz on the radio. He really has been brilliant, Alan, a real help. We'll never forget how much he has helped keep Mandy's spirits up during the long trips to Oxford and back. Whilst the lengthy hours he works might make it tricky, I really hope we stay in touch once Mandy's treatment is complete.

Today Alan was asking about when and where we got married, and so we shared with him the whole Mandy winning the Bride of the Year story. To be honest, whilst we were incredibly fortunate with Mandy winning that, and we had an amazing day as a result, what we weren't so lucky with was the weather. It was appalling. As the lads and I drove down the M4 that day (my last night as a free man was spent at my Best Man Andy's house), the clouds just got darker and darker. And then it started to rain. Biblically. And it didn't stop all day. Actually, it did stop briefly, and the sun even came out for 30 minutes, which was lucky as it was just as we were having the photos taken. But it was a lovely wedding at our local parish church, and Mandy looked jaw-droppingly gorgeous.

My Uncle Ray had kindly brought his vintage Mercedes down from Colchester, and along with another beautiful old car provided for us as part of the Bride of the Year prize, delivered Mand, her bridesmaids and her mum to the church in some style. The lads and I were, of course, already inside by then, looking a little worse for wear having got soaked whilst seeking some pre-wedding Dutch courage at a local pub during the heaviest of the rain. But all the key parties turned up, we both said "I do" in the right places, and although in the photos my hair very clearly reflects the drenching I got from the rain, it was great. My memory of the day does start to get a little hazy from the point we moved onto a local hotel for both the afternoon and evening receptions - as my nervousness over my speech saw me consume even more Dutch courage - but our wedding video suggests we, and everyone else present, had a fantastic time.

By this time, I was pretty sure Alan had wished he had never asked about our wedding, but it was a nice chance to reminisce about a lovely, lovely day. Alan did chuckle however when I explained that, due to the sheer terror I had felt at the prospect of my groom's speech, I wasn't able to eat any of my meal at our wedding reception. He chuckled even more when Mandy offered her alternative view that nerves were nothing to do with it, it was just all the Dutch courage I had drank. Either way, we returned to the same hotel for our first anniversary, and they kindly arranged the exact same menu for us, so I got to eat it after all. We enjoyed it so much we did intend to return there every year, with Best Man Andy, and girlfriend Gwen. However, with them having long-since emigrated to Australia, and (newly lactose-intolerant) Mandy now having more complicated dietary requirements than a vegetarian polar bear, it's never quite happened.

Thursday 25 November 2010
Mandy had her last radio session on Monday, hurray. That means, aside from the Tamoxifen tablets which she will need to take every day for five (possibly ten) years, her treatment is hopefully at an end. She'll shortly have a scan to ensure everything is hunky dory but, please God, that's the end of it. Mandy is walking around with a huge smile on her face and has already ordered most of the contents of the Next Directory, as she revamps her work wardrobe in readiness for getting back to normal. In fact "normal" is a word she has been using more and more. It's not that we have an exciting life normally, or that she particularly loves her job, I think it's just that at times this year normality has seemed a million

miles away, and regaining it will be the surest sign that the cancer is behind her.

After the unpleasant experience of the Cold Cap, I'm pleased to say Mand's hair still looks okay too, thanks in part to her continuing use of her trend-setting head scarves. She looks incredibly good considering what she has been through, and even the fact that she effectively has a "comb over" before me hasn't dampened her spirits. And now it's all slowly growing back, there's even talk of her getting a trendy new "pixie cut" hair-do in the New Year. It will only be an interim style I'm sure, as Mand has always worn her hair long, just as her dad always liked it, but it's good to see her thinking about such things, and a clear sign she is slowly regaining her confidence.

So Operation Fatten up Mandy is back in full swing, and hopefully it won't result in the collateral damage of me acquiring a spare tyre, as it did earlier in the year. We also have a month of rest and recovery until we have the normal Christmas Mandy is adamant she will put on for our parents and me. But we'll see. Given that Mandy steadfastly refuses to eat out this Christmas, I'm secretly hoping our siblings will invite the parents to theirs for a change. But as I say, it's getting back to normal that Mandy wants more than anything, and Christmas Day here with our parents has become the tradition, so I'll abide with her thoughts on the matter. It would be nice to have everyone there, so we can celebrate both Christmas and the end of Mandy's treatment, together. At the very least though, I will just urge Mandy to implement a few short cuts to ensure a smaller, simpler Christmas this year.

Saturday 4 December 2010
Last night, Mandy went on her team's Christmas outing to London, and although she has been asleep most of today as a result, she had a really good time. Transport there and back was provided in the shape of Mand's boss Ann's people carrier, and the outing only stretched to a meal and a show, but she's chuffed to bits at having felt strong enough to go. If the show they were seeing hadn't been her favourite (Les Mis, obviously), and the girls at work insisting all year that they would keep Mandy's place for her right up until the last minute if necessary, I think she may have pulled out some time back. But the whole thing acted as a bit of an added incentive in the end, and kept her from overdoing things.

Mandy's also now on the daily Tamoxifen tablet and she says things are mostly okay so far. Because the tablet effectively stops the female hormone oestrogen being produced, it's likely she'll get side-effects. And that's already looking to be the case in that the hot flushes, which she started experiencing part way through the chemo, have now increased in both regularity and severity. But she's handling them fine, and although they mean her sleep is regularly interrupted by them, at a time when she is already shattered from the radio, her fatigue is slowly easing.

Monday 13 December 2010
We went for dinner at Mac and Michaela's at the weekend, and considering how knackered we both felt beforehand, we had a great time. We very nearly cancelled, as although Mandy is improving daily, I'm still really struggling as a result of accompanying Mandy on more of her trips to Oxford, for radio, than was wise. But I knew Mac and Michaela would understand if we didn't stay long and, actually, I think we both just needed to have a laugh after all the stress and worry. And as if reading my mind, Macca had invited his dad, Brian, along to provide the entertainment.

You see, Brian is the life and soul of any event and a genuinely funny man. He is a proud Glaswegian who loves to tell a few stories over a drink, and has that rare ability to hold court in just about any company. Macca and Michaela, bless them, have heard every story a hundred times before, and frequently tell him as much, but for us, just being able to sit there and listen to anecdote after anecdote was great. We were both too tired to offer much in the way of scintillating conversation (nothing new there then), but laughed so much my head hurt. Macca knows from old to just sit back and let his dad get on with it, but Michaela, who as usual was taking the brunt of Brian's humour, gave him it back in spades. Their mock love/hate relationship makes for quite the double act, and had Mandy practically wetting herself. It was only a few hours, but it was just what we needed. Laughter really is the best medicine.

Tuesday 4 January 2011
Mandy went back to work today, albeit on a part-time basis. She's only doing two days this week and then three days next, but I'm not sure she's ready as she still gets tired really easily. She had felt a little pressure from her employer to go back quickly, but I think it's more to do with this "normality" thing, and her wish just to get back to how things were before she was ill. I urged her to be cautious but so far the

advice I was given right at the beginning of all this to "do what Mandy wants, when she wants to do it" has stood me in good stead, so I'll go along with it for now.

There is also the phenomenon known as "chemo-brain" to consider, which results in Mandy thinking slowly or incorrectly, which combined with my CFS ensuring similar traits in me, makes us quite the pair. However, this should improve, and as long as neither Mandy nor her employer expect too much too soon, it will hopefully be okay eventually.

Thursday 20 January 2011
Mandy and I went to see her oncologist, Dr Cole, today for her first follow-up appointment. It was all good news, due to Mandy's recent scans being clear and her steady recovery from the chemo and radio. In fact, Dr Cole explained that now she's on the mend, he and Dr Galea will only see Mandy alternately every six months, with a mammogram to take place annually. I think Mandy was initially hoping they would scan her more often than that, as a clear scan offers peace of mind. However, at the same time she wants to put the whole experience behind her if she can, and the more often she has a check-up, the more often she has to revisit the subject. I'm sure that's all natural, and in time her anxiety will settle down, but for now it's totally understandable, I think.

One other thing we discussed with Dr Cole is the ongoing effects of the chemo-brain, as not just Mandy but myself, and others too, have all noticed she's really forgetful. The way Mandy describes how she feels some days is not unlike the foggy feeling I get with the CFS, and she finds she's unable to think on her feet. But Dr Cole says it's all quite normal, so she's comforted by that and knows it will take her body some time to recover from what it's been through. Fortunately, between us we manage okay mostly. Although the irony of me, with my own (now legendary) short-term memory issues, pointing out to her when she's forgotten stuff, isn't lost on her. What a pair!

Friday 11 March 2011
Mandy and I jumped on the train to Bath today and had a lovely lunch at one of Jamie Oliver's Italian restaurants. The food and service was excellent and well worth the journey. We were only in Bath for a couple of hours, but having not been there for some years, Bath was a real treat in itself. Having grown up just down the road, I know it well, and Mand has always really enjoyed it there too.

While we were there, I had arranged to pop in and say hello to one of the people I had got to know on the cruise forum, a lady called Jacqui who works in Waitrose. It seemed silly not to, given we would be walking straight past her shop, and although I'm guessing it's always a little scary meeting someone you only know from the internet (and a small part of me wondered whether she might actually turn out to be a lorry driver called Nigel), I'm pleased we made the effort.

With me not knowing what she looked like, Jacqui had assured me that she was the tallest lady in the shop and so would be easy to spot. Well, after two circuits of the shop, the only tallish lady working there that I could see was very young and very blonde. Mand had obviously reached the same conclusion as she said to me "if that's her you are never going on that bloody internet again". Luckily for me, Jacqui was then pointed out to us as the lady just coming back from (i.e. hiding in) a store room, and whilst she turned out to be lovely, she wasn't quite as young or blond, so I was safe. Anyway, we had a brief chat and a chuckle with Jacqui, and it was nice to put a face to a name and establish that she isn't in fact the supermarket-based ~~cereal~~ serial killer that others on the forum would have me believe. All in all a really good day.

Monday 21 March 2011
Mandy is slowly getting back to her old self, and it's good to see. Her hair has grown to collar length now, and she's put a small amount of weight back on, both points which are making her feel less self-conscious, I think. There's still the occasional person who perhaps we've not seen for a while, who fails to recognise Mand, or is shocked when they do, but she's looking better every day.

Although the tiredness, and the hot flushes are still affecting her, Mandy's doing really well overall. This week she is increasing her working hours to a four-day week for the first time, as she is again feeling a little pressure from her employer to increase her hours. Also, they seem hell-bent on giving Mandy more work to do than she was able to do even when she was full-time and well. But she knows that she's not back to herself yet, and so she is trying to pace her gradual return to work according to what she feels she is able to do, rather than what anyone else wants her to do. We have a cruise coming up in a couple of weeks, so at least I can make sure she gets a much-needed breather.

Monday 29 March 2011
In recent months I have been reflecting on what Mandy has been through this last year, and just how incredibly well she has handled everything. I have also been thinking about how "small" her life has become due to <u>my</u> illness and <u>my</u> limitations. I want to try and change that. Life is just too short, and if there is one thing I have learnt this last year, it is that whatever our circumstances, we need to make the most of life. Sadly, that doesn't mean we can just down tools and start travelling the world, as neither health nor finances permit that. However, there are changes we can make for the better.

The first one is in respect of my illness, and although I'll never stop wanting to get back to full health, and therefore employment, it's time to accept that this may be as good as it gets. I know the level I can operate at without causing significant fluctuation in my symptoms, and it's okay: it's liveable. If staying at this level avoids the emotional and physical turmoil that it causes to not just me, but Mandy too, whenever I try to push consistently beyond it, then so be it. It's about having a better quality of life now rather than constantly striving to maybe have a better quality of life in the future.

The second change is ideally for both of us to try and live a little. As incredibly lucky as we are to have the cruises, there's another 50 weeks each year where, despite the difficulties the CFS presents, we need to try and do some of the things we want to do, and go to places we want to go. That won't happen overnight, and it's not going to happen just because I want it to. But by tempering my daily activity level, it should give me more energy for the events and moments in life that matter. Not always, obviously - distance, crowds, noise etc. remain major obstacles in themselves – but sometimes. And accepting the fact that yes, I will need to rest lots beforehand, and will feel rough afterwards.

Clearly, I could fall flat on my face or, who knows, even miraculously get better, but we have to try to change things. I refuse to let Mandy's life be as totally focused on me and the CFS, as it has been this last decade, even though I love her for it. Hopefully Mandy's breast cancer won't ever return, and there's a good chance it won't, but both of us need to live for the moment. It's not being morbid, or giving up on me getting better, and we're still young enough for our Bucket List of things to do before we die to only have one entry (i.e. Number 1, "Draw up a Bucket List"). It's just trying to live for today and not letting life pass us by.

Chapter 13 - The Little Ship with The Big Heart

Tuesday 12 April 2011
Well, to say there's been a lot of water under the bridge since we booked this cruise in autumn 2009 is an understatement. But that just makes us all the more grateful to be on board, especially as, back then, this cruise sold out in just 17 minutes. That was on account of this being the farewell voyage of P&O's much-loved Artemis, so we're pretty lucky to be here. And having loved our mini-cruise on Artemis in 2005, we're delighted to get a second chance to cruise on her, and also give Mandy a well-timed break, before this beautiful old ship is sold off.

It was a good start today, with a much quicker-than-normal journey down to Southampton, and us arriving so early we were handed boarding cards C. In fact, had we not needed to sit in the car for three minutes more at the car drop-off point than I personally thought necessary, I'm pretty sure we would have got a B card and boarded ten minutes earlier. But oh no, apparently it's unlucky to leave the car when Dido's singing "I will go down with this ship" on the radio. Fortunately, it wasn't busy, and we'll probably never see either the waiting luggage porter or the car valet lady again, so ongoing embarrassment was relatively contained.

Better still, "Arty's" final Southampton sailaway was accompanied by a bigger-than-normal quayside band and also fireworks, which were a nice touch, if not fully visible at 5pm. Even the passengers of Arcadia gave us a standing ovation as we sailed past her in the Ocean Terminal, with so many camera flashes going off on her balconies it almost looked like another firework display. Attending that sailaway and a bit of the party that followed, meant it was one hell of a rush to make first sitting dinner at 6.45pm, but we have a nice corner table with Richard and Joyce. We tagged on the end of that the first post-dinner show from the Headliners, before we turned in for my traditional embarkation day early night. I know, I'm just crazy me.

Wednesday 13 April 2011
First thing this morning there was a real sense of excitement around the ship because amazingly....wait for it....there was a "90% off all Artemis Merchandise" sale. It turned out to be absolutely mad, with people lined up three deep all the way around the Atrium, waiting for it to start. And then utter bedlam when it did. If you can picture the first 20 minutes of

Saving Private Ryan, it was a bit like that, only bloodier. Strange how a few towelling bathrobes at £2.50 a pop seem to bring out the worst in people. I did alright though; I picked up a casual jacket, a couple of t-shirts and a fractured rib all for under a fiver.

I've made a new friend already too. I was a little wary at first on account of the very bright designer shell suit he was wearing, but adversity brought us together when we were both on the receiving end of an elbow from the same lady at the sale. We must have both admitted defeat at that point as, with us both giving the other a "sod this for a game of soldiers" type shrug, I retired gracefully to the bar only for the unmistakeable sound of a shell suit to follow a minute later. And as our wives bravely carried on fighting the hordes to see who could get the last Artemis fridge magnet, we got talking and shared a couple of war stories from the massacre going on next door. He seemed a nice fella actually, and conveniently for me, his name is Russell which is easy to remember because, due to his shell suit, he does!

At lunch today we joined a table which included a couple who each had one of those "walkie-talkies" for keeping in touch around the ship. Turns out they have two kids in their late-teens on board, and it enables them to keep tabs on them. It seemed to me that every other word transmitted on them got lost in the interference the things tend to experience. Also, it seemed a bit rude to leave them turned on during a meal, and some of those at our table clearly found the strange noises annoying as there was a bit of an atmosphere. At one point I joked "if I'd wanted crackling for lunch I'd have ordered the pork". It fell as flat as a pancake, not a glimmer of a smile from anyone. Then out of nowhere, their teenage daughter nearly had me spitting my lunch across the table, when in response to her dad saying into his walkie-talkie "You should be here with us, we agreed we would have meal times together, over", her very clear and considered reply was:

"Whatever ….. over". It was Priceless!

Aside from that, it was a quiet first day at sea today, and then another great dinner in the restaurant. The dress code was semi-formal which was well adhered to, as you would expect in a ship full of P&O devotees. All the gents I saw had a jacket or blazer on (most with ties) and the ladies looking very glam too. It's funny though, watching different people's attitude to dress. Two fellas got into our lift on the way to dinner and one was trying to convince the other to accompany him back to his cabin and borrow a tie off of him. But the tie-less one suggested his friend should "stick your tie where the sun don't shine". I very nearly pointed out that actually, there are no inside cabins on Artemis, but on reflection, I'm not sure that's what he was referring to.

Dinner was excellent, as I say, and even the newly dairy-intolerant Mandy (a result of her recent medical treatment) has loved every single course so far. What was even better was that a lady at the next table came over and told Mandy she looked beautiful, and reminded her of her granddaughter who is a professional model. I could have kissed her, what a lovely thing to say; it made Mandy's night and gave her a timely jolt of confidence.

Thursday 14 April 2011
It was a nice sunny day today so everyone took to the sun decks en masse. And together with a barbeque on deck at lunchtime, it's feeling like summer already. I did my usual, and intermittently left Mandy to her sun worship to avoid me uttering the "Mand, I'm bored" whine that generally results in her latest paperback hitting me across the head at speed. But that was fine, and it's not like Mandy spent a huge amount of time out on deck, as she has to limit direct exposure to the sun following her radiotherapy.

At one point I went off to a really interesting talk on the Titanic by another new friend, Ken Vard (a fellow insomniac who seems to be the only other person awake at 5am), but ironically, I fell asleep for the last 15 minutes – anyone know how the Titanic story ends? It's actually the 99-year anniversary of Titanic today, so a perfectly timed talk in every respect, except for my requirement for sleep. I did apologise to Ken at the end and promised to make his re-running of the same talk later in the cruise.

Mandy's daily shopping 'fix' was met by the jewellery sale in the Atrium. The usual fare, from what I could tell, and Mand wasn't tempted (which has got to be a first), but she did say the poor shop lady's patience was wearing very thin, based on the sheer number of passengers who were asking "Is it still 90% off?" Bless her, Mand said she had only been open half an hour and she was already gritting her teeth.

Then, early evening, we had the Welcome Aboard Gala Night. As usual I'm afraid I was still asleep in the cabin when the captain's reception side of things kicked off at around 6pm. But I can say that the formal dress code was observed impeccably, and even Shell-Suit Russell looked especially smart, which was a relief as I've now seen him in three different designer shell suits in as many days. He's a really nice bloke, and very funny, so he's alright in my book, even if his dress sense does generate some odd looks from other passengers.

Saturday 16 April 2011
Well, after a brief visit to the duty-free shops of Gibraltar yesterday morning, the clouds cleared to give us a lovely sunny afternoon, and a rip-roaring send-off of a sailaway party. The party was great actually, if a little loud (I guess one man's loud is another man's "rocking dude"), and all the crucial ingredients were there - sunshine, cocktails, "Tragedy" by Steps, and a small pale guy doing lengths in the pool (oh come on, it was the first time I had seen it empty!). The Americans next door on the Holland America ship just watched open mouthed as the their noisy cousins sang along to all four British national anthems – Danny Boy, 10,000 miles, Delilah and Summer Holiday. It was good fun.

The other highlight of yesterday was last night's show, where four gorgeous young ladies called the Pavao String Quartet, produced an hour of the most beautiful music. They were fantastic. In fact they were so good Mandy says they've inspired her to once again pick up the violin she last played as a child - which could be tough, as I suspect it's rotting away in her mum's attic alongside her Charlie's Angels annuals and her "I hate boys, they smell" t-shirt. I was inspired by the string quartet ladies too, but for me it was the sudden inspiration to become a Mormon in order that I may propose to all four of them.

We are in Alicante today and there is some kind of boat race going on. We were able to view some of it at quite close quarters, from a window seat at the top of the Atrium. Indeed, at one point some of the Spanish royal family and a bunch of very senior looking naval officers cruised right past us on a Spanish Navy frigate thing - I mouthed an exaggerated "hola" through the window at a few perceived royals, but to be honest I could have tripped over them in the playa and not known them from Columbus.

Later, after a breezy stroll along the seafront before returning to the ship for a rest, I was stopped and asked if I was Dennis The Menace. Now, as tired as I was, my head told me that the fella asking had to be doing so for one of two reasons; either he knows me from the cruise forum or - and this was slightly more worrying - he is working as security for the Pavao String Quartet, and they had come up with that nickname following the multiple proposals of marriage I had dropped off at the reception desk earlier. Luckily for me it was the former, which still begged the question how he recognised me, but then I have been making occasional visits to the Cyber Lounge where the computers are, to post on the forum. And Ray, as my new friend and fellow passenger introduced himself, confirmed that was exactly how he guessed. Fame at last.

Anyway off to dinner now, and based on the quick look I had at the menu earlier, I think it'll be mussels, tiger prawns and monkfish for me tonight. I'll be growing gills at this rate. I know, too much seafood, but what's a fella to do when it all sounds so nice?

Sunday 17 April 2011
When I got in the lift a moment ago I got mistaken for a dancer. It's shallow I know, but I'm really chuffed with that, despite the obviously failing eyesight of the lady concerned. In fact, now I'm in my early 40s and more wobbly and wrinkly than I've ever been previously, it's really made my day. It also means I can finally take off the leotard and leg warmers I've been wearing all week. Anyway, it's Palma today and the weather is looking great, so following a nice lie-in this morning, we're now thinking about having a stroll in the sunshine.

Oh, and I ran into the dad from the walkie-talkie family earlier, and as with every other time I've seen him, he was taking the whole walkie-talkie thing very seriously. He was very animated, and repeating the same phrase again and again at increasing volume, attempting to be understood. Credit where credit is due though, he knows all the radio lingo and appears to have the whole family unit organised to the point that they could very easily mount a co-ordinated assault on the buffet at a moment's notice. Don't know what his name is, but in my head he's a "Roger" because he says "Roger" a lot......over!

Monday 18 April 2011
Yesterday in Palma was the best day of the cruise so far. We were only planning a stroll around the cathedral area, but almost immediately we

jumped in a horse-drawn carriage, which was a really nice start. When we subsequently wandered along to the cathedral there was a massive "everyone welcome" service going on for Palm Sunday. We were immediately beckoned in by two ladies stood at the door, handed a palm leaf each and quietly guided to seats at the back. It was an absolutely beautiful service and I'm pleased we stumbled across it.

Leaving the cathedral, we next sat and listened to a street performer who played classical Spanish guitar. He was outstanding, so we bought one of his CDs. Luckily for us his English was good, as I didn't fancy having to hum The Godfather theme tune he had been playing earlier to find out which of his CDs that was on.

After that it was back on board for some lunch, which included an Asian Platter to start, which was so nice that on the suggestion of our waiter (honest!) I had a second one. I hugged him on the way out. All the waiters we have had have been great actually, many of them in very good moods because, as you would expect on a farewell cruise, most of them go home at the end too.

In the evening, after a number of us couldn't get in the first show, we were fortunate to get seats for the second of the very popular Tom O'Connor shows. It was very good. He's a really funny man and still has really sharp delivery. And it was great to finally see a comedian on a cruise ship that doesn't roll out Mother-in-Law jokes all night. Apparently he's just flown to Sydney and back twice within a week, so given he must be knackered, he was amazing.

So all in all, a really nice day yesterday, and as it was hot and sweaty around the Balearics yesterday, we even managed a couple of hours by the pool in the afternoon.

Tuesday 19 April 2011
Breakfast this morning didn't half prove hard work, when we sat down with a very nice, but hard-of-hearing, couple with really posh accents. Chuck into the mix a waiter whose own accent was very Indian, and me, with a strong West Country accent having to step in to translate, and I was soon wishing we had just had room service in the cabin. Before you judge me too harshly, please bear in mind the following "juice" discussion is just one example of many over the course of a very, very long hour:

Posh Lady : *What jice do you haarve?*

Waiter : *Ice Madam? We have cold ice Madam.*

Posh Lady : *What jice?*

Waiter : *Cold ice Madam.*

Posh Man : *Cold eyes, who's got cold eyes?*

Waiter : *No, cold ice sir, your wife wants cold ice.*

Posh Man : *Ice, this time of the day, are you mad?*

Posh Lady : *Orange, do you haarve orange?*

Waiter : *Orange and grapefruit segments Madam?*

Posh Lady : *sorry, what jice was that?*

Me to waiter : *I think you'll find, my lover, that the lady is sayin' she do want some of that there oringe joose.*

Waiter : *Ah, I see, I'm very sorry Madam, I didn't understand. You would like some orange juice?*

Posh Lady to me : *What's he saying, what was that?*

Me : *He says he be getting some of that there oringe joose for you Misses.*

Posh Lady : *Oh good, why is it taking so long?*

Me : *Please God take me now.*

Waiter : *And do you still want ice with that Madam?*

Me : *humpff* (muffled whimper as I stick a fork in my thigh).

Anyway, it was another formal night last night and a number of gents wore the white jackets, which I'm personally not a fan of. It's just that they remind me of the blokes who worked in 1950s American ice-cream parlours, and some take offence it you repeatedly ask them for two 99s and a Magnum. There again, it might just be that, being as pasty as I am, if I was to wear one you wouldn't be able to tell where the jacket stopped and I began.

I was pleased with myself as I wore a proper bow tie for the first time ever, but boy, tying one of those is a complicated business, isn't it? However, as well as being more comfortable to wear, I was able to loosen it when I got hot late on, so that the bow tie hung around my neck in that cool way that only self-tie bow ties can. In fact, when I later caught my reflection in the mirror behind the bar, I fully expected to see James Bond looking back at me. Sadly I looked more like Odd Job. But that's okay because, based on her normal drinking-to-toileting ratio, Mandy's not so much Miss Moneypenny as Miss Spendapenny.

We're in Sorrento today and our cabin was literally shaking at 6.45am this morning. It meant that the rather pleasant dream I was having about Kylie Minogue ended rather abruptly, which is a shame as by my reckoning I had been doing rather well up until then. As I awoke fully from my slumber, I realised the origin of the shaking was just the tender boat outside of our cabin being lowered, and that the repeated shouts of "more" were not from Kylie at all, but just the crew indicating how much lower the tender had to go before splash down. Anyway, having now breakfasted and showered, our tender number to go ashore is due to be called next so I must go.

Wednesday 20 April 2011
Yesterday, Sorrento was as beautiful as we thought it would be, although in my mind's eye I had pictured it a little sleepier. The tenders dropped us at a quiet little port area, but once (via shuttle bus) at the top of the cliff in the town centre, it was hustle and bustle a-plenty, almost city like. The town itself is formed around a busy central piazza lined by open-fronted cafés which (aside from the traffic, parked cars and mopeds) is really nice. It must have been even better in decades gone by before the advent of all those motor vehicles.

Of course that didn't stop us jumping on one of said vehicles as we grabbed the final carriage on one of those little tourist "trains" to see a bit more of Sorrento. Despite the fact that we were followed around some very tight bends so closely by the bus behind us that I could see what the bus driver had had for breakfast, it was an enjoyable ride. But we certainly saw a lot of Sorrento, we really liked it. As Captain David Perkins said during his announcement this morning (he had never sailed into Sorrento before either), it looks spectacular from the bay. Viewed from the sea, Sorrento just grows out of the rock face with the most beautiful plants and flowers, and the grandest of hotels and houses, just seemingly draped across the cliff side.

When we got back on board the weather was still great so we relaxed on the Sun Deck for a while and read our books. I'm reading one about Artemis herself actually, co-written by a lady (Sharon Poole) that I know from the cruise forum, and it is very informative. Did you know for example, that Artemis in her previous guise was one of three ships on which they filmed The Love Boat? Or that Arty, or Royal Princess as she was called then, was launched by Princess Di on her very first solo-engagement. And that she was once Cary Grant's favourite ship? The book has the photos to prove all of that and more.

Thursday 21 April 2011
A good day in Rome yesterday. Not only did my intended day of spoiling Mandy rotten nearly go completely to plan, but we didn't get lost once and the temperature was warm and sunny without it being uncomfortably so. Having been to Rome a few times now, my plan was to do something different, firstly by taking Mandy to the Villa Borghese for a stroll around the park and a rowboat around the lake. Then I hoped to take her to lunch and see the supposedly incredible views over the city, at the nearby Hotel Eden, before a slow stroll back to St Peter's via a couple of our favourite sights. And it nearly worked perfectly.

On joining our coach it became clear where Nancy Dell'Olio has been since being dumped by Sven Goran Eriksen a few years back. She was our guide. This lady literally didn't stop speaking from the point we got on the coach until she left us at the drop-off point in Rome. Now admittedly she's there to give some pointers for our "on your own" trip, but ye gods she went on - to the point where there was even talk amongst the passengers of us bribing the driver to break the microphone for the trip back. Her pronunciation wasn't the greatest either with regular references to the importance of "poop", to which I nodded enthusiastically having myself just taken on board extra roughage over breakfast. The penny eventually dropped when she said she had personally seen "poop" at the windows many times - "Oh, Pope" said the coach in unison.

Anyway, after the whole coach embraced their release from Nancy with some delight, Mandy and I headed for the Villa Borghese, the park up above the Spanish Steps. Sadly, although beautiful the park is having a lot of very noisy work carried out at the moment, so after sitting for a while in one of the quieter spots, we cut our visit short and walked down the road to Hotel Eden. Now Hotel Eden is a real gem. It's a five-star hotel and reminded us a lot of the Beverly Wilshire in Los Angeles/Pretty Woman, but with the added benefit of its rooftop restaurant and bar having terrific panoramic views overlooking all of Rome's seven hills. As we got there a little earlier than anticipated, and had had a hearty breakfast only relatively recently, we settled for a pot of tea each in the Garden Bar, with a great view all the way back to St Peter's. The teas came in at nine Euros a pop, and if you wanted a light lunch, then a Club Sandwich or Cesar Salad is about 25 Euros, but it's worth the expense I think, a real find.

It must have been about 1pm when we left Hotel Eden in the end, so we took a slow stroll down to the Trevi Fountain, which was really quiet and we took a few more "us at the Trevi" type photos. Mandy bless her, nearly came a cropper on some loose cobbles, which caused her to utter the immortal words "bloody Romans, didn't they build anything to last". She was joking obviously (?), but I took that as a sign it was perhaps time to eat after all. And so after another short stroll we were seated at one of the restaurants lining the Piazza Navona, having lunch and doing some serious people watching at a table perfect for both.

Mandy was as happy as a happy thing from Happysville by this time, especially when I found her some dairy-free Gelato ice cream a little further around the piazza. True, she wasn't quite as enthusiastic when, due to her choice of flavour, some clown launched into a chorus of "Mango Italiano (hey mango)", but to be fair, the song was a bit too big for me! Even the ice cream seller looked at me with a certain wariness, although in his defence, he was still a little stunned from my attempts to communicate dairy-free to him by "moo"ing at him and simultaneously signalling the severing of my jugular in the (surely?) universal sign for "no".

Anyway, by this time our day of exploring (and regular stops to recharge) was coming to an end, so we headed back to meet up with Nancy and the others. Although there were a few latecomers (there's always a couple isn't there?), this gave the rest of us a chance to coordinate our efforts into working out how to keep Nancy quiet on the way back to the ship. Cunningly, the chosen method of attack was for us all to pretend to be asleep within minutes of leaving Rome, so that faced with a sea of closed eyelids, Nancy would take the hint. And it worked. Although in my case there wasn't much pretending going on.

So another great day and I was chuffed that it went mostly to plan, as Rome is one of Mandy's two favourite cities. She was over the moon too, if completely knackered, so mission accomplished, even if it meant that it was straight back to the cabin after dinner for an early night and some much-needed rest.

Today we're in Monte Carlo, home to the mega rich. And talking of wealth, do you know, Mandy has always said to me that she wanted to be in Monaco and living tax-free before she reached the age of 50. Well, thanks to today's port of call, and the Cash ISA I arranged for her a couple of weeks back, I've made all her dreams come true with a good few years to spare.

Friday 22 April 2011
I've just popped in here to the Cyber Study for a bit of peace and quiet, while the rest of our group are finishing the Musicals quiz in Tiffany's. I know it's Easter, but one of the entertainment officers has just absolutely crucified the song "Summertime". She's a nice lady, and the dodgy microphone didn't help, but I'll never be able to listen to that song again without it bringing tears to my eyes. *"And the living is easy"*? The blessed release of death seemed like a whole better idea, I can tell you. So I thought I would come in here and do a quick update on yesterday.

So, yesterday we breakfasted in Monte Carlo, don't you know. Well actually, we had breakfast in Artemis' Coral Dining Room, but in a window table overlooking Monte Carlo harbour. And for a while there we nearly didn't make it any further, due to a serious swell preventing the tender boats from operating. However, Captain Perkins gave the tenders the go ahead from about 10am, and we had a really enjoyable couple of hours ashore.

After all that walking in Rome the previous day, we initially opted to explore on four wheels. Yes, this morning I thought I had died and gone to heaven, as I got to drive around the Monaco Grand Prix circuit. We hired, for an amazing 15 Euros for one hour, one of those electric smart-car things. It was brilliant. I knew the street circuit fairly well anyway, being an avid Formula 1 fan, and easily got three laps in (would have been four but Mandy needs to perfect her tyre changing) before needing to stop for a rest.

I'm not sure my car racing was quite the level of relaxation Mandy had anticipated on her holiday, as she seemed very concerned about our speed, pedestrians and a whole string of other vehicles. It's also true that as an electric car, I had to provide my own sound effects, but no biggy: "brummin" and "screeching" are my forte, and I could tell the locals were impressed. Someone even said I drove a little like a young Ayrton Senna, although, actually, maybe that was me. Doesn't matter, the main thing is someone said it! It was absolutely brilliant, and a lifetime's ambition achieved. It might have only been 15-30 kph, but in that tiny little thing it felt more like 120.

Next, having utterly terrified Mandy and probably everyone else in Monte Carlo, I suggested we chill out in the area around the Casino and Hotel De Paris. We basically just kicked back and people (and seriously nice car) watched over a glass of wine in the Café De Paris. We were joined by some friends from the ship, Michael and Nina, who were just wandering past until we led them astray. But with the great sunny weather continuing again today, and a perfectly located table in one of the world's most iconic spots, it was perfect for a few drinks and a chat.

Coming back to the ship, the tenders proved a little dicey as the swell had got a lot worse. The nose of our particular tender dipped under the waterline at one stage, so much so that the windscreen started to resemble one of those glass-bottom boats. I'm sure I saw a fish swim past the cockpit at one stage. Great fun though, and everyone seemed to enjoy it (ish).

Petula Clark provided the entertainment last night, and fair play, two 'capacity crowd' shows of 70 minutes or so, which for a lady of 78 is pretty good going. Being a relative youngster, I didn't know many of the songs, except for Downtown and Couldn't Live Without Your Love, but I promised my dad I would go along (still trying for that autograph, Dad) and Petula still looks absolutely lovely.

Anyway that's it for now, I suppose I best get back to this quiz, and, literally, face the music.

Saturday 23 April 2011

Good news and bad news in rainy Barcelona yesterday. On the good side, a little Spanish girl taught me two new Spanish (possibly Catalan) words – "Splishy" and "Sploshy" - shortly before sending the contents of a very muddy puddle in the direction of my beige-coloured trousers. On the downside, Arty's last ever sailaway party had to be moved into the Horizon Lounge, as the rain just wasn't going to ease off.

Actually, energy-wise I was struggling a bit so wasn't planning to go to the sailaway party anyway, but Mandy insisted on dragging me up La Rambla like a reluctant puppy to the vets (i.e. arse flat to floor, legs stretched out horizontally in front). She tried to bribe me by saying she would buy me a Barcelona football shirt, but I know her game, she just wanted me to have the name "Messi" on my back to forewarn potential dining companions of my eating habits.

She deserves some fun though, so as much as I despise shopping, I tried to be enthusiastic and join in. I accompanied her to one shop called "Jesus" (pronounced "Hey Zeus" in these parts), but it turned out the Jesus with his name above the shop was actually an overweight chain-smoker with a roving eye for the ladies, so I'm pretty sure he wasn't the son of God. Then, in another shop I pointed out to Mandy one particular dress as being "nice", but Mand just rolled her eyes and said the (admittedly petite) item concerned would "barely qualify as a bloody undergarment". To be honest, whilst I was keen to assist, I was now gradually losing the will to live, so took a vow of silence from there on in, revoked only at the end of our little expedition, when she went in not one, but two of those big El Corte de Julio Inglesias shops. Hey Zeus woman, have a heart!

Fortunately I later recovered sufficiently to attend my first-ever cruise forum meet up. I missed an earlier one due to it being held on the day after embarkation, when I was pretty knackered. But Fiona, who organised both that one and today's meet, recognised me in the Cyber Study the other day, and invited me along. And although I didn't recognise many of the names from the forum, they seemed a nice bunch, and I also learned a little forum-related gossip, so I'm glad I went along. So a good day, and we now have three very welcome sea days before home.

Sunday 24 April 2011

It's 4am, I can't sleep, and none of my fellow insomniacs are around to play with. So I thought I would take a few photos while no-one is around. Trouble is it's very choppy indeed and many of the photos (in slow shutter/night mode) are coming out blurred. So instead, I'll do an update on yesterday's events.

A relaxing day at sea yesterday. A little breezy at times but really warm if you sat in the right places, and scarily, Mandy seems to have an (un)natural instinct for exactly that. As usual, when I wasn't dragging her along to the four visits a day to the restaurant that I am insisting on for the final days of the cruise, I left her to the sun-worshipping. It meant I was able to attend another one of Ken Vard's excellent presentations.

Ken's talk this time was about Artemis herself, and it was really interesting. Did you know for example, that Artemis, or Royal Princess as she was then, was the last cruise ship out of New York on the morning of the September 11 attacks? And just the previous day, many of her passengers had been in the twin towers, either up top on the observation deck or having lunch in the Windows On The World restaurant that has since featured in the many 9/11 documentaries. Ken's talk included lots of really interesting little snippets in fact, and it's clear he thinks a lot of old Arty. A really good talk.

Later, on our way to dinner I saw Roger Roger struggling to communicate, via the walkie-talkie, with his wife. I tapped him on the shoulder and pointed just 30 feet across the Atrium to where his wife stood having similar difficulties understanding him. He did then walk across the Atrium to her, as I thought he would, but not before twice saying into his radio, "it's okay, I can see you, I'm coming over, over." Go figure!

The Headliners show last night was Down the Old Dog & Duck (or something like that) which promised to be a "right old sing along, me old cock and sparra". We normally love anything Headliners-related, but beforehand we weren't sure about this one at all. In fact, we dillied and dallied, and dallied and dillied! As it turned out, we were right. The most up-to-date of the songs in the show had to be a good 30 years before I was even a spark in Ma and Pa's newly-installed central heating system. That said, most of the older passengers seemed to enjoy it, and it was funny in places.

Monday 25 April 2011
We've seen some really spectacular sea swells over the last 36 hours, which has been good to watch but it's made it tricky getting around. Amazingly it's much better this morning since we entered the Bay of Biscay (I know, how's that for irony?), and Captain Perkins has confirmed that we're due to arrive late back into Southampton tomorrow, as he opted to slow Arty down a bit to ensure everyone was comfortable. Not a big problem: it's a farewell cruise so it's not as if more cruise passengers are waiting to board the ship this time, and frankly, I'd like to stay on here as long as possible. The latest indication is we'll disembark in Southampton about five hours later than originally planned.

Earlier today I walked the length of the ship just behind the captain (not in a stalker way, just in a 'people to see, things to do at t'other end of ship from our present location' kind of way), and just in that short period, the poor man was subjected to two enquiries of "who's driving the ship?" and three lots of "it was a rough one yesterday Captain". Now I'm a tolerant(?) person, but even I was contemplating self-harm by that stage. How the captain puts up with that every day without pulling out a couple of skewers secured from the on-deck BBQ for such occasions, and sticking them in his eyes, I don't know.

Oh, and I was chatting to Roger Roger today and he said, in hindsight, he thinks the whole walkie-talkie thing simply gave his kids a whole new medium through which they could ignore him. He then asked me what I do when I lose Mandy around the ship - I said that's easy, I just start talking to a young, attractive female member of The Headliners, and as if by magic Mandy appears out of nowhere. It never fails!

Thursday 28 April 2011
Apologies for the delay since my last entry, Mandy managed to throw herself down the stairs on the last night of the cruise, so we've been a little bit busy sorting out her very swollen, plum-coloured ankle. We were on our way to dinner at the time, so it was classic Mandy, focusing solely on the food and forgetting she was wearing the kind of shoes most established circus performers would have trouble staying upright in. She was a bit shaky afterwards, but after dragging her way to the restaurant (multiple fractures wouldn't have kept her from her dinner), Roy, our wine steward, "nee-nar, nee-nar'd" his way through the tables with a stiff brandy in his hand, which was just the job.

In actual fact, our final dinner was well worth Mandy dragging herself along too. It was excellent, and was followed by a hugely well-deserved clappy and twirling-napkin reception for the chefs, on their restaurant walkthrough. Funnily enough all that napkin waving was perfect for Mandy, as the draught it caused saw off a particularly fierce hot flush. Our head waiter said, had he known, he would have arranged for the whole restaurant to do that on a nightly basis for her. Anyway, that brandy meant any pain from Mandy's ankle was quickly forgotten, and she was soon swaying away to the "We Are Sailing" finale to the show. Sadly, when it came to lugging the hand luggage around the next morning, she was about as much use as an ashtray on a moped, but at least she hurt her ankle at the end of the cruise rather than the start. And what a cruise it was, we had an amazing time on what was a massively important cruise for us, Mandy especially, after the horrible twelve months that proceeded it.

In terms of Artemis, it's true you don't have to look too hard to see how old she is. One of the junior officers told me that, on the bridge, there are nearly as many buttons that don't work as do, but somehow a mental picture of Scotty from Star Trek up on the bridge saying "I canna make her go any faster Captain" seems quite apt. She's still a beauty though, and although the continually repeated tag line "The Little Ship with the Big Heart" had already started to grate with me before we had even left Southampton (and once, memorably, the whole restaurant groaned good-naturedly at its use during a captain's announcement), again it seems kind of apt. It's sad to think we'll never cruise on her again, but I think Third Officer Paul Shepard summed up everyone's final thoughts very well in the Cruise Log when saying "Artemis, may you find your way without us".

Chapter 14 - An Emotional Rollercoaster

Tuesday 10 May 2011
It was Olly's funeral today. After seemingly being on the road to a full recovery, Olly had phoned us some months back to say his cancer had returned and that he had decided against further treatment. It was terrible news to hear, let alone tell, but Olly joked his way through that phone call, even as Mandy tried to disguise the obvious emotion she felt at the other end. We knew, therefore, that the end was near for Olly, but that doesn't ease the sadness at Olly dying in his early 40s. Life can be so unfair. With Olly having been treated for cancer at the same time as Mandy, and particularly with him having selflessly talked her through her own treatment, it just made his passing even harder to take.

Olly arranged his funeral as a celebration of the full and rewarding life he led. Indeed, after spending his entire working life at sea, and having cruised around the world more times than he could remember, he travelled further, and saw sights, than most of us would struggle to fit into a dozen lifetimes. It seemed apt therefore that Olly's coffin was carried into church to a live rendition of the Les Miserables song "Bring Him Home". Rest in peace Olly.

Friday 10 June 2011
Mandy returned to the hospital last week for a check-up to make sure her chemo and radio treatment hasn't left her with any ongoing problems. The main check was for lymphoedema, which is a swelling to the arms and legs, caused when someone's lymphatic system doesn't drain away fluid within the body like it should. Because of her cancer treatment and the removal of some of her lymph nodes, Mandy's lymph system is at greater risk than normal. However, the check-up confirmed that Mandy isn't showing any signs at all of lymphoedema, so all good.

Thursday 21 July 2011
I've recently been having a recurring nightmare about being trapped or suffocating. Is there some deep psychological reason for this, you ask? Do the dreams, for example, denote a subconscious fear of me being stifled by my CFS and the limitations it forces on me?? No, that's not the cause at all. It's actually down to Mandy and, on being partially awoken by a particularly strong hot flush, her suddenly throwing her half of the duvet off of her, and onto me. Or more specifically, such is the arc of her throwing arm, onto my head.

Not to worry though, it's only ten subsequent minutes of terror-driven nightmare before I awake in a panic, and my head surfaces gasping for breath, through a good foot and a half of piled-up duvet. Of course, by then a much cooler, post-flush Mandy has returned to a deep sleep completely unaware of her attempt on my life. Our two (by now meerkat-impersonating) cats, on the other hand, look daggers at me from their end of the bed, clearly unhappy at being awoken from their own slumbers and beseeching me to, if at all possible, suffocate a little more quietly please.

Mandy is actually doing really well. She still gets incredibly tired, and as you can tell, the hot flushes are not reducing in either strength or regularity, but both these points should improve with time. A few weeks ago I went along with her to a breast cancer "day" run by the local hospital where Mandy had her chemo. What was nice was that we got to see Pat and Rebecca again, Mandy's two chemo nurses. It was also a good and very informative day, covering such things as retaining bone health (use of Tamoxifen can mean the opposite), but I could tell Mandy didn't enjoy it. Her way of coping with having had breast cancer is to try and put the experience behind her, and so I'm not sure she'll want to attend such events in future, as they just bring it all back.

Monday 29 August 2011
At the weekend we held an afternoon tea for our friend Marion, who kindly took Mandy to some of her radio treatments in Oxford last year. Two other old friends, Lynn and Max, also joined us, and although Mandy had baked and sandwiched her heart out for them as a way of thanking them for all their help and support last year, the tea soon turned into more of a mini-celebration of Mandy's return to health. From the point they clinked their way into the house, due to the copious bottles of champagne and wine they brought with them, it was one long, boozy celebration. It was brilliant.

For my part, with Mandy having spent the previous 24 hours preparing everything, and then presenting it all beautifully on her newly-acquired Queen Anne bone china tea set, I was given the job of waiter. In practice - for cakes and sandwiches galore were already laid out - I just had to keep the tea cups and wine glasses topped up, a task for which Mandy handed me a pair of white silk gloves in the hope I would at least look the part. However, I'm pretty sure I failed to achieve the Downton Abbey look she was hoping for, especially when I later (rather sensibly in my opinion, given my propensity for spillage) added an apron to my ensemble, albeit one depicting the life-size torso of Michelangelo's David. Which, actually did the job splendidly, and wasn't anyway near as pornographic as it sounds, thanks to a carefully placed post-it note halfway down.

As I say, the afternoon was brilliant. The five of us first worked together 23 years ago, and so with us laughing and reminiscing our way through a whole table full of delicious home-made grub, not to mention numerous pots of tea and bottles of plonk, the afternoon just flew by. All too soon though, we were pouring the ladies into a taxi for their journey home, and unanimously concluding that we should make it an annual event. Marion, bless her, who enjoys afternoon teas everywhere from the Cotswolds to The Ritz, said that it was the best afternoon tea she had ever had. But then, like the Earl Grey, we were all bit stewed by then.

Saturday 15 October 2011
I met my newly-arrived great-niece Callie today, and I think it was probably a lot more monumental for me than it was for her. You see, as beautiful a bundle of joy as she is, and as pleased for my niece Jessica and her husband as I am, it's all a bit of a shock to the system. I mean, I'm a great-uncle! And as much as I have always tried to be a great uncle, I'm now a GREAT-uncle – i.e. the uncle equivalent of a grandfather!! At 42 !!! That hardly seems right.

Seriously though, it was lovely to meet Callie, and also see my mum and dad, the new great-grandparents, looking so happy and instantly falling in love with her. It was only a small gathering that my sister Caroline, had put together so that everyone could come and say hello and meet the new addition to the family. However, it meant it was uncrowded and not too noisy, so not only was Callie on best behaviour, but I was too. Even if I am still getting my head around this great-uncle thing.

Tuesday 15 November 2011
I phoned Father Colin today about the renewal of our vows, as things are getting a little complicated and I'm starting to feel a little anxious about it. You see, in the summer Colin had a big disagreement with the head priest for our parish, Father Derek, which caused Colin to move to another church about 60 miles away. That in itself wasn't a problem, as Colin assured us he would come back especially to do our renewal of vows ceremony in May. That was good to hear, as with Colin having

been so supportive last year Mand and I have wanted him to do it all along. The trouble is, it now appears that Colin never gained Father Derek's agreement to come back for the ceremony, and it seems Father Derek is now unwilling to permit this. As I say, it's getting complicated.

To try and resolve the problem, I had a chat with Father Derek and explained how our renewal of vows had come about, and why we wanted Father Colin to do the ceremony. Father Derek instantly agreed to let us go ahead, but asked for two things in return. Firstly, he wanted us to have as small a ceremony as possible, as he didn't want other parishioners to hear about him permitting Colin to return. Secondly, he wanted Colin to personally phone him and ask him for permission. That was frustrating to hear as we had planned to invite everyone who had helped us through a tough 2010. Also, his second point felt more like a point-scoring exercise which I wasn't even sure Colin would do. But as ridiculous as all that sounds, it would mean I could still give Mandy the ceremony she planned so carefully, so it was worth a try.

When I explained all this to Colin he said "no problem", he would phone Father Derek as he had requested. That's a huge relief, and although I think it's best to delay sending out the invites until I know for sure everything is okay, hopefully it will be fine. I don't know, it doesn't seem too much to ask to have our renewals at the church we got married in, and the ceremony conducted by our friend Father Colin, when us, the church and priest were all still in the same parish until very recently, but boy it had started to feel like we were asking for the earth.

Saturday 26 November 2011
Our old friend Charley took Mandy to Cabot Circus shopping centre in Bristol today, as a bit of a girlie day out, and they had a great time. I hate shopping (but don't mention it much!) so it was good that they got to spend a day, free of male company, just wandering from shop to shop. Add in breakfast at Carluccio's and lunch at Raymond Blanc's, and I think they both felt like they had thoroughly spoilt themselves. It was a well-timed shopping trip actually, as due to those severe hot flushes Mand is still having, she has found she's had to change much of her wardrobe in favour of loose fitting, and wide-necked, sleeveless tops. Easily removable layers help, but when she feels like she's ready to "blow" (which is often) cool and breathable clothing seems to be the best option. Please note however, Mandy doesn't sweat, she just "glows". Two completely different things, apparently!

Mandy says she's keen to put on some more weight having not fully regained that which she lost last year. I'm hoping therefore to get her out and eating at places, and with people, that will encourage her to overindulge. So today's outing with Charley, and their double stop off at celebrity chef owned restaurants, was well timed. Mand was totally knackered when she got home, mind you, and it's clear that she still gets tired really easily. However, we are using the unused holiday entitlement which she was permitted by her employer to carry forward from 2010, to give her regular rests, and that's been crucial now that she's back to working five days per week.

It means that I have to be very careful with how much I do, as I just can't afford to be too ill myself, and then have an already exhausted Mandy coming home to, effectively, be my carer. But that's okay; my normally constant need to be getting better has been well and truly parked for now. It's been a long time since I attempted to consistently push beyond that glass ceiling, and I feel better for it. It also continues to mean that I can be there for Mandy when she needs me, or at least not be the drain on her physical and emotional resources that I fear I and the CFS have been in the past.

Friday 16 December 2011
It's my birthday this weekend, so Mandy and I went to Bath today and had lunch in a great little place called the Firehouse Rotisserie. It was recommended by Jacqui, my friend from the cruise forum, and actually, as it turned out, she and hubby Ian ended up joining us, which was great. The house speciality, as the name suggests, is meat cooked on their rotisserie, and given it's nearly Christmas, they had a turkey option which was fantastic. I can definitely see us going there again.

It was nice to get to know Jacqui and Ian a little more too. We've met them a couple of times now, but normally it's just been for a quick coffee. I know from our time on the forum that we've all got a lot in common and a similar sense of humour, so unusually for me, I wasn't too nervous beforehand. It was great food, excellent company and a good start to my birthday weekend. Which is just as well, as other than a few friends and family popping in, we've deliberately kept the rest of the weekend quiet.

Friday 23 December 2011
I phoned Father Colin again today as it's all gone very quiet since we spoke last month. I also had a call from our local parish office last week

and they mentioned that they have Father Derek down to conduct our renewals ceremony. So, given we have been sitting on the invites for a while now (we had planned to send them out with the Christmas cards) and Mandy too is starting to stress over it, I phoned Colin to see how he had got on with speaking to Father Derek.

Colin was his normal jovial self initially, but as soon as I mentioned the renewal of vows ceremony, something in his tone changed. It turns out that Colin hadn't phoned Father Derek last month after all, but instead had written to him and received no reply. There seemed more to it than that though: it almost sounded from the way Colin was speaking that he no longer wanted to come back and conduct the ceremony. When he then used the phrase "I'm happy to do your renewal of vows but…" (and with the emphasis very much on "but") it confirmed it for me that he wasn't keen. It wasn't anything personal at all, just that due to the fall-out between him and Father Derek, he no longer felt comfortable returning for the ceremony. I can understand that, I just wish he had let us know much earlier.

So after talking it over with Mandy, we have decided to cancel our renewal of vows for now. It was always supposed to be a happy occasion and it has instead become a bit of a hassle. Ironically, given they are both men of god who preach the importance of forgiveness every day, Father Colin and Father Derek just don't seem to be able to forgive each other. With Mandy and I seemingly getting caught up in the periphery of their fall-out, it means our renewals ceremony feels less and less like the celebration it was intended to be. And do you know, now we have decided to cancel it, and we don't feel caught in the middle of a spat, it's quite a relief. Besides, we still have a brilliant cruise to Venice in May to look forward to, so trust me, we'll still be celebrating.

Monday 9 January 2012
We recently returned to see Dr Cole and the good news is Mandy is showing no signs of any further problems. She's also feeling a little bit sharper now, which is helping her at work particularly. But one year on from finishing her treatment, she still gets incredibly tired. Mand describes it as just a wave of exhaustion that comes over her, which combined with the hot flushes constantly interrupting her sleep at night, means she gets more tired the longer the week goes on. It's something she's trying to get used to, and rarely complains, but it means her weekends are largely spent recovering.

Dr Cole explained that it is very much the continuing side-effects of the Tamoxifen which is giving Mandy very strong menopausal-like symptoms. He said these usually settle down over time, but the general rule of thumb is that the further away a patient is from a natural menopause, then the more severe such symptoms can be. That certainly seems to hold true as the relatively young Mandy is having hot flushes so frequent, and so severe, that she's been our main source of heating this winter. But it's a small price to pay in the overall scheme of things, so she'll put up with it, she says.

One thing we do need to think about, due to those ongoing side-effects, is possibly reducing Mandy's hours at work. Last year she was able to take lots of extra rests, due to that extra holiday entitlement she was permitted to carry forward. However, this year that situation reverts to normal and so she could really struggle. Dr Cole says he will happily support us in any such request to Mandy's employer, and so despite the obvious financial implications, I think a three-day weekend would really help her. Not just with the side-effects of the Tamoxifen, but also the chemo-brain which still impacts even now. Definitely something to consider.

Tuesday 10 January 2012
I've been reflecting on us cancelling our renewal of vows, and whilst I think it was the right thing to do, I've got a couple of ideas on how I can still make our 15th wedding anniversary extra special for Mandy. With a couple of really nice surprises, and the cruise to Venice we have booked aboard Arcadia, I'm sure she will have a fantastic time.

Mand and I did recently discuss if we should instead renew our vows on board Arcadia, but whilst Richard and Joyce will be there, our (non-cruising) parents wouldn't be. We also wondered if we should take up the offer of Father Colin's replacement, the lovely Father David, to conduct the ceremony before we go, but Colin was, and hopefully still is a friend and so it wouldn't feel right to just replace him like that. No, the more we think about it, it was the right decision to cancel. In our eyes, it was the celebration element that was key and we can still do that, and at the same time thank those people who have helped us through a difficult time, by meeting up in smaller groups over a few drinks, or some nice scoff. Which let's face it, with my aversion to group situations, will help me no end.

Tuesday 24 January 2012
I spoke to a lady called Sam at the local hospice today to see if I could help them on a casual basis, whereby if I was too ill to come in at certain times it wouldn't cause them any problems. It's not that I'm suddenly doing any better health-wise or want to push my luck, but more that I'm trying to accept that this may be as good as I will get, and so I want to try and do something constructive with the energy I do have. I've supported the hospice in a number of ways over the years, and whilst all that had to stop, I still know some of the people who work there and so I'm hopeful they can find something for me that's not too demanding. And Sam was really positive. She suggested a couple of possible roles for both of us to go away and think about in light of my limitations, so fingers crossed.

Tuesday 7 February 2012
I was back at the local hospice this afternoon, helping a nice lady called Maggie serve afternoon tea – or at least a cup of tea and a cake – to the patients. It's something that the hospice try to do every day, and they have a small number of volunteers who try to brighten up the afternoon of the patients, and any visitors, by providing this service. It's only a trial to see how I get on, and all the food preparation is done by the kitchen, but I think this could be manageable, especially as we have a trolley to carry the food and beverages around on.

This afternoon actually went okay, and Maggie seemed pleased with what I did. It was about two hours from the point that I left my front door to when I was back home and prostrate on my sofa, which is a bit too long, but there is minimal travelling involved and I was able to grab a short rest in the middle. There's some interacting with the patients and the staff, which I enjoyed, but it's all pretty quiet and at a relaxed pace. I noticed I was a little bit shaky when handing out the drinks, so will have to test that aspect further, but I wasn't directly handing anything to a patient today, so not an issue yet. I really hope I can finally put myself to some use, and in a good cause, even if it's only once or twice a month.

Wednesday 14 March 2012
I went back to the hospice last week to do the induction training I need to do (for health and safety purposes) before I can start trying to do the afternoon teas on a regular basis. It was really hard going. Sam and I had tried to break down the normal day-long training session into three, more manageable, chunks, the first one being last week and the others to

follow in the summer. Trouble was, I found even this smaller version so hard that my brain just felt like mush by the end of it, and I was a little shaky too. Actually, it was that bad, I think I've probably scared them off, and based on how rough I felt in the days that followed, maybe that's not such a bad thing.

I'm disappointed obviously; I thought this was a way I could try to use the small amount of useable energy I do have, in a worthwhile way. But I'll wait and see if they contact me again, or even have a think about what else I could do - maybe something at home where I can manage the situation better. It is so disappointing though, I thought I would be okay with the training once it was broken up into smaller segments. However, not only was it too much information to take in, but a room full of about 15 others also training, questioning and interacting, just seemed overwhelming. I think it might be back to the drawing board.

Monday 9 April 2012
Today I had a phone call from Damon, Yeti's brother-in-law, to say that Yeti is very ill. I had thought there might be something up, as we were planning to visit Yeti a couple of days ago, but when I made my normal phone call to check with his nurses that would be okay, they said I should talk to his parents. We've visited Yeti a lot over the years and that's the first time they have said that, as his parents had already approved our visits many years ago. Failing to then get hold of Yeti's mum and dad over the weekend meant I was already anticipating bad news.

Damon explained that Yeti had caught an infection and that they have been told to expect the worst. Whilst Yeti had survived two similar scares in previous years, this time it had turned into Septicaemia which means, realistically, he doesn't have long at all. That was hard to hear obviously, and I really felt for them all. At the same time, Yeti has effectively been in a coma for very nearly ten years, and a big part of me wishes that would end. I don't believe for a second that he's been in any pain or discomfort these last ten years, in truth I believe he's only been "there" at all in very brief moments, but for his sake - and his family's - I can't help thinking that it's time for him to say goodbye.

Tuesday 16 April 2012
You know how when you've got a number of metaphorical balls in the air at the same time, things rarely come together perfectly. Well, I can tell

you that when you are a couple consisting of one very dopey, very wife-reliant, CFS sufferer, and one chemo-brain-fuzzled wife, things never come together. Or at least not anywhere in the same ball park as perfectly. But on Saturday it all did. Honestly. And even despite my inevitable attempt to cock up one very important aspect, it was a brilliant, brilliant day where everything just worked. Perfectly.

First off, a few weeks back the Curry Night lads (Macca, Kenty and Skelts) reminded me that last year I had asked them to keep April 14 free for a possible mini "stag" do. Obviously, these days I personally drink like an eight-year-old girl and have the stamina of new-born foal, but my idea was for us to pop down to Bath for a couple of hours and just have some boys time, given that four weeks later Mandy and I were due to renew our vows. Silly really, but I obviously don't get to do that much lads stuff now, and I thought if I got plenty of extra rest beforehand, it would be a good way to kick off the renewals celebrations. Anyway, as we subsequently cancelled our renewals way back, I had forgotten all about the Bath trip, and not even mentioned it to the other fellas I hoped would join us. But the curry lads said they still had it in their diaries, so why don't we still go to Bath and also take the girls with us. "Cracking idea" said I.

That had all proved quite handy too, as I had recently been talking to the jewellers in Bath, Clive Ranger, where we bought Mandy's engagement ring many years ago. In short, I wanted to buy her a surprise eternity ring to give to her on our cruise, but I needed an extension to their normal exchange period as a) we aren't back from the cruise until the end of May, and b) my CFS-related recovery time could even mean an additional month on top before we can get back to Bath. By pure luck Richard, the Managing Director, answered my phone call and couldn't do enough to meet my unusual requirements. The only issue was getting down to Bath without Mandy, to pick up the ring in the first place, as it's not a journey I could do on my own. So actually, the lads resurrecting the Bath trip not only ties in nicely, but I will also have some help from the other Curry Night wives in gauging Mandy's ring size. Sorted!

And so on Saturday, Macca and Michaela, Kenty and Claire, Mand and I all jumped on a lunchtime train to Bath where we met Skelts and Tabs, who had made a similar journey up from Exeter. It was a bright sunny day, and having rested for some days beforehand, I was feeling good. It was also a rare chance to spend some time with all the Curry Night wives, who between them managed to take along just about every form of designer handbag I could think of.

After a swift drink in the bar opposite the station, we shot off to Bath's "happening" place of the moment where, against their normal strict policy, Michaela had somehow convinced them to reserve a table for us in a quieter area off to one side. As soon as we got there the staff started smiling at us inanely, so I started to think something may be up. I'm used to a "he must be the one that is ill and I'm unsure how to act" smile, but this was different. All was soon revealed as the manager walked over saying "you must be the anniversary couple", with multiple bottles of Prosecco following in his wake. Yep, we had been well and truly set up for a surprise celebration of our 15th wedding anniversary.

Now, I normally see things like that coming a mile off, but neither Mandy nor I had had a clue. We were speechless and really touched: what a lovely thing to do. It had all been so well arranged too – a quiet table in a nice bar/restaurant, just the right number of us so as not to cause me any issues, and loads of Mandy's favourite bubbly, Prosecco. The only problem was that, other than a glass each for the nicely-worded toast that followed its arrival, no-one was really drinking the Prosecco in volume. And so with Mand feeling obliged to drink as much of it as she could herself, and her normal alcohol intake being two, possibly three, glasses (she's only small), she was soon feeling very merry indeed. Which was quite useful when first Michaela, and then even I was able to try on one of Mandy's rings as part of a concocted discussion about Mandy's slim fingers, without her getting the least bit suspicious.

We ended up having such a good time in that bar, and the quiet corner table was so well situated for me, that we stayed all afternoon. Our waiter kept us well topped up with drinks (well, seven of us topped up, I suspect Mandy was necking Prosecco from the bottle by then) and we were having such a good laugh, that the time just shot by. In fact it was only when I looked at my watch that I realised it was 5.27pm already, which was a big problem as Clive Ranger, the jewellers, closed at 5.30pm. With Mandy facing the other way, I made a hasty exit from the bar and tried to cover the two-minute walk to Clive Ranger as fast as I could. As I got there I could see the final few trays of jewellery being removed from the window displays and my heart sank: they must be closed. But my watch said 5.29pm and their door sign still said "Open", so I tried the door a couple of times. It didn't open. Bugger. As I tried a third and final time, thank you God, the door opened. Now I'm not sure if I just wasn't pushing hard enough the first two times, if someone unlocked it that third time, or if it was just a mixture of desperation and alcohol, but that final time I tried the door I pretty much fell into their shop.

"I'm Dennittth, I'm here to pick up an etuuuurnity ring!" I said to the nice-looking shop lady from my now semi-prostrate position on the carpet. Luckily for me, they had been expecting me all afternoon, and based on a conversation I had with Mandy outside their display window a couple of years ago, I was able to quickly select a simple gold ring with its top half inset with diamonds. I explained that, as far as Mandy knew I had just popped out to the Gents and so they were really helpful, sorted out my credit card payment quickly, boxed up the ring and sent me on my way asap. I did still manage to walk back in the front door of the bar just as Mandy was swaying back from the ladies, but with a swift and discrete offload of the ring to Michaela, and a cock-and-bull story about me having just popped out to talk to a passing Jacqui, I just about got away with it.

After that, the rest of the day passed in a bit of a blur. A fantastic, really having a good time kind of blur, but a blur all the same. I remember holding a giggling Mandy upright at times, and also restricting my own alcohol intake by cheating with alternate mineral waters when I could get away with it, but other than that I don't know where the time went. Normally, part of me would have been counting down the minutes until I could return to the peace and comfort of my own living room, but on Saturday this only happened at the very end. Obviously I was really ill on Sunday, I was worse still on Monday, and today every single muscle hurts. But it was so worth it. I couldn't do it very often, and wouldn't want to even try, but on Saturday everything just came together so well, we absolutely loved it.

Monday 23 April 2012
My friend Yeti died last week, ten years and one day since he was last truly with us. That's typical of Yeti, hanging on in there to clock up a milestone even though he was given just hours to live over a fortnight before. It's very sad obviously but he is now, without any shadow of a doubt, at peace, and I just hope his mum and dad, and sister Sharon, can somehow find the strength to move on. They've all been through so much in those ten years, I really feel for them.

Two days before he died, Mandy and I made a quick trip down to see Yeti to say our goodbyes. It was also goodbye to all the nurses who have taken such good care of him all those years. I was surprised just how upset one or two of them were too, as they had never had the chance to really know Yeti. And in some ways it's a shame they couldn't have had just one conversation with him to see what a great lad he was, but then I guess they realised that from getting to know his family and friends. As sad as it was driving away from his care facility, and knowing it was the last time we would see Yeti, I also felt relieved it was coming to an end for him.

Damon, Yeti's brother-in-law who's been kindly phoning me regularly with updates, phoned me again last night. This time is was to ask, on behalf of Yeti's mum and dad, if I would be a pall-bearer at Yeti's funeral and help carry his coffin into church. My immediate thought was "wow, what an honour", and whilst trying to hold back a tear, I hope I said as much to Damon. But I know that physically I'm just not up to it, and my foggy old brain was also telling me that there are a number of Yeti's old mates that deserve to be there ahead of me - both points which I also said to Damon. In hindsight, I wish I had asked Damon if I could think it over, as although I think he understood, I didn't want to leave him with any other impression than I was honoured and humbled to be asked. I hope Yeti's mum and dad understand too.

Friday 27 April 2012
Some brilliant news today. Mandy and I went to see Dr Galea today for Mandy's first annual check-up and mammogram, and it all went very well indeed. The scan was clear and Dr Galea is really pleased with how Mandy is doing. We had lots of new questions for him, reflecting a mind-set of very much cancer "survivor" rather than cancer "patient" now. I'm sure he had heard them all before though, as he fired off answer after answer in his normal efficient and professional manner.

Mandy has pretty much put the breast cancer behind her, but these follow-up appointments, as reassuring as they are, do still bring the subject very much back to the forefront. Given that this latest one included her annual scan too, and therefore had increased potential for bad news, she handled the additional anxiety well. I do notice a change in her in the run up to these appointments, but I'm proud of how she's handling them so far, even if it does mean her getting her breasts out in front of other men on a regular basis. Only joking, she's doing and looking great, and long may that continue.

Dr Galea is a little concerned about just how much Mandy is still struggling on the Tamoxifen, but it now looks less and less likely that the side-effects will ease significantly. Therefore, as with Dr Cole, he's keen to support Mandy if she feels she needs to reduce her hours at work. So having also discussed it with our GP, we will now look to put that in place formally, as Mandy has found working four days per week on a trial basis recently has helped massively.

Thursday 3 May 2012
It was Yeti's funeral yesterday and I'm pleased to say that, with six other mates carrying his coffin, I was invited to lead them into the church. It was a moving occasion anyway, but with Yeti's family, and the other lads, fixing it so that I was able to help Yeti on his final journey, it meant a lot. And aside from being a little wobbly on my feet, and therefore confirming I had made the right decision not to be a pall-bearer, I was deeply honoured to do it.

After a religious service at the church, in which we all remained suitably and respectfully attired, the six pall-bearers and I changed tops as soon as we arrived in the crematorium car park. We then assumed the same positions as before to see Yeti's coffin safely into the chapel, but this time, due to Yeti being a devoted Ipswich Town fan we all wore Ipswich shirts with "Yeti" printed across the back. He would have loved that, and for us it was the most emotional part of the day.

Yeti's family, on the other hand, were immense, and exercised so much control over their emotions, it put a number of us to shame. Theirs was by far the greatest loss and yet they were dignity personified. I think it helped that, after ten long years, Yeti was still thought so much of that something approaching 300 people squeezed into the church for the service. It was a great send off for a great lad.

Chapter 15 – A Time to Celebrate

Thursday 10 May 2012
Well, it's our 15th wedding anniversary and, being back on board Arcadia today, we intend to spend the next two-and-a-bit weeks celebrating. What's more, my new "life is too short", "live for the moment", "annoying over-use of cliché" approach to life resulted in me recently upgrading to our first ever balcony. With our midday sail-in to Venice in mind, I had to bide my time for a starboard cabin to become available, but I got there in the end and am chuffed to bits. I had planned it as a surprise for Mandy, but that particular cat got out of the bag some weeks ago. No matter, as soon as we entered the cabin her attention was 100% on the biggest bouquet of flowers I have ever seen, a gift from our friends Charley and Andrew.

And the surprises didn't stop there, as for the first time ever I helped Mandy with the unpacking. Well, when I say helped, I mean I placed my bucket and spade and inflatable crocodile on the balcony in readiness for some decent weather. Mandy was a little dis-chuffed about the crocodile, until I informed her of the alternative (adult only) inflatable device one of my mates has provided for its possible life saving properties - let's just say she's called Lola and she has a permanent look of surprise on her face.

At dinner tonight we were reunited with regular cruise companions Richard and Joyce, and our table this time is right at the back of the Meridian Restaurant, overlooking the wake. A terrific first Headliners show followed, and as you will have gathered, we've really rated all the Headliners troupes we've seen. And this lot seem better than ever, with a five or six song medley which sounded as good as anything I've seen in nearly ten years of cruising - and that's saying something. Anyway, enough for now, I need my bed and an early night.

Friday 11 May 2012
Good Morning from a calm Bay of Biscay. It wasn't quite this calm at 5am this morning when I was first up and about, but I'm pleased to say it's lovely now. Not quite balcony weather yet, however it's great having the curtains open and watching the sea. Although, having unintentionally given the Isle of Wight ferry an eyeful yesterday (apologies to anyone on Red Osprey), I must remember to close those balcony curtains when I'm a) in the buff, and b) close to land.

Anyhow, after my usual embarkation day struggle yesterday we have a lazy day of recuperation planned, although I did pop along briefly to a meet-up of P&O cruise forum regulars. It was fun, and nice to put a few faces to names. Of those present, I knew Sue Kersh, Jack Sparrow and Cotto a wee bit, which was good as I'm a little nervous in such situations. But they all seemed a good bunch and it's always good to have some familiar people on board for a chat and a chuckle.

Saturday 12 May 2012
A nice first sea day yesterday. I'm still struggling a bit health-wise, as our recent emotional ups and downs have hit me a bit. That's okay though; I will just go steady for a while so that I'm good for Venice. I'm okay in short bursts, I just need to pace things a bit and fit in regular quiet spells, so apologies if things get a bit repetitive - e.g. watching movies, sleeping, sleeping at the movies etc.

So just a quick update for now to say that the food has been excellent so far, and I'm a very happy chap as I've had mussels already, which were mighty fine. After dinner last night we ran into Jack Sparrow again, and she confided in me that as the only female in her team at work she is known as "No Balls". This meant we had something in common, because courtesy of yesterday's swim in the coldest pool I have ever been in, mine appear to have gone AWOL too.

I also ran into Frank Manning from the forum, who missed the forum meet-up, but who I know from our online chats. He's a real gent and lectures part-time at a local college, so he is enjoying the rest too. Personally I think these academic types should be made to get a note from their parents before taking time off during term time, but he's bigger than me, so will leave someone else to raise that one with him.

Other than that it was all a bit of a blur yesterday to be honest, as my foggy old brain spent most of the time in a neutral gear. One thing I do remember clearly was being woken in the early hours by what sounded like the whole New Zealand rugby team in the cabin next door, doing the Haka. God only knows what was going on.

Sunday 13 May 2012
I had a narrow escape yesterday as Mandy visited the on-board jewellery shop. There we were, Mandy looking at the diamond rings, me trying to subtly nudge her out of the shop inch by inch, when this young

sales assistant came up saying how the item concerned would really suit Mandy, and generally buttering her up. Then he asked "did we have any questions?" So I hit him with;

"Aren't diamonds immoral due to the trade's imperialistic roots, and its calling for a ruling white minority over a subjugated black majority forced to provide cheap labor, not to mention its more recent financing of warlords, mercenaries and corrupt politicians, all of which result in widespread hardship or death to the populous, including thousands of drug-dependent child soldiers who are too dosed up to know any better?"

His mouth dropped open for a second or two and then he immediately rushed off to assist another, imaginary, customer on the other side of the shop. Sorry if that sounds a bit harsh, but unbeknown to her, Mandy is already getting a diamond ring on this cruise and I don't want anyone or anything else to steal the limelight.

The weather was a bit misty yesterday morning, so we went to see the movie. It was War Horse, and whilst I can't vouch for the middle bit (zzzzzzzz), the first and last hours were great. When we came out of the cinema it was sunny, so virgin balconiers that we are, we sunbathed on our balcony for a while. The angle of the sun meant I pretty much had to hold my ankles behind my head to achieve the all over sunning I desired within the smaller, non-shaded part of our balcony. But, hey, I'm nothing if not determined and my inflatable friend Lola didn't seem to mind.

Next it was time to get ready for our first formal night, and unusually there had been no mention of it being a Captain's Welcome Aboard Gala Night. That's no problem, I'm sure there will be one later, and by the time I had disentangled everything from my contortionist sunbathing, we just had time for a drink and dolphin watching in the amazing Orchid Bar before going onto dinner.

Today we are in Malaga and it really feels like we are cruising now. I do love the sea days, but to me, it never feels truly like we're cruising until we have our first port under our belt. We had a walk along Malaga's seafront this morning, and it instantly became clear that they've done a lot of work since we were here last. The port and harbour areas especially look terrific, with lots of brand new bars, restaurants and shops along the new purpose-built promenade.

Having parked ourselves on the beach, watching the locals having their Sunday strolls, runs and bike rides, Mandy's attention was suddenly drawn to a very tanned Spanish fella with his shirt off, who stopped to use the exercise apparatus just off to our right. "Wow, he's lovely" she said with some delight, before claiming she was talking about the Golden Retriever and not his firm, mahogany-coloured owner with the bulging muscles. The man was an Adonis and must be an athlete of sorts, as his short exercise regime was amazing - supporting himself solely with his hands to first lift himself up and then very slowly moving his whole torso 360 degrees, akin to a parallel bars gymnast.

At this point my masculine competitiveness got the better of me, so I puffed out my chest, sucked in my belly, and my sandcastle building took on a far more challenging and complex tone. By the time Raphael Nadal's more muscular brother had finished his exercises, I had created a sandcastle version of Gaudi's Sagrada Familia, and I was lying nonchalantly on my side with my head resting on my hand, chewing an imaginary piece of gum. Oh yes, he may have had me on the looks front, the muscles front and physical dexterity front, but we both knew who was the better at sandcastles.

A swift lunch followed, including a memorable "when I become a widow" conversation with Mandy (which I was never going to come out of well) in which Mandy, in the event of my death, basically lives on a cruise ship. Then a bit of sun snoozing up by the Aquarius Pool, and now Lola and I are in the Globe ready to watch Man City try and get the win they need to clinch the Premiership title. They are also showing the Man United (who could also win the Premiership today) game in the pub, but the whole ship seems to be behind City so let's hope they do it.

Monday 14 May 2012
Well, that turned out to be a hell of an ending to the footy season; Man City never do anything the easy way do they? The best atmosphere I've known on a cruise ship for a football match, partly because many of the Man United fans on board, rather than watch their own game in the Rising Sun, came to watch the City game instead. And boy they were gloating for most of the second half when it looked like City had blown it. Strangely, they went very quiet at the end when City scored twice in injury time. The place erupted when the winning goal went in, even the Indian waiters joined in the celebrations, as 99% of the ship turned into City fans for the day. Absolutely brilliant.

Anyway, dinner in the Meridian was excellent last night after a couple of not-so-good nights. The food itself has been good throughout actually, it's just everything got a little slow, food was turning up cold, and we were having to leave the restaurant so late that we missed a show. Our waiters are nice lads and keen to please, but just seemed to have too many tables to look after. However, fair play to them and our head waiter, they were clearly addressing this and we had our best dinner to date - mussels, sea trout and citrus tart for me, and dairy free versions of the same for Mandy. Nice.

Precautions have been put in place on board today to avoid a spread of that occasional little visitor to cruise ships, the Noro Virus, so a number of small but noticeable changes. That means that communal touching of items is reduced where possible (e.g. salt and pepper pots replaced by individual paper sachets) and passengers encouraged to wash their hands extra carefully. All sensible steps, with minimal impact on passengers, to avoid them catching a nasty if short-lived virus.

After dinner we decided to go to the Crow's Nest for the first time, and after a few drinks, the four of us, plus new friends Rob and Gill decided to enter the Syndicate Quiz - bad idea! It was fun, but we were appalling. Nearly as bad as Team Kersh, made up of cruise forum members. We really struggled. Would you believe there were no football questions, Beano questions or even anything on the life and career of Ms Kylie Minogue? Just what sort of quiz are these people running?!? A good laugh though.

Tuesday 15 May 2012
Mandy has forced me to have another lazy day today, as from tomorrow we have six consecutive port days. So today, given that we're passing Sicily, then taking a sharp left after the boot of Italy, we've been doing what the Italians call "il dolce far niente", which I believe means "the sweetness of doing nothing". In practice that means we have been laying around all morning in the comfy chairs in the chill-out area next to the Aquarius Pool, where every morning feels like Sunday morning – that is easy-listening music, the smell of coffee while you read a good book, and surrounded by the beautiful blue Mediterranean.

Anyway enough about today, it was a great Captain's Gala Dinner last night with, for me, lobster, sea bass and rack of lamb. We didn't have the Captain's Welcome Aboard Party as I understand officers are required to restrict their passenger contact when the anti-infection protocols are at a raised level. But still a good night with everyone dressed to the nines.

Then after dinner and a drink, we found ourselves in the Crow's Nest again, and against our better judgment we entered the Syndicate Quiz once more. In short, after a strong start (three out of three correct) and some heckling from Cotto and the rest of Team Kersh, our form dipped alarmingly. We're still learning stuff though (for example, the ring leader in Guy Fawkes' Houses of Parliament gun powder plot wasn't, amazingly, Ms Catherine Wheel, but it was worth a guess) and it's good fun. I must confess however, that rather than take our defeat to Team Kersh gracefully, we opted to instead boo them repeatedly when, on our way to bed, the doors of our opposing lifts opened simultaneously at every floor.

Incidentally, whilst I think of it, it turns out it wasn't the New Zealand rugby team waking me up by doing the Haka the other day. Having heard it a couple of more times since then, and given that I now know that the couple next door are getting married later in the cruise, I'm pretty sure it's them getting in some last-minute "practice" – pre-match training if you like. Not a problem, good luck to them. Anyway, off to fall asleep in a movie. Toodaloo.

Wednesday 16 May 2012
Right then, today we are in Kotor in Montenegro, and it is a little gem. The place where Kotor is situated looks like a fjord. What's more, the P&O in-cabin guide says it's a fjord. But if we're being pedantic, it's not a fjord (and many a local tells you it isn't) as I believe the ice cap that made the fjords didn't come anywhere near this far south. But it's lovely, and to me Kotor looks a little like a mix of Norway and the Cote D'Azur, and well worth getting up at 7am to watch the one-hour-long sail-in from your balcony.

We stayed on the balcony for a long lazy breakfast actually, which meant we disembarked later than most of our fellow passengers. So late in fact that we immediately ran into Sue Kersh and hubby Garry on their return journey to the ship, with Sue highly recommending the local beer and ice cream (and I thought I was the uncultured one). To be fair, we later found her to be right on both counts. Then, before we had completed the short walk to the city gates, we also ran into Frank Manning and his lovely wife Sue who were equally euphoric about the local paninis. As you can tell, all my fellow forum members seem to have very successfully found my level.

Anyway, after eventually entering the old town via the city gate, we were immediately struck with just how Dubrovnik-like it was. Smaller streets and squares, but still very Dubrovnik-esque. It also has a city wall that can be walked, and I do love a wall walk as you know, but this one is very steep and a bit beyond me. So steep in fact that it disappears so high up the mountain, I half expected to see an exiled Dalai Lama coming down it. It does look a great walk though, with amazing views, if you are up to it.

Another thing I would like to have done was kayaking on the "fjord" which looked very easy on the millpond-like water. There was a group of about 20 kayaks go out mid-morning, and it, and they, looked great. I was really tempted, but with one arm still considerably weaker than the other I would probably have ended up going around in circles. So instead we had a nice gentle walk inside the walls of the old town, where there were bars, restaurants and shops galore. As well as stops for ice cream and beer, me being the last of the big spenders, we also secured a Kotor thimble for Mum's collection.

After a relaxing afternoon back on board, we went to the Classical Sailaway Party. I was a little dubious beforehand, as whilst I don't mind a bit of classical music, you don't often see the words "classical" and "party" in the same sentence, so I said as much to Mandy. From where I was stood, out on the balcony, I didn't quite hear all of her reply, but I definitely heard "Nut Cracker" and "Sugar Plum Fairy". So, not willing to risk the words I missed being "use my" and "turn you into", I agreed to go along. And actually it was great, and a nice change from the norm.

And now, after another excellent dinner in the Meridian, and then the best Headliners show so far, we are back to the cabin for an early night as we now have two days in Venice. And I have a little something up my sleeve for tomorrow.

Thursday 17 May 2012
Did I say I had a little something up my sleeve today? Well as it turned out, I had a little something in my pocket, but either way, today's midday sail-in was really special. We have been lucky enough to have witnessed dawn and midnight sail-ins and sailaways in Venice before,

but this just about topped them. It was simply beautiful, all basked in lovely midday sunshine, and viewed from our own perfectly-located balcony. And of course I had this eternity ring to surprise Mandy with as we sailed past the Grand Canal. I had toyed with the idea of just casually slipping it on Mandy's finger, but was concerned that any sudden move could send the ring over the side. So I opted to put it in my trouser pocket, realizing that although our balcony was on the best side to view the sail-in, it was also on the cooler, shaded side of the ship, and so Mandy would want to stick her hands somewhere warm.

"And whose bloody ring is this?" she said accusingly a few seconds after popping her cold hands into my pockets. Luckily the penny dropped almost immediately, as she recognized it as the style she had pointed out in the jewellers' window a year or two back. As you can tell, I'm not a big one for romantic gestures, but it all seemed to work out okay, as her initial tentative smile of realisation slowly developed into a huge toothy grin. Mandy loved the ring, it fitted(ish) and, as I said a few words about how much she meant to me, our eyes started to very slightly well up. In my case, that was due to the chilly cross wind of the Venice basin obviously, but it was clear Mandy was really moved by the whole occasion. A few minutes later Richard, who along with Joyce had been in on my plans all along, popped in with a bottle of champagne, and then just as swiftly left us to enjoy it. It truly was, for many reasons, a wonderful arrival into Venice, and one that we will never forget.

After the midday sail-in we grabbed a quick lunch and headed for our (unlimited use for 18 Euros) cruise launch, which then took about 20 minutes to the drop-off point just to the right of St Mark's Square. We immediately realised that to our left, towards St Mark's, it was just a heaving mass of people. So we decided to save the touristy bits until it was quieter, and instead turned right towards the Arsenale area. This area of Venice is lovelier and quieter the further you walk. It was like one long seafront meander. And then, after a while, we just sat down and mellowed-out on a bench overlooking the lagoon.

On our return to the launch things had thinned out people-wise, so we carried on straight past it with the aim of going to Harry's Bar for one of their famous Bellinis. We had never been there before as everyone seems to think it's overrated, overpriced and just trading off its famous past, but we decided to give it a go. Unfortunately, although I was wearing a collared shirt, tailored shorts and smart shoes, my shorts meant I didn't meet the dress code so I didn't get far. However, what I did get to see inside was a small depressing-looking place, and the decor, tables etc. just reminded me of Rene's café out of 1980s sitcom Allo Allo. Even the windows were frosted, so no view. So I won't be popping back with trousers on as, if I'm going to spend 15 Euros on a beer (and God forbid that ever happens) there are much nicer places in St Mark's Square.

Having then instead gone to the ship for a nice long rest, and subsequently dinner in the Meridian Restaurant, we grabbed a launch back into town to find once again that evening time in Venice is just magical. It's quieter but still has a buzz about it, without that daytime feeling of someone having kicked a massive, tourist-filled hornet's nest. Parts of it are lit up beautifully, and St Mark's Square especially is just great at that time.

Next we took a quiet stroll to the Rialto Bridge, stopping off at a few shops and bars on the way, which was great but tiring. By then, having meandered ourselves to exhaustion, it was time to shoot back to the ship. We did briefly stick our heads in the late Headliners show when on board, which looked great as usual, but we were knackered so it was straight to bed for us. A really special day which will be the highlight of the cruise, if not the year, I'm sure.

Friday 18 May 2012
The America's Cup was taking place in the Venice lagoon this afternoon, so we decided we would get up and go ashore (and back) early, to avoid the "crazy" which we suspected would happen later. So at 8.30am, having breakfasted, dressed, and somehow found the will to put one foot in front of the other, we left Arcadia in search of the first launch of the day. After yesterday's efforts I felt like I had been hit by a train, but every step got a little easier, and when we got to St Mark's it was well worth getting out of bed for. It was nice and quiet, the early morning sun was creeping over the buildings, and there were some fantastic smells coming from the cafés.

We had nothing planned as such, so just wandered aimlessly as we got to appreciate a more relaxed version of Venice in daytime. Alas, after a while it started getting a little busier, so we sat and people-watched in a spot we found last time we were here, close to one of those "Traghetti" Gondolas that simply take (mostly) locals over the Grand Canal for a Euro. We were disappointed not to see the little Dachshund who patiently sat guard on the Traghetti last time we were here, but we're fairly sure it was him we saw later on one of the more traditional Gondolas, so he's clearly been promoted.

Next we trudged back to pick up the launch back to the ship. By this time it was getting really busy, especially around, and between the Bridge of Sighs (so called, and I'm serious this time, because of the sighs of the prisoners when they crossed it for the final time) and the Bridge of Groans (so called because of the groans the tourists make when they realise it's not the Bridge of Sighs they are looking at, situated on the next canal along). But we got past them all and jumped on the 11am launch back to the ship and boy, I felt the better for it.

After a kip, lunch, and an even bigger kip, I am now writing this before hitting the Sun Deck for another kip. Oh, and while we were ashore earlier we bought masks for the Venice Ball tonight, where I intend to make the most of my anonymity (laughs wickedly). Mandy's mask is very tasteful and sophisticated, and she looks amazing in it. Mine however, is one of those ridiculous Casanova masks with a long droopy nose, but you know what they say about men with long droopy noses? No me neither, but surely it's got to be something to do with virility, hasn't it?? Or maybe such a mask just suggests the wearer's real nose is long and droopy too??? Either way, I've got one, and whilst we may be the only ones at the ball that can't dance, I'll look great! And virile!!

Saturday 19 May 2012
"Kje Je Banka" from Sunny Slovenia! We've been in Koper (pronounced Ko-Pour) today, and in many ways it's the perfect post-Venice port - quiet, small and close to our berth. In fact, although we only raised ourselves briefly last night to go and see the midnight sailaway, and were still breakfasting in the cabin at 10.30am today, I'm surprised we made it ashore at all. However, as soon as we got off the ship, it was just a short walk up to Koper's old town.

As I say, Koper isn't huge, with small winding and cobbled streets that reminded me a little of Cornwall in places. We wandered around most of the old town in just 30 minutes, which was about my limit. When we got back to the ship we found a horse-drawn carriage on offer, the two horses really beautifully turned out, as was the young lady driver in her dressage blazer and plaited hair. So we jumped in, and judging by how much time they spent necking with each other, the two horses enjoyed it as much as we did. The round trip was only 30 minutes, and ten Euros each, but was a real bonus. Anyway, time for me to negotiate with Mandy if I can watch the Champions League final later. Wish me luck!

Saturday 19 May 2012 (Part 2)
Okay, the good news is I'm sat watching the footy. Fingers crossed the satellite reception holds out. All the comfy seats were gone in the main venue, the Rising Sun, so as I need some serious back support after yesterday's efforts I am on a comfy sofa in the Electra nightclub watching the game. That's okay, it's much quieter in here. However I reckon I might take Mandy along to the Venetian Masked Ball in a minute if Chelsea don't buck their ideas up. There's a rumour that some fella is going to streak around the dance floor wearing nothing but a Casanova mask.

Oh, and before I forget, Mandy has been flashing her new ring around the ship so much, to just about anyone that will stop and look at it, that a couple of the Entertainment Team have started calling her Frodo. I think it was actually Gollum that had the fixation with the ring in the Lord of the Rings, but based on my increasingly haggard features and receding hair line, I fear they may have already allocated that name.

Sunday 20 May 2012
Morning all, from sunny Dubrovnik. I did indeed leave the football at half-time last night, so that I could take Mandy to the Masked Ball. Everyone looked fantastic in their masks, and Sue Kersh from the forum looked so good she won a prize. It was good fun, and you'll be pleased to hear that there was no streaking across the dance floor, due primarily to my muscles aching so much that taking my shoes and socks off is now a two-man job. Logically, the Masked Ball was timed to coincide with a formal night, so masks or no masks, everyone looked great in their posh frocks and dinner suits. Sadly, no matter what I wear, next to my stunning wife I still tend to look like someone has kitted me out with the contents of a charity shop. But I do still try, and for once, thanks to my mask no-one was quite sure it was me.

Next we saw the late showing of another terrific Headliners show - my favourite numbers being the amazingly high-tempo Can Can and a Lion King one (I'm a sucker for a grass skirt me) which I think was called "He Lives in You". The show finished perfectly in time for me to catch the penalties in the football, so over a medicinal Whisky Mac (I've got a wee bit of a sore throat) I stayed and really enjoyed watching that, after first walking Mandy back to the cabin. Didier Drogba eh? Who would of thought he could stay on his feet long enough to be a match winner?? Well done Chelsea, it's about time an English team beat a German one on penalties.

Oh, and at dinner the salt and pepper pots etc. were back on the table, so all looking good now, I guess, as far as that small Noro Virus outbreak is concerned. They really seem to have handled it well actually, some very sensible steps taken with minimal impact on passengers.

So Dubrovnik then. Well, it's our third time here and it's got busier every time. When we first came here I walked the city walls by accident (just went up some steps) and completely missed the little window you were supposed to pay at. Now there are big iron gates you have to go through, a sizeable admission fee (about seven Euros I think) and there's so many people up there that the walk apparently takes two to three times as long as it used to. It's worth it though; a nice walk with some great views and I wish I could have done it again, but a bit beyond me today.

Another thing that's changed is the sheer number of people wanting to sell you an excursion, especially around the old town's harbour. When we first visited the harbour six years ago it was so quiet that we heard that sickly little kitten meowing away, and took him off to the vets. These days we would never have heard him. However, as anyone who has been here will testify, it's a nice place, Dubrovnik, and although it gets busy once you are inside the walled old town, there are always quieter spots to be found if you try, especially if you go early like us.

The harbour area was the first place we headed to again and, whilst busy, it was lovely and the gorgeous morning sun just added to it. One of the excursions involved going on a replica of an old galley ship and this sailed (chugged really) into the harbour just as we arrived. Sadly it was all booked up already, but it looked like fun. Next we wandered around one of the little markets that seem to appear around every corner here. We bought some really nice locally-produced olive oil and some grappa, after first having a decent sized free sample of both. The grappa especially was terrific, and had such a kick to it, it instantly cured (well, numbed really) my sore throat - and at just 40 Kuna/£4 a bottle you just had to "grappa" it while you could.

By that time the old town was turning from busy to outright "loco" and I know what a scramble getting back on a shuttle bus can be like here (regularly up to eight buses servicing multiple cruise ships, and all trying to squeeze into the same lay-by), so we bid the locals "Dovidenja" and headed back for lunch.

Monday 21 May 2012
It was a little overcast in Corfu today but the temperature was still in the 20s and so we had breakfast on the balcony again. The crew then carried out a safety drill, and I'm pleased to report that the lifeboats next to us were all released and lowered very efficiently and correctly.

One point that got me thinking during the exercise, concerned the instructions they give over the tannoy when they want certain members of staff to go to their designated lifeboats. Now I'm sure "photographer 5" and "Spa 3" take a nice photo and paint a lovely nail, but if Captain Keith Dowds takes requests for such things, and should disaster befall us, could I possibly have an officer and a Headliners dancer in my boat? An officer so that we have someone who knows their way around a compass, and a Headliners dancer in case, having needed to eat the officer, she and I find ourselves marooned on a desert island with the future of the human race depending on our fornication. Obviously I would tell her about my vasectomy eventually, but until then, important to keep the lass motivated, I feel.

Anyway, it was a nice slow morning in Corfu today. Well it was slow for us, but due to today being the anniversary of Corfu being re-Greeked, some places were heaving. Many of the locals were out in force, including a number of marching bands banging and trumpeting their way around Corfu's narrow streets. Some of them were a little rag-tag in appearance whilst one band in particular, thanks to their glorious brass helmets, were literally more polished. It was nice as long as you didn't get too close. I SAID IT WAS NICE, AS LONG AS YOU DIDN'T GET TOO CLOSE!

There were loads of shops and restaurants open, despite it being a Corfu Bank Holiday, and some real bargains were to be had. Admittedly many of the "designer" goods were fakes, including hundreds of handbags (gulp), but Mand stayed strong. In fact the major purchase was mine (I know!), as I got a solid silver cross and a chain. We bought it from a tiny little shop not much bigger than the elderly gentleman owner himself, and had his cat not been nursing her kittens in his doorway, we would have missed him completely. A cunning marketing ploy obviously, but it got our attention, and I'm well pleased to have made a good deal with a clearly knowledgeable and cat-loving proprietor.

After a short stroll around Corfu town we headed back to the shuttle bus and I surprised Mandy by complementing the, up until then, solely Greek-speaking bus-coordinator lady on her lovely Scouse accent. Turns out I was bang on - she's a Liverpudlian originally, and in fact her world champion swimmer of a son had been the first bearer of the 2012 Olympic Torch. She said that although he's Greek, he was interviewed by a UK-based news programme and asked to "do a bit of Scouse" to which he said something like "no way, me mam would kill us". His name is Spyros Gianniotis, and as I say, he's Greek, and we said we would keep a look out for him in the London Olympics next month.

Tuesday 22 May 2012
A nice lazy one this morning, and even though we had an extra hour in bed, courtesy of leaving Greece, we only just made the 9.30am cut-off for breakfast in the Meridian. We timed it well as it turned out, as we got a table for two overlooking the wake, which due to a combination of the low morning sunshine and a really decent sea-swell, looked quite spectacular. Then we sat reading our books in the comfy chairs at the top of the Atrium and hurray, I finally finished mine. I've been reading one of Donna Leon's Venice based Commissario Brunetti novels, whereas Mandy, perversely for a cruise, has been motoring her way through a trilogy called The Hunger Games!?!

And talk of the devil, my good lady has just walked back into the cabin carrying a sizeable handbag purchase and announcing "right that's the first one bought!"

Wednesday 23 May 2012
Good morning from a calm and sunny Mediterranean, and very nice it is too after yesterday's wind and movement saw all the sun decks empty, aside from the covered pool area. With everyone keen to make up for lost time today, the sun-loungers were soon full up and the dreaded sun lounge "hoggers" reserving perfectly good, empty loungers for their long, often lost, friends and relatives. One fella close to us regularly rebutted, for well over an hour, any enquiries made about the four empty beds he was reserving, with a bolshy "they're in a class, they'll be

back shortly". Hmmm, they must be in a class every day then, because he does the same thing each time. Well done to one lady though, she told him exactly what she thought, in no uncertain terms. I was so impressed I helped her secure a couple of beds close by shortly afterwards.

Anyway turning back to yesterday, and the sea being a little choppy as I say, we had a lazy afternoon in the cabin. We borrowed the Rise of the Planet of the Apes DVD from the library and watched this whilst stretched out on the cabin sofa with a soya latte. With the balcony curtains wide open for a full, floor-to-ceiling, view of the spectacularly choppy sea, it was a great way to spend a few hours, especially as it was too windy to sit outside yesterday.

Then after relieving a bit of muscle stiffness with an awesome swim (it was like Bondi beach up there yesterday it was so choppy) and a sauna, we showered early and hit the Intermezzo Bar for pre-dinner drinks. It was the formal Black and White Night so everyone looked great, even one fella in his flashing bow-tie. This one brought a smile to my face, as generally they do, but wow it was so bright and flashy it should have come with a warning of possible seizure inducement.

Next we went to the show, Killer Queen, which was terrific - a seamless medley of Queen classics with great songs, great singing, great dancing, and culminating in a brilliant all-round performance delivered at a phenomenal pace. Both showings (I know because we went to both either side of some drinks) got a thoroughly well-deserved standing ovation from the audience. I'd wager the Headliners enjoyed it too as, on account of them leaving the ship at the end of this cruise, this was the very last time they would perform it, and they clearly went for it.

After that I walked Mandy back to the cabin and then headed for a Whisky Mac nightcap in the Crow's Nest to see how Team Kersh had done in the quiz. I just missed them as they left with their tails between their legs having finished second yet again. Always the bridesmaids that lot.

Thursday 24 May 2012
A strange mix of weather yesterday on board Arcadia as, even though it was dry and sunny throughout, for most of the day it was really windy again. So windy in fact, that the roof over the Crystal Pool was partly closed despite the clear sky and bright sunshine. Luckily for us however,

we somehow managed to sit on two of only four sun-loungers around that pool that was still left in direct sun, as the opening in the roof was directly above us. We had the best of both worlds - sheltered from the wind but still getting the sun. How lucky was that? And I didn't even go that pink!

Then come the evening, the wind dropped completely and we decided to have an evening drink on the Prom Deck. The sea was so beautifully calm that not even Arcadia was causing a ripple. It was so pleasant and warm on the Prom Deck that six of us sat there, drinking and chatting until 10pm, watching numerous pods of dolphins and an amazing sunset over southern Spain, which made for some great photos.

Today we were up at the crack of dawn, and after a swift breakfast on the balcony overlooking "The Rock" we were in the centre of Gib just after 8.30am, and bumping into the Kersh's on their tour of the shops. After Garry Kersh and I practically high-fived each other, in recognition of us both deciding to take our good ladies shopping at a time when most shops are closed, we stopped for a coffee in the square. Then it was a nice stroll back to the ship, stopping to occasionally rest or chat to those we recognised going in the opposite direction.

After lunch we heard the announcement that "all passengers are required to make their way to the Aquarius Pool for The Great British Sailaway". Now admittedly we were a few minutes late, but when we walked through the door out to the Aquarius Pool area it was just a mass of people and flags - by far the busiest sailaway I've been to. It was pretty overwhelming to be honest, and not just because my large Piña Colada and Mandy's Cosmopolitan was £11 a round. But we found a "quiet" spot at the back which gave us an incredible view of everybody partying Arcadia style.

Friday 25 May 2012
As the two of us had not had a chance to really celebrate our anniversary alone, and with no Gary Rhodes venue on board Arcadia now, last night I took Mandy off to the Orchid Restaurant for dinner. We immediately recognised the maître d' as one of the lads who used to work in Arcadian Rhodes, which was nice as we had a quick reminisce as he sat us at our "usual" table - or at least the one we sat at every other night on our seven-day cruise to the Fjords in 2010 - right next to the full-length glass window overlooking a nice calm sea. The food, as usual, was excellent,

and for what I think is normally a £10 a head cover charge, great value. However, we had been given a gift package which waived the cover charge and included a free bottle of wine, so having also had those cocktails yesterday we were pretty merry by the time we left.

We then wobbled down to meet Richard and Joyce, and continuing my cunning plan to do something different every night for the last few nights on board, we all decided to go to the Rising Sun for the first time. Now if we were a little tipsy then some of these lot were real drinkers. All good harmless fun though, nobody overindulging to silly levels, and I was actually sat there thinking this is okay, why haven't we come here before? Then the live music started, which was so loud Mandy could barely hear herself slur. The music, especially the singing, was good, it was just really loud, so being the delicate flower I am, we retreated to the Spinnaker Bar. Nothing wrong with the Rising Sun at all, it seemed like a good atmosphere in there, just a bit loud for me.

Anyway, all that remained after that was for me to walk Mandy to the cabin, then pop up to the Crow's Nest for my medicinal Whisky Mac nightcap, and to congratulate Team Kersh on finishing second in the quiz. They were only halfway through the quiz at that point, and joint first at the time, but by now we all knew the inevitable outcome.

Sunday 27 May 2012
Despite yesterday's occasional thick cloud, most of us used our last day to top up our tans on the sun decks, where we also got to see a serial sunbed hogger get his comeuppance. It was the same guy I mentioned the other day, again keeping four empty sun beds whilst the rest of his party did God knows what, God knows where. After an hour or two, one of the drinks waiters, having seen this fella turn away many a request for his very empty beds, said to him "I'm very sorry sir, but the reserving of sunbeds is not permitted". The man made a bit of a fuss, but with the other passengers metaphorically lining up behind the waiter, he sulked off like a naughty child. The waiter got a round of applause.

After a relaxing afternoon, we joined Richard and Joyce for dinner in the Meridian, and then another very good Headliners show which involved famous numbers from the movies. The dancers stole the show this time, keeping up an amazing pace and looking great in such things as Bunny Girl outfits, black rubber catsuits, not to mention pole dancing in sparkly gold hot pants. The girl dancers didn't look too shoddy either.

Then the four of us from dinner met up with our two other regular companions on this cruise, Rob and Gill, and headed for the Orchid Bar. Over some drinks we all agreed it had been a fantastic cruise, and as a sign of just how good the crew have been, we all said we have never before wanted to search out so many of them to say thanks and all the best. In addition to Rob and Gill, we also made a number of other new friends, especially those we met from the P&O cruise forum, who were all good fun. The highlight of the cruise for me however, was undoubtedly that sail-in to Venice, and giving Frodo that ring, but every single day has been a good one. It really has been a special cruise.

We all then decided to have an early night in readiness for disembarkation day tomorrow. Or that was the plan anyway. Mandy and I made the mistake of walking past the nightclub, when all of a sudden out popped Cotto, shaking his fists in the air and shouting "yes, we did it", and trying to convince me that he and the rest of Team Kersh had finally won the Syndicate Quiz. Then, with me still querying the validity of his claim, and suggesting the normal winners didn't turn up, he dragged us into the nightclub to celebrate with him and Jack Sparrow. It wasn't for long, and the music wasn't too loud to cause me any issues, so it was good fun. I even danced with Mandy. She was over the moon, suggesting that I hadn't danced with her properly since our wedding day - "well just don't expect it every 15 years" I said.

Chapter 16 – Reflecting

Friday 22 June 2012
As ridiculous as it sounds, as I write this final entry I'm not sure I will ever be comfortable sharing this book beyond close friends and family. That said, the two people outside of that circle that I have been brave enough to show a draft to were both very complementary. They also said the book didn't have the happy ending they had hoped for. I can understand that: I am after all still ill, and Mandy remains on medication to help avoid the return of her cancer. But, in my head, the book does end happily in that Mandy and I are both still here and very much enjoying life. We have also both learnt what is most important in life, and of course I still have an income, for which I am incredibly grateful and fortunate. I hope therefore, if you have read this far it feels like a happy ending – sort of.

That said, I have found myself reflecting a lot of late. Reflecting on the fact that I've now been at home trying to get better, trying to get back to work, for over a decade. I've also been thinking a lot about Mandy and everything she has been through with her breast cancer. But rather than contemplating how different things might have been had we both instead been healthy, I found myself focusing more on the positive factors that have seen us through such a tough period.

The first thing that occurred to me was just how much our cats Frisco and Maui (and the much missed Cosette) have meant to us. They really have been a constant presence these last ten years and I don't know what we would have done without them. Sadly, recent vet visits have made it painfully clear that their time with us is coming to an end, and I just know it's going to break our hearts when the time comes to say goodbye. They've been with us ever since we came back from honeymoon (to San Francisco and Maui, in case you hadn't guessed), and been such a presence. I never envisaged they would enrich our lives in the way they have. They really are our best friends and we will love them always.

Speaking of friends, that's an area that has been a real eye-opener in the last decade. They say that it's at times like these when you find out who your friends are, and I guess there is some truth in that. Indeed, a few people who I honestly thought were lifelong friends, disappeared very early on. And that's not meant as a judgment – God knows my CFS, for example, makes me hard work to be friends with – it's just what happened. But the biggest realisation by far was finding out that there are others who I didn't realise were as good a friend as they have subsequently shown to be. They, our families, and some of the newer friends we've since met through CFS, cruising, or the church have really come through for us, and I will be forever grateful.

Then finally, something brilliant that came out of these last ten years, and which we may never have discovered but for the CFS, has been the cruises. From our very first one in 2003, the cruises became a shining beacon of hope and positivity at the end of what, at times, felt like a very dark tunnel. Just having a cruise booked, no matter how far in the future, gave us something on the horizon to look forward to and aim for. We've been lucky enough to have now cruised in each of the last ten years, and we absolutely love them.

So all in all, I think we've been pretty lucky. Well okay, the CFS is unfortunate. And Mandy having breast cancer, especially at such a young age, was awful. But, debilitating and life-threatening illnesses aside, we've been pretty blessed I think. And especially with our new-found outlook of trying to enjoy life as often and fully as possible, I pray that will remain the case. I am increasingly determined to live for today, and despite the CFS, still try to realise a few goals. And who knows: whilst health-wise it might not be all plain sailing, maybe we could even do a world cruise one day? I might just need to sell a kidney first to pay for it!

Mandy has the Last Word (as usual!)

I am in total awe of Rich for writing this book. I was already immensely proud of him for the way he has dealt with his illness, and how he adapted to such a massive change in his lifestyle. But writing this book, over so many years, and overcoming the significant CFS-related barriers he faced in completing it, really is a huge accomplishment. I have seen, more than anyone, just how physically and emotionally hard a task the book has been for him, and also, no matter how hard it got, how determined he remained to finish it one day. Although it doesn't feature me anywhere near enough, and makes me cry every time I read it, I love it. He is - and always will be - my inspiration.

Whether you know Rich (as Dennis, DTM, Rich, Richie or even Sicknote) or not, I hope you can see from this book that he's a good (sometimes grumpy) man, trying to do his best in difficult circumstances. Even though his plans and dreams were forever altered when he became so ill with CFS, he remains one of the most positive and warm-hearted people I have ever met. He is also my husband, and I am so very proud of him for writing this book.

Rich, I love you.

Mandy

p.s. Rich only permitted me to write the ending to his book if I also pointed out that not all of the events covered may have taken place on the exact dates indicated. Either due to his failing memory, or in his attempts to make the book an easier read, it may be that some dates are incorrect, or in one instance two very similar cruises were amalgamated to avoid too much duplication. However, it all formed part of his story at some point, and so I hope you'll excuse him that little bit of poetic licence and the occasional exaggeration for (hopefully) comedic effect.

Sicknote Goes Cruising

Acknowledgements

Before the book acknowledgements, I must first thank Martin Lee for all his help in connection with my CFS. Martin, you are a wonderful man and your arrival in my life at such a crucial time was immense, and something I will be forever grateful for. In learning to live with CFS I have also been very fortunate to have access to the considerable knowledge and talents of Hanqiao Sun, Jane Catchpole, Richard Carter and the ME Association. To them, and to our friends and family who have stuck with us this last decade, thank you all so much.

In terms of my book, there are three people who damn near qualify for co-author status, such was their contribution to it. The simple fact is that there is no way that I could have written the book without Mandy my wife, and our friends Charley Liddle and Helen Kent. George and Deb Williams were a massive help too. Sincerely, thank you all.

In addition, I owe a debt of gratitude to everyone on the cruise forums that encouraged me and gave me the confidence to write the book. It was only when some of you started saying you really enjoyed my cruise reports and my style of writing that I started to think the occasional diary, which I had started primarily for the purposes of mental exercise, could possibly be of interest to anyone else.

Thank you also to those who kindly agreed to me writing about them or their loved ones, in particular Roy and Maureen Yeates, and their daughter Sharon.

Cheers too, to Jim Naylor for allowing me to reproduce the caricature he did of me in circa 1999, and use it on the cover of this book. It just seemed kind of apt.

Oh yes, and a massive thank you to everyone who helped us through an incredibly hard 2010.

Finally, our sincere and heartfelt gratitude to the staff and crews of P&O Cruises.

Printed in Great Britain
by Amazon.co.uk, Ltd.,
Marston Gate.